Bayonet to Barrage

Bayonet to Barrage
Weaponry on the Victorian Battlefield

Stephen Manning

Pen & Sword
MILITARY

First published in Great Britain in 2020 by
PEN & SWORD MILITARY

An imprint of
Pen & Sword Books Ltd
Yorkshire – Philadelphia

Copyright © Stephen Manning 2020

ISBN 978-1-52677-721-8

The right of Stephen Manning to be identified as Author of this work has been asserted by him in accordance with the Copyright, Designs and Patents Act 1988.

A CIP catalogue record for this book is available from the British Library

All rights reserved. No part of this book may be reproduced or transmitted in any form or by any means, electronic or mechanical including photocopying, recording or by any information storage and retrieval system, without permission from the Publisher in writing.

Typeset in 11/13 point Palatino

Printed and bound by TJ International

Pen & Sword Books Ltd incorporates the imprints of Pen & Sword Archaeology, Atlas, Aviation, Battleground, Discovery, Family History, History, Maritime, Military, Naval, Politics, Social History, Transport, True Crime, Claymore Press, Frontline Books, Praetorian Press, Seaforth Publishing and White Owl.

For a complete list of Pen & Sword titles please contact

PEN & SWORD BOOKS LTD
47 Church Street, Barnsley, South Yorkshire, S70 2AS, England
E-mail: enquiries@pen-and-sword.co.uk
Website: www.pen-and-sword.co.uk

Or

PEN AND SWORD BOOKS
1950 Lawrence Rd, Havertown, PA 19083, USA
E-mail: Uspen-and-sword@casematepublishers.com
Website: www.penandswordbooks.com

Contents

Acknowledgements ix
Abbreviations xi

Introduction 1
1. The Bayonet – Sobroan, 10 February 1846 7
2. Percussion Rifled Muskets – The Crimean War, 1854–6 41
3. Breech-loading Rifles – Amoaful, 31 January 1874 65
4. The Martini–Henry Rifle – Gingindlovu, 2 April 1879 95
5. A Wall of Bayonets and Fire – The Sudan Campaigns, 1884–5 125
6. Technological Slaughter – Omdurman, 2 September 1898 147
7. Barrage – Pieter's Hill, 27 February 1900 175
Conclusion – Lessons Forgotten 203

Notes 212
Bibliography 220
Index 227

To Samuel Hudson, a true friend who has been so supportive

Acknowledgements

I would like to thank the staff of following institutions that were all so helpful in assisting my research: the National Army Museum, London, the Royal Marines Museum, Portsmouth, and the Lancashire Military Museum in Preston. At Exeter University I would like to express my gratitude to Professor Jeremy Black and Doctor Bob Higham for their encouragement and advice.

    I would also like to thank Anthony Gratton-Cooper and Will Churcher for their informed, and helpful, criticism and proofreading skills.

Abbreviations

ASHM	Argyll & Sutherland Highlanders Museum, Stirling Castle
HMSO	Her Majesty's Stationery Office
KZNA	Kwazulu Natal Archive, Durban, South Africa
LIM	Lancashire Infantry Museum, Preston
NAM	National Army Museum, London
OIOC	Oriental and Indian Office Collection, British Library, London
QLRM	Queen's Lancashire Regimental Museum, Preston
SA	Shropshire Archive
WO	War Office Records Office held at The National Archives, Kew

Introduction

Queen Victoria's long reign (1837–1901) witnessed a transformation within British society that saw Britain become the paramount imperial power of the age, both industrially and militarily. The Industrial Revolution altered the British landscape; factory chimneys and colliery wheels became common features, whilst canals and railways carved their furrows across the land. The lives of tens of thousands of rural inhabitants were changed forever as they left the land in search of work in the ever-growing urban areas. The blight of inner city squalor was one of the many prices to pay for the growth generated by rapid industrialisation; yet, it was economic advancement that paved the way for Britain to become the world power of the nineteenth century and establish an overseas empire which, by the end of Victoria's reign, 'governed roughly a quarter of the world's population and covered about the same proportion of the earth's land surface'. As Niall Ferguson has so succinctly recorded, 'The British Empire was the biggest Empire ever, bar none'.[1]

Although some of the gains were acquired by peaceful settlement many required the intervention of the British armed services. The battle flags of numerous regiments displayed the names of far-off battlefields on which the British Army had fought. As the century progressed, politicians resorted, more and more frequently, to the might of the British Army and Royal Navy; to win its Empire, to gain territory before an European rival, to right perceived wrongs and, in the case of India in 1857, to punish those who dared to try and free themselves from British administration. The British soldier, whether clad in scarlet or khaki, fought in such distant places as New Zealand, Burma, Canada, the North West Frontier and throughout the continent of Africa. Varying terrain imposed different challenges and this, of course, led to the adoption and adaptation of tactics to suit the difficulties faced by the British soldier. Above all, advancements in weapon technology throughout the nineteenth century dramatically altered the Victorian battlefield.

The improvements in weaponry can be viewed as an evolutionary process, with one improvement, in say barrel rifling, leading to further enhancements as the years progressed. Yet, when considering the technology available at the start of Victoria's reign, such as the smooth-bore flintlock musket, compared with that used at the end, the machine gun, the advancement can be viewed a revolution.

However, this revolution got off to a slow start for as Hew Strachan has so admirably demonstrated in his work, *From Waterloo to Balaklava* in the period from the end of the Napoleonic War (1815) to the battles of the Crimea, the weaponry, both in terms of muskets and artillery, had altered little, nor had the tactics changed significantly.[2] There still remained an over reliance on the final mad assault, with bayonets fixed, which was such a feature of the Anglo-Sikh wars of the 1840s. As General Charles Napier declared, 'No troops can stand a charge of bayonets, and whoever charges first has the victory . . . Firing is a weapon . . . of defence, not of attack'.[3] Yet, as will be shown in Chapter 1, in a study of the Battle of Sobroan (10 February 1846), and from research into the effectiveness of British weaponry in the pre-Crimean army by D.F. Harding, the tactics used by the British were as much forced upon them by the limitations, and the inferiority, of the weapons available to them, as they were a historical tactical legacy.[4]

From his earliest work (*The Tools of Empire*), to his most recent (*Power Over Peoples*), Daniel Headrick has convincingly argued that technological superiority powered European imperialism and, as Headrick has recognised, this is clearly apparent on the Victorian colonial battlefield.[5] According to Headrick, 'The nineteenth century saw more innovations in firearms than any period before or since. Innovations that increased the ease of loading, the rapidity of fire, and the accuracy and range of bullets gave those who possessed new weapons the ability to dominate and coerce those who did not'.[6] Whether it was the introduction of the percussion cap, the magazine rifle or even the machine gun, colonial powers possessed huge advantages in tactical weaponry over their 'savage foes', which, as Headrick has argued, virtually preordained imperial expansion. By the end of Victoria's reign, 'Any European infantryman could now fire lying down, undetected, in any weather, fifteen rounds of ammunition in as many seconds at targets up to half a mile away'.[7] The indigenous peoples of Africa simply could not compete in the arms race of the nineteenth century.

From the end of the Crimean War, in February 1856, to the beginning of the Second Boer War, in 1899, the British Army was largely faced with the challenges of colonial warfare. Such 'small wars' were still fought along eighteenth-century lines, for the demands of inhospitable terrain, and the huge distances involved, forced British commanders to resort to long lines of communication and supply, where infantry boots and wagons, pulled by oxen, dominated. At a tactical level, troops were frequently deployed in Napoleonic formation, such as the square, which reflected the mobility of the enemy as compared with the British, and allowed fire to be so concentrated that the technological advantage, such as the rapid fire of the machine gun, could be decisive.

This book, *From Bayonet to Barrage*, aims to enhance the work of Headrick by placing technological superiority firmly in the context of battlefield success. It examines seven Victorian battles, or campaigns, that epitomise how the factors of advancement in military technology, changes in tactics and the adoption of new ideas combined throughout Victoria's reign to defeat her enemies. These examples will demonstrate how British commanders, and their troops, used the tactical advantages they possessed to gain significant victories over their foes.

British battlefield successes were sometimes achieved after a reversal, whether partial, as in the case of Tamai (13 March 1884), or after a complete defeat, as at the Battle of Isandlwana (22 January 1879). However, it will be shown that after such setbacks British commanders were able to amend tactics or adopt new ones so as to overcome their enemies. The traditional view of Victorian commanders being slow to adapt to a rapidly changing world will be shown to be largely a myth. Howard Bailes claims that the 'die-hard' individuals were, thankfully, in the minority. Bailes has argued that too much attention has been given, in both the contemporary press and subsequent histories, to traditionalists, such as the Duke of Cambridge (1819–1904), who stifled change and 'derided the significance of technological development'.[8] British military thinking was not always driven by character and tradition, but by professionalism and intellect in which officers were determined to keep pace in an era of ceaseless change. Lessons for the British High Command from colonial warfare could be rather ambiguous and 'it was recognized that the conduct of small wars formed a distinct art, diverging from regular warfare'.[9] Colonel Charles Callwell in his work of 1896, *Small Wars: Their Principles and Practice*, became the leading expert on imperial warfare, yet he was not the first to consider the lessons for the British Army. Several serving officers, such as Colonel Gawler and Lieutenant R. da Costa Porter, had earlier recorded their thoughts on the lessons to be learnt from 'small wars' and such debate indicates that, at one level, the professionalism and intellectual vigour within the nineteenth-century British Army remained healthy.[10]

At another level, the fact that Callwell, a mere subaltern, became the authority on 'small wars' perhaps suggests that the commanders of Whitehall were rather slower to consider their profession.[11]

In addition, throughout the Victorian period Britain was generally on a par with her continental rivals in terms of military hardware and equipment. For example, magazine rifles were introduced into British regiments a matter of months after they had been sanctioned in the German Army.[12] On many occasions, even in the Crimea, the British Army possessed far superior weaponry than that used by its enemies.[13]

The British Army was portrayed as too slow to change or adapt in Leo Amery's seven-volume *The Times History of the War in South Africa*, which was published between 1900 and 1909. Amery freely admitted that the work was primarily written as propaganda devoted to the cause of army reform.[14] As such, the work was largely critical of the performance of the British Army. Again, Howard Bailes has written, 'For two generations these [Amery's views] have tended to colour the lens through which the Victorian army is viewed. Echoes of Amery's blanket indictments may be found in dozens of popular military histories.'[15] Although examples can always be found of military folly and stagnation, and the Victorian army possessed examples of both, the history of Victoria's campaigns is also one of innovation and adaptability, as will be shown.

From the late 1880s onwards, 'modern' weaponry entered the battlefield; howitzers, quick-firing artillery, magazine rifles, cordite and lyddite explosives and Hiram S. Maxim's reliable machine gun, with the unprecedented rate of fire of 600 rounds per minute. Maxim's weapon was 'destined to revolutionize small arm tactics'.[16] So great were these innovations that in his posthumously published work of 1910, *The Science of War*, G.F.R. Henderson described this period as 'the second tactical revolution'.[17]

This 'second tactical revolution' is strikingly illustrated in two late Victorian battles, both of which are examined in this work. First, Omdurman (2 September 1898), which is perhaps the ultimate imperial battle. Here, all the technological superiority and industrial power of the British Empire was used to convey, by boat and train, British, Egyptian and Sudanese troops to the battlefield. By using the latest tactical weaponry of magazine rifles, artillery and machine guns, this diverse imperial force decisively defeated the Mahdist army. As the young Winston Churchill wrote, the victory was 'the most signal triumph ever gained by the arms of science over barbarians. Within the space of five hours the strongest and best-armed savage army yet arrayed against a modern European Power had been destroyed and dispersed, with hardly any difficulty, comparatively small risk, and insignificant loss to the victors.'[18] Second, the Battle of Pieter's Hill (27 February 1900) saw the British finally defeat the Boers in a set-piece battle which allowed for the relief of the besieged British force in Ladysmith. After such earlier defeats at Modder River (28 November 1899) and Colenso (15 December 1899), the British were able to adapt their battlefield tactics and fully utilise their tactical weaponry of long-range rifle fire, artillery barrage and the machine gun to overwhelm a defensive position, with concentrated decisive fire used to support an infantry advance. As Edward Spiers has written, 'Buller's forces clearly demonstrated more effective field craft and co-ordinated artillery/infantry operations in their assaults upon Cingolo, Monte Cristo, Hlangwane, Inniskilling Hill and finally Pieter's Hill before relieving Ladysmith.'[19]

Pieter's Hill had clear messages for the future battlefields of the Western Front; yet, by 1914, the lessons of this successful attack had been largely lost to the British High Command in the midst of a series of debates that followed the end of the Boer War.

Whilst concentrating upon the battles themselves, some background to the conflicts in which the engagements were fought has been provided. Both primary and secondary sources have been used to research this work and, wherever possible, the words of those who fought in the individual battles have been included, bringing a degree of authenticity and realism to the book. Although this work is primarily concerned with technological advancement in weaponry and with this tactical development on the battlefield, it also focuses on the bravery and fortitude of the British soldier, something which should never be overlooked in any age.

Chapter 1

The Bayonet – Sobroan, 10 February 1846

Our swordmen next assailed the Seikhs, Regarding not their dreadful shrieks; Our gleaming bay'nets next they saw, Which made them dread us more and more . . .

Private J.W. Baldwin, HM 9th Foot,
participant at the Battle of Sobroan

On the evening of 18 June 1815, as the British and Allied troops advanced against the remnants of the Old Guard, the general order was given to fix bayonets and draw sabres. The resultant butchery of those resolute and brave Frenchmen was the price paid to allow for Napoleon's flight from the battlefield of Waterloo. The butcher's bill for the day was appallingly high. Over 47,000 men, British, French, Prussian, Dutch and Belgian, lay dead or wounded in an area of just 3 square miles. The fallen had been slashed by cavalry sabres, felled by musket fire, blasted by artillery and stabbed by bayonets. Later on in the evening, the victorious Duke of Wellington stated to his wounded military secretary, Lord Fitzroy-Somerset, that: 'I have never fought such a battle, and I trust I shall never fight such another.'[1] Although this was to be the Duke's last campaign, he would live to read of equally bloody encounters in which British troops fought using very similar uniforms, tactics and weapons to those at Waterloo.

The military thinking and tactics of the Napoleonic era were to dominate for the next three decades or more. Young British officers present at Waterloo were not to command large formations of British troops in action again until the Anglo-Sikh Wars of the late 1840s. It was in these conflicts that the folly of outdated tactics, now made antiquated by improved weaponry, were evident in the exceptionally high battlefield casualties. Yet, despite these high numbers of fatalities and injuries, many of those senior British officers failed to comprehend that the battlefield formation of two lines of infantry firing volleys of barely aimed musket fire proceeded by frontal bayonet attacks had to be modified and perhaps even abandoned. In addition, few commanders realised that the weaponry then available constrained their battlefield options.

D.F. Harding has even claimed that a 'Wellington doctrine' existed amongst the seasoned British veterans that 'the sooner British infantry were allowed to close with the bayonet, the sooner the action would be won . . .'.[2] In his 1903 autobiography, Field Marshal Viscount Garnet Wolseley wrote of this doctrine:

> He [The Duke of Wellington] believed in the volley delivered at close quarters, and quickly followed by the bayonet charge, in which the superiority of the British soldier was instantly apparent. It was a mode of fighting peculiar to us, and had won many a victory for England. Our military histories had taught us to believe in 'Brown Bess' as the soldier's fetish. With a bayonet fixed, it became the clumsy pike with which we had so often charged and overthrown Napoleon's finest legions, and, above all things, it was believed to be the weapon best calculated to develop the hand-to-hand fighting qualities and spirit of our men.[3]

By the 1840s the chief advocate of such Napoleonic tactics was General Sir Hugh Gough (1779–1869), who commanded British and East Indian Company Forces throughout the First Anglo-Sikh War. Gough's battlefield mentality was clearly seen in his early bloody encounters during the Peninsula War (1809–14). His reckless bravery, for which he was to become so renowned, was demonstrated at the battles of Talavera (23 July 1809), Barrosa (5 March 1811) and Vittoria (21 June 1813). However, it was at Tarifa, where he was in command of the besieged British garrison, that Gough's willingness to order the bayonet was amply demonstrated. On 29 December 1811, French forces breached the city's walls. Gough commanded the regimental band of the 87th Prince of Wales' Own Irish Regiment to strike up 'Garry Owen' and screamed to his men, 'Whenever there is an opportunity, the bayonet must be used.'[4] In a brief, intensely fierce action, the British bayonets were put to hard work and the French were beaten back. Throughout the remainder of his long career, Gough was never reluctant to repeat such an order. Indeed, Gough was convinced that the eventual issue of every battle 'must be brought to the arbitrament of musketry and the bayonet'.[5]

The brief First Anglo-Sikh War was, arguably, both one of the bloodiest and most intriguing of Victoria's reign. The conflict can be said to have started with the Sikh Army, the Khalsa, crossing the Sutlej River on 11 December 1845 and was formally ended by the Treaty of Lahore on 9 March 1846. The roots of the war can be firmly traced back to the unification of Sikh confederacies of north-west India into a single Sikh state under the leadership of Ranjit Singh (1780–1839). By the turn of the nineteenth century the British East Indian Company, with its military forces, comprising both British and native Indian units, had gained territorial control of all of India, with the exception of the Punjab, Kashmir and Sind. Within these regions, after years of Afghan domination, Ranjit Singh rose, from a list of several contenders, to prominence through a combination of cunning, guile, bribery and ruthless ambition. In numerous small-scale engagements, the Afghan yoke was overthrown and Ranjit exerted his own authority over a loose confederation of Sikhs.

Conscious of his own perilous position, Ranjit determined upon a two-pronged course of action. Whilst acting ruthlessly against his internal rivals, he knew that, militarily, the Sikhs were ill-prepared to withstand an assault upon them by the massed organisation and forces of the East India Company. Ranjit thus agreed a pact of non-aggression with the British in a treaty signed at Amritsar in 1809. This treaty accepted British suzerainty south of the Sutlej River, including the Sikh states of Cis-Sutlej, but crucially allowed Ranjit to form a single unified Sikh state to the north of the Sutlej River. In the intervening thirty year period before his death in 1839, Ranjit, without the threat of British intervention, was able to consolidate his own position, and that of the fledgling state, in a number of military victories which eliminated all Afghan influence over the Punjab. The Sikh kingdom expanded from Tibet in the east to Kashmir in the west and from Sind in the south to the Khyber Pass in the north, an area of 200,000 square miles.

At the heart of Ranjit's success was the Sikh Army, the Khalsa. Using the Khalsa as a tool to promote his own authority, to unite the Sikh states, and to conquer and protect, Ranjit reorganised the army away from its dependence on ill-disciplined cavalry formations to a strong core of well-drilled, trained infantry regiments, supported by powerful, professional artillery. Organised and drilled in European techniques, the Khalsa became a formidable force which, by the time of Ranjit's death, numbered 47,000 regular infantry and around 16,000 cavalry, supported by nearly 500 guns.

Ranjit's death left a power vacuum in which a state of anarchy prevailed. The Khalsa quickly appreciated that their inherent strength made them the arbiter of power and, as one newly appointed ruler after another fell at the hands of assassins, the Khalsa, via its military committees, which were elected by the common soldier, gained more say in the running of the country. Each new nominal head of the Sikh nation had to pay ever increasing bribes to the Khalsa to ensure its support, only to be discarded when a more ambitious individual promised more. Such a situation prevailed until September 1845, when the Khalsa brutally murdered Vizier, or Prime Minister, Jowahir Singh, the brother of the Queen Regent Maharani Jinden (1817–63), mother of the young Maharajah, Dhulip Singh (1838–93). This act was to bring to the fore two individuals who both feared and despised the Khalsa, Lal Singh (d. 1866) and Tej Singh (1799–1862).

Following the death of her brother, Maharani Jinden appointed Lal Singh as the new Prime Minister. Apparently, Lal's only qualification for this important and dangerous position was that he was the Maharani's lover. Tej Singh was persuaded to accept the poisoned chalice that was Commander-in-Chief of the Khalsa, whilst in Kashmir power rested with Gulab Singh and his private army of 10,000 men.

Across the Sutlej River, the British administration, headed by the Governor-General Sir Henry Hardinge (1785–1856), with Sir Hugh Gough as Commander-in-Chief, viewed the chaos of the Sikh state with both apprehension and with an eye on a potential prize. The local British political agent, Major George Broadfoot (1807–45), supplied Hardinge with regular reports of the situation within the Sikh kingdom and was also able to establish clandestine links with Tej Singh and Lal Singh, both of whom clearly feared for their own wellbeing. The chain of invincibility that had surrounded British forces in India had been weakened by the British military humiliation during the retreat from Kabul in 1842, which had given some in the Khalsa the belief that they too could inflict a similar crushing defeat upon the British. In addition, border clashes along the banks of the Sutlej River, particularly Broadfoot's unilateral seizure of two villages near Ludhiana for the British under the weakest of pretences, enflamed a fragile situation. Although the British were beginning to believe that war with the Sikh kingdom was inevitable, it seems there was a belief, from the Governor-General down, that war would be fought at a time of British choosing. This view was clearly reflected in the disposition of British troops along the Sutlej frontier where the number of soldiers rose from 2,500 men, in 1836, to 14,000 strong, in 1843.[6]

As the year 1845 entered its final months it was clear to the British, via reports from Broadfoot and his assistant Captain Joseph Cunningham

(1812–51), that the Sikh Army had become a law unto itself, with the Sikh leadership having only nominal control. The Sikh state became weakened by the rampaging acts of the Sikh Army; soldiers robbed, looted and extracted money from the general population, leaving it unable to pay taxes to state officials. In turn the court's coffers diminished to such an extent that the army could not be paid, which further increased the army's riotous behaviour. To the likes of Lal and Tej Singh, the safety of British rule seemed the only way to escape the lawlessness and killing that was running rife within the state and the complete destruction of the Khalsa became the target and ambition of these men.

Thus the First Anglo-Sikh War was to be one of the most politically intriguing of all of Victoria's war, for those in nominal command of the Sikh Army did everything in their power to contrive its destruction and provide the British with as much intelligence as to its movements as possible. As early as March 1845, Gulab Singh confided to Major Broadfoot of his hopes that the British would invade the Punjab and he even offered his own troops to assist them. By November, it was decided by the ruling clique of Lal and Tej Singh that the army must be led to war against the British, not to conquer, but to be annihilated. The thought of war was met with enthusiasm by the Khalsa, whose soldiery had a firm belief that they would be victorious and, perhaps, their victory might even see the end of British rule in India. Even though the British were rapidly becoming aware of the likelihood of war, their preparations were far from complete. Lal and Tej Singh thus conspired to ensure that if any opportunities for victory were presented to the Khalsa, they would do everything in their power to restrain the army.

Once the Khalsa had crossed the Sutlej, the army was to be kept in a defensive posture, so as to allow the British to converge its own strength from across the numerous garrisons of northern India. The campaign was to be hampered as much as possible, short of raising the suspicions of the common soldier. Both food and ammunition would only be sent fitfully from Lahore, and the Sikh Army was only to be used on the defensive. Furthermore, communication channels, already opened between the British and Tej and Lal Singh, would be maintained and as much intelligence as to Sikh battle plans, details of defensive entrenchments and movement of Sikh forces would be provided as possible. Despite all the help given by this intrigue, the Sikh Army was to offer a stern and sobering test to the British forces that were entrusted with its destruction.

Throughout the First Anglo-Sikh War Gough was judged harshly by many of his contemporaries, in both Britain and India, who were shocked by high British casualties. Some later historians, such as Donald Featherstone, also viewed Gough as an unimaginative commander, who was too quick to resort to the use of the bayonet charge to carry an enemy position. However, these opinions miss several crucial points. First, the Sikhs were a highly trained and skilled professional force, who were both brave and confident of their own abilities and were thus resolute in battle. To defeat such a foe the British would most certainly have endured considerable battlefield casualties, whatever the tactics employed. Second, for political reasons, it was vital that the Khalsa was utterly defeated in battle and this meant that wherever Gough located the enemy he felt obliged to attack. British flanking movements might allow the Sikh forces to evade battle and thus Gough always favoured the direct assault. Finally, and crucially, Gough would have been fully aware of the deficiencies of British arms, both musket and cannon, which meant that a close-action engagement, in which the bayonet would be decisive, was inevitable.

The British flintlock muskets of the Napoleonic period were known by the generic name of 'Brown Bess', although the proper title is that of the Baker rifle, which saw service from 1800 to the 1840s. This smoothbored weapon, designed by London weapons maker Ezekiel Baker, had a limited range of 100m and was wildly inaccurate, prone to misfire and slow to use, two to three shots per minute in combat being the average. Although the Baker rifle was highly regarded by the crack shots of Corps of Riflemen (later to become the Rifle Brigade), its deficiencies were not so well understood by troops of the Line and mass production of this rifle saw a falling of standards across its component parts which further highlighted the rifle's failings.[7]

The major advance in musket technology was the adoption of the percussion system of ignition. This development saw the ignition of the charge within the barrel by the fall of a hammer upon a percussion cap, which was simply a small copper cylinder lined with fulminating matter, stamped into the approximate shape of a top hat. This set fire to the charge by a flash through a hollow nipple. Such a system removed the need for priming, thus making the process of loading shorter and more reliable. A percussion lock was first patented by the Revd Alexander Forsyth in 1807, but the end of the Napoleonic conflict, combined with the need for economy, meant that this new improvement was not adopted for military use until the late 1830s. Comparative trials at Woolwich in 1834 between flint and percussion locks clearly showed the advantages of percussion, with the Brunswick rifle demonstrating its accuracy over all other types.

With percussion, many of the dangerous disadvantages of the flintlock disappeared; for example, gone was the need to regularly change the flint or adjust its size or shape, as was the problem of how much powder went into the pan and how much into the barrel and gone also was the ever-present danger of personal injury from a misfire.[8] From the Woolwich trials, the flintlock was shown to misfire every 6½ shots, whilst the percussion misfired, on average, 1 in 166 shots. With percussion ignition the soldier had only to make sure he pressed the copper cap firmly in place on the nipple, to be virtually certain that his musket would fire. The percussion was demonstrated to be faster to load and also marginally more accurate.

The Brunswick rifle acquired its name from a design by Captain Berners of the army of the German state of Brunswick. Berners' ideas were improved upon by George Lovell in 1831 and, following the successful Woolwich trials of 1834, the Board of Ordnance made the decision to re-equip the army with this new percussion arm known officially as 'Lovell's Improved Brunswick Rifle.' Its barrel of 98cm in length had two rifling grooves and fired a very distinctive 'belted ball', a bullet with a raised rib around it, which fitted into and gripped the deep rifling.[9] Rifling of the barrel, simply put, meant that the barrel was made with two, or more, tiny grooves along its length. On firing, the belted ball would grip this rifling which would result in it spinning from the barrel. This effect improved the accuracy of the rifle.

Although the Brunswick rifle went into large-scale production in 1837, the issuing of the new weapon across the British Army was to be a lengthy and somewhat complicated process that was hampered by a disastrous fire at the Tower of London, in 1841, which destroyed many thousands of flintlock muskets that were awaiting conversion to percussion. Pattern 1838 was made entirely as a new arm, with no converted parts being employed, whilst Pattern 1839 was a conversion from flintlock musket parts and this Pattern was generally lower in quality than the new percussion production muskets. However, an acute shortage of arms resulted in many of this Pattern 1839 remaining on issue to Line Regiments for almost twenty years. A new series of arms, Pattern 1842, the last smooth-bore Line Regiment musket in the British Army, had to be manufactured afresh and this delayed the universal adoption of the percussion musket across the British Army until the late 1840s.[10] Indeed, it was not uncommon for the same regiments to carry a mixture of both flintlock and percussion muskets, as was seen during the Sikh conflicts and in South Africa in 1846, when the 27th Foot saw action with both variants. However, it seems clear that all of her Majesty's regiments engaged during the First Anglo-Sikh War were issued with the 1839 Pattern percussion musket, although the East Indian Company Regiments largely carried flintlocks.[11]

For all the improvements offered by percussion, such as easier and faster loading with a corresponding increase in the rate of fire, the smooth-bored musket's range improved little. An effective range of just 150m hardly altered the complexities of Anglo-Sikh War battlefields. There was an improvement in accuracy between the two variants. Again, Harding has shown, in data taken from East Indian Company trials, that at a distance of 120yd the average percentage of hits for the percussion musket was 25 per cent as opposed to 19 per cent for flintlock.[12]

However, this improvement was somewhat offset by increased difficulty in loading the weapon; a mallet had to be frequently used to knock down the bullet with the ramrod, and mallets were indeed issued to troops for this purpose. The use of the mallet frequently distorted the ball, thus increasing the propensity for fouling. Furthermore, the Two-Grooved rifles possessed higher incidences of fouling, even after just four or five shots, which meant the rifle had to be cleaned, something that was clearly impractical in the heat of battle, before firing could be resumed. Again, Harding has shown that in addition to these inherent problems, Gough's army was largely issued with unsuitable ammunition, which was mistakenly loaded bare, without the use of patches of material to ease its projection along the barrel when fired.[13] This error further compounded the problem of fouling to such a degree that the Two-Grooved rifles soon became useless in battlefield conditions.

This issue was first brought to light at the Battle of Ferozshah, as described in the following memorandum:

> The circumstance which give rise to this correspondence, was the failure of those Rifles at the Battle of Ferozshah, as they had been found during this action almost impossible to load after the 5th or 6th round, by the whole of the Rifle Companies engaged, the Ball jamming in the bore of the piece & entirely destroying the confidence of the men in the weapon . . .[14]

The Nusseree Rifle Battalion of Ghurkhas was fully equipped with the Two-Grooved rifle before the start of the campaign and it is clear that the problems with the rifle were well known to its troops:

> The impossibility of loading the rifles issued to the Nusseree Rifle Corps with the cartridges, as issued from the Magazine,

the great difficulty experienced in forcing the ball down, even during the first four rounds, when detached from its paper casing, and the almost utter impracticability of ramming it down at all, after a half a dozen shots had been fired, were facts ascertained before the Corps left Jutog to join the Army of the Sutlej in December 1845.[15]

The awareness that fouling was a significant problem after a mere four or five shots was not generally known until the Battle of Ferozshah as there existed the widespread practice of only firing two or three shots during each training session for the principle was 'little and often'.[16] These inherent difficulties with the Two-Grooved rifle resulted in their withdrawal from the rifle companies, including the Nusseree Battalion, by instructions dated 10 and 19 January 1846.[17] As the change was immediate, it would seem that all rifle units were using the smooth-bore percussion muskets at the Battle of Sobroan. Clearly with such inaccurate or faulty rifles, the tactical requirement of having to close with the enemy, to use the bayonet, still remained.

The Sikh Army was largely armed with flintlock muskets, resembling the old 'Brown Bess', which were plagued with misfiring problems and had a similar range to the British weapons. In addition, Ranjit Singh purchased small numbers of muskets from the British and had them copied in his own workshops in Lahore, Amritsar and Kotli Lorahan. Both British and Sikh weapons fired a soft lead ball about 0.68in in diameter at a relatively low velocity. Upon impact the ball would spread, shattering bones and leaving a large hole in anyone unlucky enough to be hit. Such wounds were often fatal, but if not, the unfortunate soldier would be incapacitated. The amputation of shattered limbs was a common practice, which, combined with blood loss and medical ignorance, often resulted in death. Whilst the Sikhs and the British had some parity in musketry, the Sikhs excelled over the British in the efficiency and accuracy of their artillery.

Up until the 1860s, the artillery pieces employed by the British Army were smooth-bore muzzle loaders, which had altered little since 1815. The standard equipment of both the British and Indian Horse Artilleries was the light 6pdr gun and it was this that saw constant service throughout the Sikh wars. The calibre of these pieces was 3.6in and each weighed 6cwt. With the standard allowance of forty-six rounds, together with limber and carriage, the weight pulled by the team of four horses was over 27cwt. A common feature of these conflicts was the sight of the Horse Artillery galloping through a storm of fire unleashed upon them by the superior and heavier Sikh artillery. Gunners of the 6pdr had to gallop into close quarters with the enemy. Once engaged the crew could hope to unleash round shot or case into ranks of the enemy infantry, who were often only a few hundred yards away. Until the enemy infantry came within musket range or the Sikh artillery focused their muzzles on the British the gunners were comparatively safe. Once in enemy musket range the Horse Artillery would retreat to a safe distance to repeat the deadly process. These 6pdrs had a range, firing round shot, of up to 1,200yd, and up to 300yd firing case shot, with a muzzle velocity of between 1,500 and 1,700ft per second. Whilst an experienced light gun crew could be expected to fire eight rounds per minute, in practice, under battlefield conditions of smoke and sheer terror, three was more likely. Featherstone has described the British artillery, up until the 1860s, as 'little more than musketry of greater calibre and longer range'.[18] The British, particularly in the later stages of the First Anglo-Sikh War, were able to deploy 18pdrs (range 2,000yd) and 8in howitzers (range 1,700yd) as heavy field artillery, rather than in their normal roll of siege weapons. However, there is little evidence that these heavier pieces were particularly effective against the entrenched Sikh positions.

In contrast, the former Sikh leader, Ranjit Singh, in his successful attempts at increasing the military effectiveness of his army, placed great emphasis on the development of artillery. By the late 1820s, the Sikh Army had attracted several European mercenaries, many of whom were veterans of the Napoleonic Wars. With high rates of pay, opulent living quarters and unprecedented levels of power and prestige, it is easy to see what drew such men as Jean Francois Allard, Jean Baptiste Ventura, Paolo de Avitabile and Henri Court to serve in the Sikh Army. The four were the most prominent of Ranjit Singh's advisors and the Sikh ruler came to rely upon this quartet, preferring to trust these foreigners over his local commanders. Both Allard and Ventura were influential in developing a complete infantry training manual for the Sikh Army and Avitabile established a most formidable regiment named in his honour, as well as overseeing the introduction of a limited number of percussion muskets into Sikh service. However, of this famous quartet, it was Henri Court who played the most significant role. Court had been educated at the French Military Polytechnic, where he specialised in ordnance. He personally supervised the casting of many artillery pieces at the Lahore foundry as well as training the Sikhs as gunners, alongside another European instructor named Gardener.

The Sikh artillery throughout the First Anglo-Sikh war was the mainstay of the army and the professionalism, fortitude and bravery displayed by the Sikh gun crews, who worshipped their guns and could be relied upon to protect them with their lives, was much admired by their British adversaries. Following Court's lead, the gunners were trained completely to the old French Napoleonic system, with commands in French. The gunners were instructed how to lay, aim, prime and fire a gun, both at the walk and at the double, and drill lessons and tactical training were given a high priority. The introduction of firing ranges, allowing the artillerymen to gain considerable experience of actually firing their guns, all added to the skill and professionalism of the force.

In both cannon and howitzers, the Sikh ordnance factories produced brass pieces in much greater number and far heavier than the British; the Sikh 42pdrs, 32pdrs, 18pdrs all had a range in excess of the British pieces. Furthermore, even when the two opponents had artillery of an equal calibre and quality of manufacture, the Sikh weapons were far weightier in metal and could thus fire a larger charge of powder, allowing for greater range. It was said that a Sikh 4pdr was as heavy as a British 6pdr. The commander of British artillery during the First Anglo-Sikh War, Brigadier Gowan, endeavoured to rectify the British inferiority in the weight of the gun metal by enlarging the bores of the 9pdrs into 12, but the number of such pieces never exceeded sixty. The Sikhs prided themselves on producing heavy artillery pieces which often required forty or more buffalo to draw them along. Such weapons were often given names, such as 'Fatch-Jang' (victor of battle), and were covered in rich engraving and Persian inscriptions, often in verse. Such an approach added to the loyalty the Sikh gunners felt towards their charges. The Sikhs also employed numerous zamboorak, which were small canon mounted on a swivel and either carried on the back of a camel or mounted upon defences, which, when firing grapeshot, could be deadly against advancing infantry. Early difficulties in producing quality shells, shot and gunpowder were overcome with the employment of yet another mercenary, a Hungarian named Dr Martin Honigberger, who superintended the powder mill and gun foundry in Lahore. He was also responsible for creating a hangover cure for Ranjit Singh, which was, apparently, regularly consumed! By the time of Ranjit's death on 27 June 1839, the formidable Sikh artillery comprised nearly 500 guns.

Gough did possess one distinct advantage over the Sikhs and that was in the superiority of his cavalry force. Time and time again throughout the conflict the British cavalry was able to rout its Sikh counterpart and indeed the Sikh cavalry failed to distinguish itself in any of the engagements. However, when it came to neutralising the fire of the Sikh artillery, or to dislodging the stubborn resistance of the Sikh infantry, the British cavalry was less effective. Although the 16th Lancers and 3rd Light Cavalry took part in a glorious charge against the enemy infantry at the Battle of Aliwal (28 January 1846), their success has to be qualified. At the sight of the British advance, the highly disciplined Avitabile regiment formed a defensive square and, although the British were able to charge through, it remained an unbroken formation despite three attempts to break it. This Sikh regiment was able to retreat from the battlefield in good order. George Denham-Cookes, of the 3rd Light Dragoons, was present at Aliwal and wrote, almost romantically, that it was 'a beautiful sight to see the steady way the division marched forward, never hesitating as the enemy's shot tore great rents in their columns'.[19] Of course, such words do not hide the fact that the cavalry paid a high price for its bravery. Of the nearly 600 British casualties at Aliwal over 42 per cent were from the cavalry, reflecting the bloody consequences of charging disciplined infantry. This figure included Sergeant Harry Newsome, who forced his mount over the front rank of kneeling Sikhs and into the square. Here his body was later discovered with nineteen bayonet wounds.[20]

The British commander was forced to ask his troops time and time again to close with the enemy. Inferior artillery, the inability of cavalry to dislodge infantry and the limited range of the muskets then available all meant that Gough had little choice, if he wished to silence the enemy's effective artillery, but to engage at close quarters with his adversaries and quickly. It was these factors, and limitations, that defined the British tactics throughout the set-piece battles of the First Anglo-Sikh War, rather than any inherent inability on the part of the British commander. However, this is not to say that Gough was without fault as will be clearly shown in a summary of the campaign.

Despite Lal and Tej Singh's clear desire to assist the British in any way possible, the war, with the men and equipment available to the British, was always going to be a stern test for Gough and his troops. From the moment the Khalsa crossed the Sutlej River, on 11 December 1845, the Sikh Army possessed great advantages. Not only were they superior in artillery to the British, but the Sikh forces had a distinct numerical edge. Over 100,000 men now comprised the Sikh Army, including nearly 54,000 regular, well-trained infantry, over 20,000 horsemen and nearly 11,000 professional artillerymen. The best estimate is that 35–40,000 men, supported by 150 guns, crossed the Sutlej in the initial advance. By 18 December Lal Singh had supplied Captain Peter Nicolson, the assistant British political agent at Ferozepur, with detailed troop figures which seem to have supported this estimate.[21] In contrast, the British, in isolated garrisons, had much weaker forces with which to confront the invasion. Major General Littler, based at Ferozepur, had a garrision of 7,000 men and 12 guns, but of this figure only one regiment, HM 62nd Foot, was European and could be expected to offer a stubborn resistance. Similarly, the garrison town of Phillaur, near Ludhiana, had a contingent of 5,000 men, under the command of Brigadier H. Wheeler, but again only one regiment, HM 50th, was European. A rapid movement against these weak and isolated British bases would surely have met with a decisive victory.

However, military success was not what Tej and Lal Singh desired. Thus, instead of concentrating their superior forces, on crossing the Sutlej the Sikh Army was split into three separate arms. The main force, under the command of Lal Singh, was held at the village of Ferozeshah, close to the British garrison at Ferozepur. Here, Tej Singh laid a nominal siege to the British. A further Sikh army, under the command of Ranjodh Singh, was sent to Ludhiana to oppose the small British force there. Thus, as Gough journeyed north, to combine with the units at Ferozepur and Ludhiana, bringing the British force to a strength of 22,000 men, he knew, from intelligence supplied by Tej Singh, that he would not face the entire Sikh Army in battle and that it might be possible to defeat each unit in piecemeal actions. Gough's major concern was that, despite the best efforts of the contriving Sikh leadership, the Khalsa would grow impatient and attack the isolated garrisons before he could arrive with the bulk of the British force. With this thought in mind, Gough ordered a series of forced marches north and by 17 December the British were approaching Mudki.

News of Gough's hurried advance reached Lal Singh on 17 December and he ordered a relatively small contingent of the Khalsa, with few artillery pieces, south to oppose the British. Lal Singh struggled to dampen disquiet amongst the army that the Sikh force was not large enough to defeat Gough's army and this deficient force reached Mudki by midday on 18 December. Gough's main body reached the vicinity in the late afternoon, and his exhausted, thirsty and hungry troops collapsed near the outskirts of the village and began to prepare a camp. Here the thick jungle, and nature of the terrain, meant that neither army could clearly see each other's position. Only clouds of dust, raised by the movement of both cavalry and infantry, betrayed the relative locations of the opposing forces. Sikh and British skirmishers clashed, but offered no clarification as to the exact whereabouts of each army. In this confused situation, Gough acted impulsively; despite the exhausted state of his troops, the lack of firm knowledge as to what forces opposed him and the late hour, with darkness rapidly approaching, he decided upon battle.

Lal Singh's duplicity had ensured that the Sikhs were outnumbered by the British in both infantry and artillery. The Sikh commander fled the battlefield as soon as the battle commenced. Crucially only twenty-two Sikh guns took part in the engagement and although they were served well, and inflicted considerable damage, the superiority in British numbers was the deciding factor. The British cavalry routed their Sikh counterparts, allowing a general advance of the British infantry against a mere 3,000 Sikh troops. The jungle terrain and dark conditions meant that the battle was particularly vicious and terrifying, with both forces resorting to the bayonet in close combat. The battle raged from 4pm until midnight, when the superior weight of the British infantry finally dislodged the tenacious Sikhs from the battlefield, capturing seventeen Sikh guns. Both sides suffered similar casualties; the Sikh losses were estimated at around 300 dead, many of them artillerymen who had stood to the last by their guns, whilst the British claimed 215 fatalities and 657 wounded. There is little doubt that this battle should not have been fought so late, just as the light of the day was on the wane. Gough's impulsiveness at charging his force into a jungle battle in the darkness of the night resulted in unnecessary casualties and only superiority in numbers had won the day for the British. Gough expressed concern at the reluctance of the Company's native troops to engage in close combat with the Sikhs.

After a brief period of rest, Gough moved his force further north, so as to make a juncture with Littler's garrison at Ferozepur. Aware, again from compliant Sikh intelligence, of the position of Lal Singh's forces at Ferozeshah, Gough marched his army to within striking distance and instructed Littler to march his troops out at Ferozepur, under the noses of Tej Singh's men, to join him in an attack at Ferozeshah. Lal Singh secretly informed the British of the weakness of his own defensive position and even told them that the northern stretch of the Sikh camp had been left undefended. However, Gough chose to ignore this information and decided upon a frontal attack on the southern defences. It appears that Gough was dubious about Tej Singh's loyalty and feared that the delay caused by a flanking movement, so as to allow an attack on the northern side of Lal Singh's position, would leave the British vulnerable to an attack from Tej Singh, whose force was just 14km away. Gough clearly felt that if a quick victory could be won at Ferozeshah then he could eliminate the risk of the two Sikh armies joining forces. So confident was he that such a victory could be attained that he, again impulsively, urged an attack upon Lal Singh even before Littler's force had joined him. Such a move was overruled by the Governor-General, Hardinge, who, although second in command to Gough, exerted his political authority over his excitable commander.

Littler's men, after an exhausting forced march, finally made juncture with Gough's force at around 2pm on 21 December 1845, adding 5,000 men to the total of 18,000. This figure comprised 5,674 European troops and 12,053 Indian troops. The British had seventy-one artillery pieces, although most were the small 6pdr horse artillery. At the sight of Littler's approaching troops, Hardinge was reported to have given Gough permission to attack, with the words, 'Now the army is at your disposal.'[22] By the time the combined force had been assembled into battle order it was 4pm and, once more, the British would be attacking a resolute foe in the dark.

Gough's force was opposed by 103 guns, many of heavy calibre, including some 62pdrs, and approximately 25,000 troops. The initiative rested with Gough for he could launch his attack upon the Sikh entrenchments at any point in its 4km perimeter. However, Gough decided to concentrate his attack on the southern defences, hoping to bring greater numbers to bear on one specific spot and here outnumber the Sikh defenders. Unfortunately, it was just at this spot that Lal Singh had decided to place the largest number of guns.

The battle began with an opening exchange of mortar and cannon fire and the Sikh gunners soon established the superiority of their weapons and training. With heavier calibre guns and further range, the Sikh gunners unleashed round shot upon the British guns at a typical rate of fire of three Sikh shots for every two British. Furthermore, the Sikh fire proved to be more accurate and soon began to take a toll as more and more British guns were destroyed or disabled. Colonel Robertson later wrote, 'most of them [British guns] were smashed; and dead horses and broken limbers were lying about, having been completely outmatched by the heavier artillery of the Sikhs'.[23] After a 2-hour artillery duel, in which the British had been outgunned, Gough was left with no alternative but to order an infantry advance against the Sikh positions.

Gough ordered the British left, under the command of Littler, to advance on the south-west face of the camp. As the troops got to within 150yd, the Sikh gunners, with double chargers of grapeshot from their heavy guns, unleashed carnage upon the British line. The 62nd Regiment was particularly hard hit, as described by Robert Haviland, one of the few survivors of the advance, 'the Sikhs opened such a fire of grape that our men fell like rain in perfect rows on the ground'.[24] Haviland lost 281 of his comrades killed, with 18 officers killed or wounded from this one British regiment. The advance of the British left, in the face of both grapeshot and disciplined musket volleys, stalled, faltered and then retreated.

With the repulse of the left, Gough immediately ordered an attack by the stronger British right against the south-eastern corner and weaker east face of the Sikh position. Here the British had some success and were able to penetrate the Sikh lines. An attack by 416 officers and men of the 3rd Light Dragoons against the lightly defended north-eastern perimeter also met with initial success. However, once in the Sikh camp the British troopers met tenacious resistance from the Sikh infantry and were forced to withdraw, having lost approximately two-thirds of their strength. Although British infantry were now inside the Sikh position, the Sikh line still held, and despite all British reserves being thrown in, was only slowly pushed back. After 5 hours of hand-to-hand fighting, darkness had fully descended and in the confusion British units lost all cohesion. The Sikhs, having maintained their will to fight, and, despite Lal Singh's protestations, rallied and launched a counterattack which gradually recaptured the southern end of the camp. Realising that his men were hard-pressed, Gough ordered a somewhat chaotic retreat to a point 400yd south of the camp, where a defensive position was established. By 1am on the morning of 22 December the Sikhs had completely reoccupied their entrenchments and were now awaiting the order to advance upon the exhausted British.

Gough's situation was most desperate. Although a defensive square had been formed, there was little order. Regiments were mixed together, with many officers dead or wounded. The artillery had been effectively destroyed, only the British cavalry maintained some sort of cohesion. In the darkness little could be done to restore order and the troops were simply told to get some rest. Gough and Hardinge spent most of the remaining night discussing their perilous situation; several of the senior officers urged a retreat for not only were the troops exhausted, there was no food or water available, and very limited amounts of ammunition both for the British muskets and the few surviving artillery pieces. However, for political reasons both men could not countenance a withdrawal which would have been viewed by all as a defeat and a huge loss to British prestige. There were wider implications to consider; with most of the European forces concentrating towards the Sutlej there were few available to quell any potential uprising elsewhere in India that might result from a British reversal. Surrender too, for similar reasons, could not be contemplated. Thus, both Gough and Hardinge resolved that the only option was to remain and fight. Hardinge, however, ordered that state papers should be burnt to save them from reaching enemy hands.

The Sikhs were simply waiting for the sunrise which would allow their artillery to pound the British defensive position. They were unaware of the arguments that were flowing through the Sikh command. Questions were raised as to why hadn't the Sikh cavalry be ordered to attack the retreating British, and also why hadn't the order been given for a general advance upon the weak British position, and where was Tej Singh's force? In this atmosphere of recrimination and distrust, Lal Singh used all his powers of persuasion to convince his followers that it was their position that was weak and that the Sikh Army should withdraw from the field. Amazingly, Lal Singh was largely successful and, as the British contemplated their fate, the Sikh Army slipped away unnoticed. Only a small, but defiant, group refused to accept Lal Singh's orders and these brave men, several hundred strong, prepared themselves for a British attack.

Unaware of the night's intrigues, Gough assembled his depleted force at sunrise and resolved to advance once more, rather than wait to be blasted by Sikh artillery. Gough leading the left wing, and Hardinge the right, gave the order to use only the bayonet, for ammunition reserves were too low to permit long-range musketry. Expecting at any moment to receive a barrage of fire from the Sikh line, the British were amazed to discover that the enemy had largely withdrawn. The remaining Sikhs fought bitterly to the end, receiving no quarter from the British troops.

All British order now collapsed as the survivors sought out the sustenance which they had been denied for so long. No picquets were placed to give advanced warning and the first Gough knew of the advance of Tej Singh's army from Ferozepur was when a large dust cloud appeared to the west. Readying his exhausted troops as best he could, Gough could only assume that Tej Singh had changed his loyalty and that he had brought his army to finally destroy the British force.

The Sikhs unleashed a furious cannonade which forced the British out from their defensive square to seek cover where they could. With his artillery spent and infantry exhausted, Gough could not even order a general advance upon the Sikh guns. His only option was to order a feint to the left by the remnants of the 3rd Light Dragoons in the hope of drawing off some of the Sikh fire. To the amazement of the British this movement seemed to precipitate a general retreat of Tej Singh's army from the battlefield. This was surrounded by controversy at the time and there remains no clear answer as to why Tej Singh made such a decision. The British feint might have been interpreted as a flanking movement and there is some evidence to suggest that Tej Singh believed that the British cavalry were attempting to rendezvous with a force of artillery sent from Ferozepur and attack his army to the rear. Alternatively, the day, to a highly suspicious Tej Singh, was considered inauspicious for a battle. However, it can also be argued that Tej Singh was simply acting to save the British force so that it could be used another day to destroy the Khalsa. Whatever the reasons behind the withdrawal, Tej Singh managed to convince his disunited followers to return towards the Sutlej.

Gough, Hardinge and the rest of the British force could not believe their fortune and now set about burying their 694 dead comrades. A further 1,721 were wounded, compared with around 3,000 Sikh casualties. Although the British had lost the majority of their artillery, the Sikhs had suffered too, with over seventy pieces lost or abandoned, along with vast stores of ordnance. Gough could claim a pyrrhic victory, although the high casualties began to raise questions as to his ability to command. He was unable to advance further north for his army was too crippled to continue the offensive. The force needed rest and reinforcement, both in terms of men and ordnance. The Sikh Army remained static on the Sutlej, with dwindling supplies and no new reinforcements. The troops could only watch as the British used the break in hostilities to steadily increase their strength.

With the Ferozepur theatre largely quiet, the focus of activity switched to the Sikh army of Ranjodh Singh (d. 1872) stationed at Phillaur, near Ludhiana, 90km to the east. Ranjodh Singh displayed a similar hesitance to engage the British and this area remained largely static for much of December and into early January 1846. However, a movement of the Sikh force further south from the Sutlej threatened the route of Gough's long re-supply chain. To counter this Gough despatched Lieutenant General Sir Harry Smith, with one brigade of cavalry and one of infantry, towards Ludhiana. The Sikhs were kept well informed by the local population of Smith's movements and, as the badly strung-out British force of 4,000 men and 18 guns approached the village of Bhudowal on 21 January 1846, they ran into a large Sikh force, 10,000 strong, with 40 guns, which was ready for battle. On appreciating the size and strength of his enemy, Smith decided to avoid direct contact and tried to veer south away from the Sikh force. However, the sandy nature of the terrain made progress slow and difficult, whilst the accurate fire from the Sikh artillery claimed many casualties. Mercifully, the main Sikh force did not advance to engage with the exhausted British, who were largely able to reach the sanctuary of Ludhiana. However, the baggage train was plundered by the Sikh cavalry and nearly eighty men were captured, along with seventy killed.

Although he had escaped destruction, Smith had suffered a blow and British prestige across India was again somewhat dented. Ranjodh Singh failed to follow up his success and Smith was permitted to rendezvous with troops from the small British garrisons in the area. It was to be these men, along with further reinforcements, that were to meet Ranjodh Singh's army at the Battle of Aliwal. The move that was to precipitate battle was the approach of the British siege train, armed as it was with heavy guns, designed to engage the armies of Lal and Tej Singh. Even the reluctant Ranjodh Singh could not resist such a prize and, with news of further Sikh reinforcements coming from the north, he moved his army along the southern banks of the Sutlej to the village of Aliwal, to await their arrival.

On the evening of 27 January, boats ferried the 4,000 Sikh reinforcements, including the formidable troops of the Avitabile regiment, across the Sutlej to join their comrades in the camp at Aliwal, sited with its back to the river. The British force was also reinforced and, with intelligence gained as to the Sikh position, Smith resolved to engage the enemy. On the morning of 28 January the British formed battle lines and advanced on Aliwal.

Conscious of Ranjodh Singh's earlier reticence, Smith determined that the Sikh Army was likely to be maintained in a defensive posture and he decided to attack. A resolute advance upon the lightly defended left of the Sikh camp resulted in the flight of the Sikh irregulars, and dangerously threatened to outflank the remains of the Sikh force. In the confusion Ranjodh Singh fled across the Sutlej to safety where he formed a defensive line, abandoning his resolute regulars, to face the British onslaught. On the right, the British and Sikh infantry were engaged in savage hand-to-hand fighting, whilst in the centre the

Sikh artillery, firing grapeshot, caused carnage amongst the advancing British infantry. To escape the fire the British were ordered to lie down, then repeatedly rush forward, diving down again when the artillery fire became too intense. Using such tactics, the British were finally able to charge into the Sikh centre and the bayonet was employed to push the enemy back.

Elsewhere, despite the gallant charges of the British cavalry, notably the 16th Lancers, the regular Sikh troops, with the Avitabile regiment prominent, fought on determinedly and only grudgingly gave ground. However, the disadvantage of forming a defensive line with the Sutlej at the rear now became apparent as the retreating Sikhs struggled to escape the British forces, which endeavoured to close a pincer movement along the right and left of the southern river bank. Those Sikhs who fled were shot down or blasted by cannon fire as they tried to swim to the safety of the northern shore and it was here that the majority of the Sikh casualties occurred. Smith, despite having 151 men killed, was able to claim a complete victory, which had an important, and positive, psychological effect on the local population as well as the morale of the British. Furthermore, Smith's success allowed his force to rejoin Gough's main army and permitted the safe arrival of the siege train necessary to destroy the Khalsa once and for all.

The loss of so many guns, ordnance and experienced artillery men at the Battle of Ferozeshah severely restrained the options of the Sikh Army. Combined with the fact that re-supply of both men and materials from Lahore were only fitful at best, it meant that Lal and Tej Singh were forced very much on the defensive throughout the remainder of December and the month of January 1846. Tej Singh kept overall command and the army was encamped either side of the Sutlej at Sobroan, with its back, like at Aliwal, bordering the southern banks of the river. The two separated positions were connected by a makeshift bridge of boats, which was to become a central feature in the forthcoming battle. Gough estimated that at the time of the battle the river was approximately 350yd wide. The encouraging news for the common soldiers of the Khalsa was that a veteran commander, General Sham Singh Attariwala, who had achieved earlier fame and success serving Ranjit Singh, had been persuaded to join the army at Sobroan. Here the experienced commander was entrusted by Tej Singh with the defence of the left flank of the Sikh camp.

Gough, and his men, had enjoyed the luxuries of rest, reinforcement and re-equipment and, by the end of January 1846, the British were in a position of strength and were able to consider an attack upon the Sikhs. Gough positioned his headquarters at Bootawallah, 8km immediately opposite the Sikh position at Sobroan, and awaited the siege train. Like many in the British camp, Gough was frustrated by the slow progress of the heavy cannon needed to blast away the formidable Sikh entrenchments and galled by witnessing the strengthening of the Sikh position. Between the British outposts and the Sikh earthworks was a stretch of low jungle in which General Gilbert would engage in his daily passion of pig-sticking as he hunted wild boar, uninterrupted by the Sikh picquets. The lengthy column bringing the British mortars and 18 and 24pdr siege guns finally arrived on 7 February. Thus, at last, the British felt that they had parity with the Sikh artillery. Reinforcements had also arrived in the guise of HM 9th and 16th Lancers, HM 10th Foot, two native cavalry regiments and three infantry, under the command of Sir John Grey, a total of 10,000 men. Finally, on 8 February, both the Governor-General and the victorious Smith arrived from Aliwal with his force. Gough was now in a position to consider a final attack upon the Sikhs which would drive them back across the Sutlej and destroy the power of the Khalsa.

The Sikh entrenchments had been constructed under the supervision of a Spanish mercenary named Huerba who had designed strong earthworks, with deep ditches surrounding them, in a half-circle from bank to bank. Upon the higher northern bank, thirty-six artillery pieces were positioned so that they could enfilade the eastern and western sides of the entrenchment, but also protect the vital bridge of boats across the Sutlej. The entrenchments were roughly 3km in length and the total enclosed area was just over 1km^2. Approximately seventy heavy artillery pieces were scattered throughout the encampment and, on the weakest side, the north and north-western, a line of 200 zamboorak swivel guns were placed. Here the sandy soil hindered the construction of earthworks, but, again, Tej Singh may well have deliberately kept the defences weak, for no large artillery pieces were placed here and only irregular troops manned the defences. The eastern section was built so high that only the heads and shoulders of the defenders were visible and cannon were placed so as to fire out from the earthworks The strongest part of the defences was the centre, where the earthworks had been built sufficiently high to require the use of scaling ladders. Inside the encampment, trenches and pits were dug to offer some defence if the outer lines were breached. Estimates vary as to the number of Sikh defenders on the southern shore but a figure of around 20,000 troops, largely infantry, is suggested. The need to supply the garrison daily, via the bridge of boats, would seem to preclude a higher figure. Fatally, however, the defences demonstrated a want of unity of command; each commander defended his front according to his own skill and resources and, whilst some proved to be resilient, others, once the battle had begun, were found wanting.

The two opposing armies now faced each other in what was to be the final and most decisive Battle of the First Anglo-Sikh War. Gough seems to have predetermined his battle plan in the last weeks of January as he and his force sat opposite the ever-growing Sikh position. The previous battles of Mudki and Ferozeshah would have left Gough with a healthy respect for the abilities and steadfastness of both the Sikh artillery and infantry and he would have known for sure that any kind of assault against Sobroan would prove to be costly. However, the need to speedily silence the superior Sikh artillery was, no doubt, a determining factor in Gough's decision for a frontal assault upon the entrenchments. He could only hope that his recently arrived heavy artillery would at least be able to silence some of the Sikh guns before he was forced to unleash his infantry. Furthermore, and this was impressed by Gough upon all his commanders, if the Sikhs had been foolish enough to entrench themselves with their backs to the Sutlej, then the British must take advantage of this error to destroy the Khalsa on the southern banks. The possibility of having to ford the river and then campaign on the northern side was something that the British wished to avoid at all costs, for their supply lines would be further stretched and they would be operating in a very unfriendly environment amongst a population who would have been keen to have seen their destruction.

Gough was happy that he had got the Sikh Army where he wanted it and he was now determined upon its destruction. Heavy rains in February swelled the height of the Sutlej by 7in and thus rendered any flanking movement impossible. In addition, the swollen river meant that the Sikhs could no longer use the Harike ford and Gough now knew that any reinforcements, or alternatively the possible flight of the Sikh Army, would have to utilise the vulnerable bridge of boats.

Conscious of growing alarm at the high levels of casualties throughout the campaign, the Governor-General viewed the apparently formidable Sikh entrenchments with mounting concern. Hardinge took it upon himself to consult Major Henry Lawrence (1806–57), the newly appointed Political Agent and a former artilleryman, and Major Abbot, of the Engineers, as to their opinions on whether it was practical to storm the Sikh position by an infantry advance. Both concluded that with sufficient artillery support the British could be victorious. Reassured, Hardinge wrote to Gough, on 7 February, with the words, 'if the artillery can be brought into play, I recommend to attack. If it cannot, and you anticipate a heavy loss, I would recommend you not to undertake it.'[25]

On the afternoon of 9 February, Gough summoned to his command tent all his generals of division, brigadiers and heads of various departments. Here they were told of the Commander-in-Chief's decision to launch an attack at dawn the following day. Each was informed of their precise responsibilities for the advance and all left to make ready for the coming day.

At 3am on 10 February 1846, Gough's troops were woken and ordered to assemble into battle lines. Strict silence was demanded and no drums or bugles were sounded. The soldiers were even ordered to take off the white covers of their shakos, or caps, in case these might be visible to the Sikh defenders. By 4am, in a triumph of organisation, the entire British force had moved silently into position, ringing the Sikh defences at around 800m distance. The British strength was close to 20,000 troops, similar to the enemy's. The army was divided by Gough into three divisions. Sir Harry Smith was given responsibility for the British right; Major General Walter Gilbert commanded the middle; and Sir Robert Dick, a veteran of Waterloo who had led the Black Watch against Napoleon's Old Guard, was charged with leading the initial assault of the weak Sikh northern defences, on the British left.

With questions still abounding concerning the reliability and enthusiasm of the native troops in British service, Gough was able to deploy a number of European regiments in his assault. Smith's Division, formed of two infantry brigades under Brigadiers Penny and Hicks, was composed of HM 31st Foot and HM 50th Foot, along with HM 9th Lancers and two troops of Horse Artillery. The 42nd and 47th Native Infantry, the Nusseree Gurkhas and the 2nd Irregular Cavalry completed the Division. Likewise, Gilbert's Division was divided into two brigades, under the commands of Brigadiers Taylor and Maclaran. HM 29th Foot formed the core of the infantry, alongside the 41st and 68th Native Infantry and the Sirmoor Gurkhas. Finally, on the extreme left, Dick's Division was formed into two lines for the initial advance. The first, commanded by Brigadier Stacy, was composed of HM 10th and 53rd Foot and 43rd and 59th Native Infantry. The second line, commanded by Brigadier Wilkinson, was of HM 80th Foot and 33rd and the 63rd Native Infantry, whilst the reserve, placed under Brigadier Ashburnham, consisted of HM 9th and 62nd Foot and the 26th Native Infantry. Further to the rear was Brigadier Scott's Cavalry Brigade of HM 3rd Light Dragoons and the 8th and 9th Irregular Cavalry. Further back still were the 4th, 5th and 73rd Native Infantry.

To support an assault, Gough now had 108 various artillery pieces, including 18 heavy howitzers and mortars and 6 18pdr guns. A battery of eight heavy guns was placed between Gilbert's and Smith's Division on the right whilst Gilbert was to be accompanied by No. 19 Field Battery in the centre of the line. On his left was placed a further battery of heavy guns. The British artillery was commanded by Brigadier Gowan, who, on instruction from Gough, massed nineteen out of his twenty-four heavy pieces against the south-western angle, which was to be assaulted by Dick's Division. The batteries of 6pdr horse and field artillery extended round into a semi-circle, shadowing the perimeter of the Sikh entrenchments. The larger pieces were positioned around 1,300yd from Sikh defences, with the small calibre weapons at around 800yd. The light howitzers were massed off the south-eastern angle and, in addition, a rocket battery was deployed near Smith's Division.

Gough's plans were frustrated by a heavy early morning mist, which hung over the battlefield and delayed the first British artillery salvos for 2 hours. The first hours of the day were described by Second Lieutenant Thomas Haydon, who commanded one of the mortar batteries, in a letter to his mother:

> It was a very pretty sight at that time of the morning when the mist was hanging thick over the trenches and all was

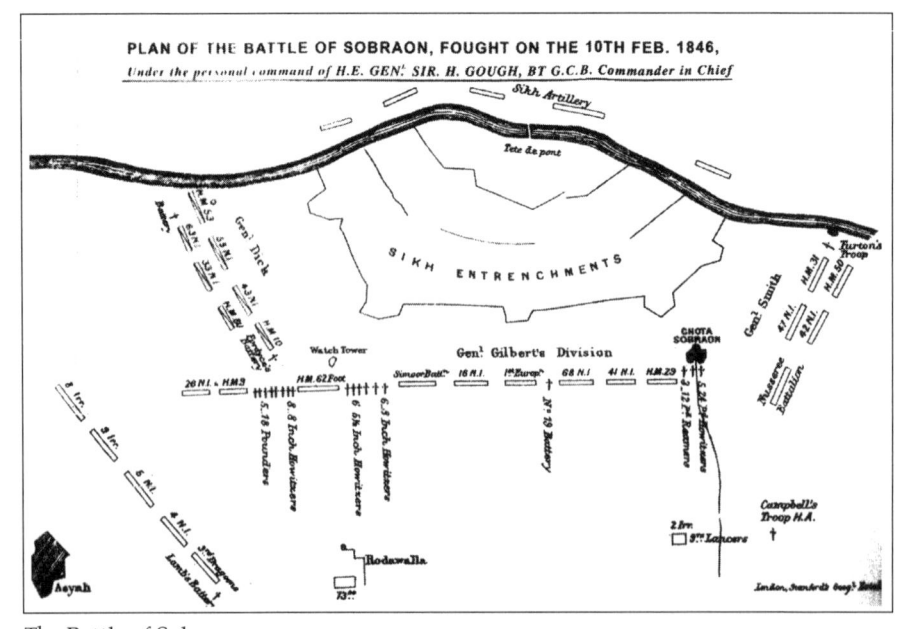

The Battle of Sobroan.

perfectly silent except just the hum of our fellows talking when we saw the flash break through the mist and heard the ring of the pieces and the whiz of the shot. Soon after that, we took our position in a small hollow when we heard the drummers and buglers of the Sikhs just as if had waken them out of their first sleep.– A Howitzer battery of our own to our left opened its fire and was returned almost immediately by the enemy. We then opened our fire, beginning regularly firing our left. . . . Well we blazed away at each other from a little after 7 till ½ past, by which time we had five men wounded in our battery, though none killed and all our ammunition expended, so we lay down under a bank which formed the front of our battery and made ourselves comfortable. The day was then beautifully clear and we could see the whole of the entrenchments from the top of this bank. It was a beautiful sight. Our batteries, heavy and light were arranged in a sort of half moon before the trenches and we were nearly in the centre, while our infantry were lying down wherever the ground afforded the best cover for them . . .[26]

The rising sun burnt through the mist and the British right first opened fire, with one of the 24pdrs. The Sikh response was almost immediate and soon a general artillery dual enveloped the battlefield, lasting for over 2 hours, until the British had exhausted their ammunition reserves for both the mortars and heavy cannon. Despite the ferocity of the cannonade, a noise louder than anything heard in India before, neither side could claim much success.[27] Certainly, the British artillery had been unable to damage either the Sikh entrenchments or silence many of their guns. Although two cannon on the north shore were destroyed, the greatest impact was upon the Sikh infantry who had been sheltering within the defensive walls. After the battle, several foxholes were found to contain thirty to forty Sikh dead, killed outright by direct hits. The British infantry, as described by Haydon, simply lay down or sought shelter in folds of ground or dry river courses or nullahs and the Sikh fire largely passed over them. The Sikhs did destroy a convoy of bullocks bringing reserve mortar ammunition forward and, according to Harry Lumsden of the 59th Bengal Native Infantry, forced the early retreat of some of the British Horse Artillery who had strayed too far forward.[28]

At around 9am the British fire began to lessen as the ammunition reserves faltered. There were some recriminations as to why the ammunition had become exhausted after just 2 hours. The artillery commander, Brigadier Gowan, received some criticism that only half the ammunition requested by Gough was brought to the battlefield and it seems certain that the commander had intended that the artillery be played upon the Sikh defences for longer than it was. The enforced silencing of the British guns resulted in a rather fanciful, and apocryphal, quotation being attributed to Gough. Apparently when news was bought that the British heavy guns would soon be silent it was reported that he responded with the line, 'Thank God! I'll be at them with the bayonet!'[29] For his troops, who loved and respected him, such a comment would have been viewed as a wholehearted invitation and something they would have expected of him. To his opponents, those who viewed Gough as an uninspiring commander with little tactical awareness, such words reinforced their worst fears.

In reality, the news of the premature silencing of the British cannonade forced Gough to act. From the observation point of a watchtower sited a few kilometres from the Sikh entrenchments, both Gough and Hardinge must have realised that the Sikh guns were still largely functioning and that the British infantry advance would be met by a hail of grapeshot and cannon shot. The battle would have to be determined by the struggle of musket and bayonet. Gough, determined on success, did not hesitate and, whilst the dwindling ammunition supply could still offer some support, he ordered Dick's Division to advance.

From the southern nullah, or ravine, where they were gaining some shelter, the Division rose and, moving to the east, headed for the northern Sikh defences. The Horse Artillery moved in front of Stacy's Brigade, and, behind Stacy, Wilkinson's troops marched 200yd further back. As the line came within 300yd of the Sikh position a body of Sikh cavalry threatened the left flank of the advance. This danger was seen off with a well-directed volley from HM 53rd Foot and the discharge of grapeshot by the Horse Artillery. Undeterred, the British marched on. With no heavy Sikh artillery to defend this area this initial advance achieved great success and drove back the Sikh irregulars, who offered little resistance. There is even a report that Stacy's men marched in 'totally unopposed with their flintlocks at their shoulders'.[30] However, other testimonies highlight the destructive power of the zamboorak swivel guns which were able to fire grapeshot into the advancing British, and Colonel J. Gough, nephew of the Commander-in-Chief, was severely wounded by such fire, just as he reached the first Sikh entrenchment. Now, with a final rush, the whole of Stacy's Brigade penetrated the enemy's first line. Here they were checked as Sikh artillerymen on the parapet to the south of the captured entrenchment turned their artillery pieces around and blasted grapeshot into the British column. Dick rushed up Wilkinson's Brigade and, after a determined attack, troops of HM 80th and 10th silenced the guns, killing their crews. It was at this point that Dick was mortally wounded by grapeshot, dying in the evening. In perhaps the only coordinated response by the defenders, the Sikhs now launched a counterattack, with troops taken from the south and east sectors.

The weight of the Sikh counterattack fell upon Stacy's Brigade. With great determination the defenders, principally the Akhalis, rushed at the British with musket and bayonet. In a desperate hand-to-hand fight the British tried to hold onto their gains. The remains of Wilkinson's Brigade was sent forward to offer support but the whole of the British left was in danger of being pushed back by the determined Sikhs. Seeing the plight of this initial advance, Gough ordered both Smith and Gilbert to throw out light troops and skirmishers from their divisions along the whole of the British line in the hope that feint attacks and diversionary movements might bring relief to the hard-pressed troops of Dick's Division. These actions were in vain, for the Sikhs paid no heed and continued to reinforce their thrust on the British left. Slowly, and remorselessly, the Sikhs pressed on as the British gradually gave ground. Volley after disciplined volley was fired into the British who fell back, away from the trenches they had gained only a few moments before. Pulling back out of musket range, the men of Dick's Division now had to endure artillery fire as the cannon so recently silenced were again directed upon them. Gough's first advance had failed.

Gough now ordered both Smith and Gilbert to turn their feints into a general attack and these divisions moved forward in line. However, they were now against new obstacles, as noted by Captain J. Cunningham, 'higher and more continuous than the barriers which had foiled the first efforts', and again the British would be faced by a most resolute foe.[31] In Smith's Division, on the enemy's extreme left, the men of Penny's Brigade, followed by Hick's Brigade, crossed rough ground to be met by a hail of artillery fire, which tore into the advancing lines. When, at last, Penny's troops reached the earthworks they were received by a merciless musket fire, along with swords and bayonet thrusts from the bearded Sikh defenders, which left gaping bloody wounds on the heads and arms of the attackers. Exhausted and battered, Penny's Brigade fell back to reform. It was now the turn of

Hick's Brigade to try to assail the barriers, only to be similarly, pushed back. Rallying, Hick's men charged forward once more, again to be met by failure.

In many battles individual acts of bravery can be enough to tip the balance of the contest. Here Lieutenant Tritton led the screaming men of HM 31st forward once more. Tritton proudly held high the Queen's colours, only to be felled, shot dead through the head. Ensign Jones, a mere boy of 14, picked up the fallen flag, only to meet the same fate. Similarly, Lieutenant Noel held the colours aloft, and when he fell, Sergeant Bernard McCabe picked up the staff and planted the flag high on the Sikh ramparts as a rallying point. In frenzy, the remaining troops surged forward, climbing on each other's shoulders to scale the walls. At this point, the Sikh soldiers sprang a mine directly underneath them, resulting in many casualties and much confusion. However, when order had been restored, the British drove the Sikhs back at the point of the bayonet only to find that some of the enemy had ventured behind the advance, where they fired into the rear of the British. Troops of HM 50th had to be sent back to neutralise the guns.

Harry Lumsden, commander of a company of the 59th Bengal Native Infantry wrote to his father after the battle and left us a vivid description of what it was like to advance against the Sikh position and the determination of the British troops to succeed:

> The instant we moved out of our cover in the nullah [dry river bed] we were saluted with an awful discharge of well-directed shot, which did great mischief in our line. This sort of amusement the enemy kept up for us with great effect until we reached within 800 yards of their batteries, when ... the Infantry closed up their half-broken line, and once more moved forward to the charge. The enemy now changed their round shot for quilted grape [grapeshot in canvas sacks], which caused even greater loss than the former but could not stop our men, who were by this time driven half mad with seeing so many of their companions killed around them.[32]

In the centre, Gilbert's Division marched towards that part of the Sikh's defences which was the most formidable of the entrenchments. The troops advanced through the most terrific artillery fire, which again claimed many British lives. Some sort of sanctuary was gained when the men reached the base of walls but here they discovered that the barrier in front of them was just too high to scale without ladders, of which there were none. As more and more troops were killed or wounded by Sikh musketry firing down upon them, the British were forced back and had to endure, not only the Sikh artillery, but also a charge by Sikh cavalry, which claimed the lives of twenty-nine bewildered infantrymen. Gough called in the 3rd Light Dragoons, who chased back the Sikh cavalry into their defences. Gilbert rallied his division and again the men surged forward, only to be rebuffed a second time. Both Gilbert and Brigadier MacLaran were severely wounded. Only Brigadier Taylor remained to lead the division in a third assault. This time the British moved their attack a few hundred yards to the left, where the entrenchments were not quite as high, but as Taylor encouraged the men forward he fell dead, struck by a bullet in the head, after he had already been wounded by a sabre cut to the face. The attackers were able to climb upon each other's shoulders and force themselves up and over the ramparts. Again, the British bayonet drove back the Sikhs away from their most formidable defences and back towards the river. British sappers now blew gaps in the earthworks and the cavalry were able to pass through in single file, led by the cavalry commander, General Sir Joseph Thackwell.

Smith's Divisions, which had gained a small hold on the Sikh left, were now hard pressed to hold on and the matter hung in the balance for some time, as described by Smith himself:

> By dint of the hardest fighting I ever saw, I carried the entrenchments. Such a hand-to-hand conflict ensued, for twenty-five minutes I could barely hold my own. Mixed together, swords and targets against bayonets, and a fire on both sides . . . We were at it against four times my numbers, sometimes receding (never turning round though) sometimes advancing. The old 31st and 50th laid on like devils . . . This last was a brutal bull-dog fight . . .[33]

As more reserves were brought-up, Smith's position became more secure and the Sikhs were pushed further back.

With the British now inside the Sikh entrenchments on both the Sikh left and in the centre, the defenders began to retire towards the bridge. This presented the troops of Dick's Division with an opportunity to press the Sikh right once more, and the three British divisions now converged on the bridge. Seeing that his escape route was in jeopardy, Tej Singh fled over the Sutlej to the relative safety of the north bank. Nominal command now fell upon the veteran General Sham Singh Attariwala, who fought valiantly until he fell under British bayonets. His bloodied body was later found where the fighting had been the thickest. At some point during or immediately after Tej Singh's flight, two of the boats in the bridge of boats were cut loose. There is general confusion as to how this happened; some, such as historian Amarpal Sidhu, believe that Tej Singh ordered the bridge to be damaged so as to stop the retreat of the Khalsa and thus ensure their destruction. Another view is that Sham Singh commanded that two boats be cut away so that the Sikhs would rally to him in one final defiant stand and push back the British, whilst an alternative is that the bridge was damaged by British troops from Dick's Division. Whatever the truth, there is no doubt that the bridge of boats had been fatally weakened.

Inside the entrenchments, mayhem and death now abounded. The British cavalry, principally the 3rd Light Dragoons, having filed in through breaches in the mud walls, now reformed into line and charged towards the Khalsa, cutting and running down any who tried to make a stand. Similarly, the British infantry, with bayonets at the ready, advanced towards any Sikhs offering resistance, whilst the Horse Artillery pulled their guns across the weaker entrenchments on the Sikh right to fire grapeshot into the massed ranks of retreating defenders. Those Sikhs who stubbornly held on to their positions in the numerous foxholes or ditches were despatched by concentrated musket volleys, or by cannon fire angled down into their defences.

The scene of death and carnage was vividly described by Private J.W. Baldwin of HM 9th, 'armed Seikhs we killed without any compunction whatever; yet how revolting to see the poor victims lay before us in such intense agony – struggling on their backs – with the hemorrhage gushing from a bayonet prick in the heart – their flashing eyes rolling most frightfully and menacingly staring us in the face'.[34] Such was the reality of death at the point of a British bayonet.

Robert Burford also left a vivid description of the intensity of the struggle; 'They [The Sikhs] fought nobly hand-to-hand with their assailants, selling their lives dearly and disputing the ground inch by inch, but it was useless, nothing could stand against those formidable weapons the bayonets, in the hands of the heroes who wielded them.'[35]

Fighting continued inside the entrenchment for nearly 30 minutes before those remaining defenders sought their escape across the bridge of boats. The retreat was certainly no rout and many British accounts survive of how the dense crowd of Sikhs was orderly and dignified in its movement towards the bridge, despite the continued fire from British muskets and cannons. Occasionally a brave individual would charge, sword raised towards the engulfing British, only to be ruthlessly shot or bayoneted. Once at the bridge, the sheer number of Sikhs trying to flee across this weakened and damaged structure resulted in its gradual disintegration. More and more boats broke free and men and camels fell into the swollen Sutlej. Many were swept to their deaths. Others met their end as the British fired muskets into the swelling mass of humanity. The Horse Artillery reached the southern bank and they too fired upon the Sikhs.

The battle had turned into a massacre. Thousands of Sikh soldiers trying to reach the north bank either drowned or were killed by the British fire. In some parts the bodies where apparently so thick that the British considered that they could have been used as stepping stones to cross the Sutlej. Those trapped on the southern shore expected no quarter and refused to surrender. Sick of the slaughter, some British troops attempted to encourage the Sikhs to lay down their weapons, but with little or no success. Those Sikhs on the northern shore watched inert as their comrades died. Despite the fact that the Sikh artillery was heavier than the 6pdr field guns pulled by the British Horse Artillery, they did not fire in support of their dying comrades. These guns had the power to drive back the British from the south bank and the fact that they offered no resistance offers further credence to the claims of duplicity by Tej and Lal Singh.

By 11am the bloody battle was effectively over. The Sikhs had lost up to 10,000 men, the majority of whom fell in and around the area of the bridge. All 67 guns positioned on the south bank, along with around 200 zambooraks, were captured. The total British casualties were 2,383, of whom 320 died. The losses were evenly distributed between the European and native regiments and on the whole the latter fought well, with the two battalions of Gurkhas particularly distinguishing themselves.

The British casualty figures hide the reality of the battlefield; this comes from the writings of those that fought on that fearful day. In a letter to his family, Private R. Perkes wrote of the loss of his comrades:

> I ham very sorry to say that the regiment I belong to suffered greatly the company I belong to thirty off us marched that morning to the enemys battery hand only eight off us returned in to our camp safe without being wounded hand the other companys equal the same hand it was a miracle

how any off us escaped for the balls had to come has thick as a shower off haile the same I never wish to see again . . .[36]

Similarly, Robert Cust wrote of the poignant aftermath of the battle:

> It was an awful scene, a fearful carnage. The dead Sikh lay inside his trenches – the dead European marked too distinctly the line each regiment had taken, [in] the advance. The living Europeans remarked that nought could resist the bayonet . . . Our loss was heavy and the ground here and there strewn with the slain, among whom I recognised a fine handsome lad whom I had well known, young Hamilton, brother of Alistair Stewart. There he lay, his auburn hair weltering in his blood, his forehead fearfully gashed, his finger cut off. Still warm, but quite dead.[37]

Although Gough had achieved his desired victory, there were some recriminations in Britain regarding the high casualty figures. However, such criticism failed to show an understanding of the professionalism of the Sikh Army and the technological weakness of the British artillery which meant that the British were forced to engage with their foe in close combat. Both Gough and Hardinge were under huge political pressure to achieve a decisive victory over the Sikhs, not just to win a war but to show to the whole of India that the British were still the masters of the battlefield, particularly after the recent Afghan debacle. Gough had found his enemy with its back to the Sutlej and, in such circumstances, he was not going to miss the opportunity so presented to conclusively defeat his foe. Crucially, the inadequacies of the 1839 Pattern percussion musket meant that the British were armed with essentially a defensive weapon. To achieve the decisive victory he needed Gough was forced to depend upon the only offensive weapon at his disposal; the bayonet.

This is not to say that mistakes were not made. Certainly, Gough can be criticised for the handling of his troops at Sobroan and indeed one of his subordinates, Sir Harry Smith, considered that the Commander-in-Chief had chosen the wrong place to attack. Smith wrote, 'I saw at once that the fundamental principle of "being superior to your enemy at the point of attack" was lost sight of . . .' .[38] After Stacy's Brigade had effected a footing into the enemy's earthwork, with relative ease, it was subject to a fierce Sikh counterattack, which, even with support from Dick's remaining brigade, forced the British back. It was only the stubborn fighting of Smith's battalions which reduced the number of Sikh defenders in the centre and allowed Gilbert's men to finally achieve success there. To have misused Gilbert's men in a series of fruitless attacks in the centre against the strongest defences was folly and these troops could have been more productively used to support both Stacy's and Smith's flank attacks. The strength of the Sikh position, and the tenacity of its defenders, was always going to result in high British casualties, however, a more enlightened approach might well have resulted in a breach in the defences during the first attack and many British lives could have been saved.

Despite these criticisms, Gough's decision to attack and decisively defeat the Sikhs at Sobroan was more than justified by events following the battle. The British were still very much aware that substantial enemy forces, supported by artillery, could be brought to bear against them. Furthermore, the British had neither the forces nor the will for a prolonged guerrilla-style war north of the Sutlej. Although the British victory at Sobroan failed to quash the fighting spirit of the Sikh Army, the decisive nature of that victory ensured that, politically, a settlement could be quickly reached. Both conspirators, Lal Singh and Tej Singh, benefited from the peace; the former became Vizier, or Prime Minister, although his need for conspiracy later saw him fall from grace with the British, whilst the latter was appointed Commander-in-Chief of the Sikh Army. Gulab Singh was rewarded for his inactivity with possession of Kashmir. The British gained territory north of the Sutlej and maintained a garrison in Lahore, both of which would be at the heart of future disputes.

Gough was very much aware of the criticisms directed towards him for his tactics throughout the First Anglo-Sikh War and he wrote, 'In India, I am a reckless savage, devoid of stratagem and military knowledge, because my loss is severe. . .'. It is clear that he felt such criticism was based on a limited knowledge of the difficult task the British faced in beating the Sikhs, a foe Gough described as 'peculiarly military . . . with a powerful artillery as well served as our own, infinitely superior in numbers and in the weight of metal in their guns'. However, he was ready to accept responsibility for the good of the army when he wrote, 'Let the world carp, let them call me savage, incompetent, and what they please; I am ready to bear all their taunts, rather than throw a shade over the bright laurels the Indian army have won.' Furthermore, Gough stated, 'My confidence in my army went far to save India.'[39] It is this confidence, alongside the bravery of his troops and their use of the bayonet, which were the deciding factors in the British victory at Sobroan.

Chapter 2

Percussion Rifled Muskets – The Crimean War, 1854–6

> Remember, Remember,
> The fifth of November,
> Sevastopol, powder and shot;
> When General Liprandi
> Charged John, Pat and Sandy,
> And a jolly good licking he got.
>
> *Punch*, Vol. XXVI 1855
> (Battle of Inkerman, 5 November 1854)

Whilst Lovell's Improved Brunswick Rifle can be considered to be the first percussion weapon to see general service in the British Army, and was a distinct improvement upon the flintlock rifles it replaced, it still possessed numerous failings. Although the Brunswick rifle was faster to load and less prone to misfiring than a flintlock weapon, it was only marginally more accurate. The Brunswick rifle was to see service throughout the Second Sikh War (1848–9) and the weapon's limited range again restricted British strategy throughout this conflict. The British, led once more by Sir Hugh Gough, were again ordered to advance with bayonets fixed against strong Sikh positions. For example, at the Battle of Chillianwala (13 January 1849) the attack of the 24th Infantry Regiment was decimated by grapeshot fired from the very Sikh cannons that the troops had been ordered to silence. Although the British could claim a victory of sorts, for it was the Sikh Army that left the field of battle, Gough's high casualties resulted in his replacement by one of his fiercest critics, General Charles Napier (1782–1853). However, Napier had to travel from England and by the time he arrived in India Gough's forces had defeated the Sikhs at the Battle of Gujrat (21 February 1849), other wise known as the 'Battle of the Guns', which effectively brought an end to the conflict. At Gujrat

Gough was able to bring over 100 artillery pieces into play against a strongly fortified Sikh position and, unlike at the earlier Battle of Sobroan, the artillery barrage managed to dislodge many of the enemy whose retreat was turned into a rout by a general pursuit of cavalry, horse artillery and infantry who were once more armed with the bayonet.

As in the First Anglo Sikh War, Gough's tactics had been restricted by the limits of the Brunswick rifle. Yet, within the space of just a few years British troops were to be armed with a rifle that would transform the battlefield, although the army's commanders were rather slow to realise what a potent weapon they now had at their disposal. This particular battlefield revolution began with a scientific breakthrough in the design of a bullet. Armourers had known for decades that ideally a bullet should be small enough to slip down the barrel easily, yet large enough to grip the rifling on the way out. If the bullet could be made to swell at the moment of firing, gripping the rifling within the barrel for a split second, then the bullet would emerge from the barrel spinning. It was also understood that such a spinning motion would increase both the accuracy and range as the bullet flew through the air towards its intended target.

In 1842 a French infantry officer, Captain Henri-Gustave Delvigne, patented a lead bullet with a cavity in its base. Delvigne theorised that the high-pressure gases caused by the explosion of the propellant would expand the edges of the bullet surrounding the cavity outwards and into the rifling grooves thus resulting in the spinning motion as the bullet left the barrel. However, in 1844 having examined the 1842 patent, and also work undertaken by a London gunmaker, William Greener, yet another French officer, Captain Claude Etienne Minié of the French Chasseurs, advanced Delvigne's design by deepening the cavity and inserting a conical iron plug. This new projectile, or .702 cylindro-conoidal bullet, was designed with a flat base thus exposing the maximum surface to the charge. It fitted easily into the bore and when fired the force of the propellant drove the plug forward in the manner of a tapered piston. This action resulted in an expansion at the base of the bullet which thus gripped the rifling grooves. Not only did the Minié bullet take the rifling and spin well, but its streamlined shape helped give it a flatter, more accurate, trajectory.

Claude Minié was a serving officer and had seen action in Algeria where he and his comrades had been forced to endure long-range sniping from the hand-made long rifles of their Algerian adversaries and he was determined to redress the balance.

Thus, in this particular circumstance it was the technological advance with the bullet that shaped the development of the rifle. A new percussion cap fired rifle, known as the Minié rifle, was soon being trialled by both the British and French armies. The initial results were astonishing. At 100yd the Minié rifle hit the target 94.5 per cent of the time compared with 74.5 per cent for the Brunswick rifle: at 400yd the results were 52.5 per cent and 4.5 per cent respectively.[1] The Minié rifle was 4ft, 6in long and weighed 10lb 8¾oz, with bayonet fixed. It was fitted with a 39in barrel with a bore of 0.702in, rifled with four grooves having one turn in 78in. It was the first rifle to have perfected sliding ladder rear sight and although at first glance the design of the rifle did not look much different from muskets of the time, it was this sliding ladder sight that made the rifle distinctive. Its effective range was 800yd, although targets at twice that distance could be hit.[2]

From 1849 the Minié rifle was issued to units of the French Army and two years later the Marquis of Anglesey, Master-General of Ordnance, with the reluctant support of the Duke of Wellington, initially ordered 28,000 of the new rifle to go into production to gradually replace the regulation smooth-bore musket. In addition, the British government paid Claude Minié the sum of £20,000 as a royalty for the right to use his bullet design in the British rifles. Wellington's approval was tempered by insisting it be called a rifled musket, not a rifle, otherwise 'the soldiers will become conceited, and be wanting next to be dressed in green, or some other jack-a-dandy uniform'.[3]

Again, at this critical moment for rifle development, the British government was influenced by another nation's creativity. The 1851 Great Exhibition, held in the Crystal Palace in Hyde Park, London, ran from May to October of that year. Over 6 million visitors attended this first international exhibition of manufactured products. Although British exhibitors were prominent, companies and individuals from across the Empire and, the world, showed their products and innovations to a public who were enthralled, inspired and amazed.

The American entrepreneur Samuel Colt's new six-shooter caused a sensation at the Colt stand. The fact that six rounds could be fired without having to reload the weapon significantly increased the rate of fire. British specialists who poured over the weapons at the Crystal Palace were in awe of the advances in firearms technology displayed by Colt. Although there had been repeating pistols before, Colt's innovation was to render them safe and reliable for the shooter and, above all, cheap as the parts were the result of mass production from power driven machinery, making them interchangeable and inexpensive to produce.

This interchangeability gave the user considerable advantages, especially in the field, where repair, replace or recycle of the working parts could be undertaken with negligible skill.

For British gun makers Colt's approach was something of a 'road to Damascus moment'. Under the then British system, musket parts made for the military were hand-crafted in Birmingham workshops, and then sent to the Tower of London for quality control, before being dispatched to another set of craftsmen to assemble each firearm. Such a complicated and drawn out system surely stifled innovation. As a result of Colt's impressive display at the Great Exhibition, the government sent three British artillery officers and an engineer to America to witness Colt's expertise and innovative practices firsthand. The British delegation was so impressed by what they saw that they recommended the importation of American machinery and practices. In addition, an expert from the United States armoury at Harpers Ferry, Virginia, travelled to England to supervise the introduction of mass production at the government's small-arms factory at Enfield, Middlesex.[4]

Although a huge improvement, the Minié rifle had received a number of complainants from troops, its excessive weight being one of the chief objections. In 1852 the new Master-General of Ordnance, Viscount Hardinge, ordered that trials be carried out to determine a better design which would combine lightness as well as the efficiency and accuracy of the Minié rifle. Various rifles were submitted by private gun makers, including Westley Richards, Lancaster and Purdey, as well a design from the gun makers Lovell who were working on behalf of the British government. The trials resulted in the creation of a rifle which incorporated the improvements and alterations gleaned from the various rifles submitted. The 39in barrel had a much-reduced bore from the Minié rifle's of 0.702in to 0.577in and rifling of three rather than four grooves, resulting in one half turn in the length of the barrel. In contrast to the French design, the new rifle was fastened to the stock by three iron bands, which also served to retain the ramrod in its channel. After a few further refinements of the experimental rifle the Pattern 1853 Enfield rifle-musket came into existence. This became the first large-scale massproduced rifle from the Enfield Small Arms Works, which was inspired by the manufacturing innovations of Samuel Colt.

Firing the bullet designed by Claude Minié, the Enfield had a huge advantage in terms of accuracy and range over the rifle it was replacing. The Enfield had an official range of 1,200yd and an effective one of 500yd, which was five or six times greater than the Brunswick rifle. The Enfield had a barrel 3ft, 3in long, and the entire weapon was 4ft, 6in long and weighed 8lb, 14oz. The bore was .577in, and the rifling was three-grooved, rather than four like the Minié, which made the round more stable and permitted it to expand more easily. The ladder rear sight was sighted up to 1,200yd, with the Enfield being a very accurate and reliable weapon. It remained, like its predecessors, a muzzle-loading rifle. The bullet and powder were sealed in a paper cartridge, which was thinly coated with grease to be waterproof and to lubricate the bullet. The Enfield had a streamlined, slim appearance which the reduction in bore size and the fore-end had produced. All these factors resulted in the Enfield being 12 per cent lighter than the Minié rifle, which met with general approval.[5]

The Minié rifle first saw active service with the elite Chasseurs d'Afrique in Algeria and for the British, the Minié 'Rifle Musket Pattern 1851' was first fired in anger against the Xhosa tribesmen of South Africa during the Eighth Frontier War of 1850–3. The Board of Ordnance sent out a limited number of rifles for testing in action. They were issued to the six best marksmen in each infantry company and, encouraged by their officers, who presented prizes for the best marksmanship, the troops took readily to their new weapon. Reports were made that on numerous occasions just the fire of a small number of men using the Minié rifle had dispersed bodies of tribesmen at distances from 1,200–1,300yd and the level of accuracy from the rifle astonished the new converts.[6]

Yet, the first major conflict in which both the Minié and the Enfield saw significant service was the Crimean War of 1854–6. The weakness of the Turkish Empire in the Balkans and the crushing Russian naval victory against the Turks at the Battle of Sinope (30 November 1853) provoked concerns in Britain and France about possible Russian dominance in the Black Sea and the Balkans. Britain was the most powerful naval power at the time and saw Russian naval strength as a threat to the route to India. Napoleon III of France saw an opportunity in conflict to strengthen his domestic position and to enhance France's diplomatic clout. With the French and British keen to humble Russian naval strength the primary focus of the conflict was on a naval and amphibious expedition to the Crimea in order to capture and render unusable the naval base of Sevastopol.

Whilst the Board of Ordnance had made the decision to equip the British Army with the Pattern 1853 Enfield rifle-musket the conversion from the Minié 'Rifle Musket Pattern 1851' took several years.

Indeed, when British forces were despatched to fight in the Crimean War (1853–6) many troops were armed with the Minié rifle and some, particularly the British 4th Division, were still using smooth-bore muskets. Charles Ashe Windham (1810–70) was a senior officer in the 4th Division during the Crimean War and led the attack on the Redan at Sevastopol in 1855. He was a fervent critic of the mismanagement of the Crimean campaign. Writing home he stated, 'the great advantage we have had in superiority and in the superior arming of our Infantry has been thrown away because, all of a sudden, it has been discovered that there are no more 'Minie' Rifles and many of the Regiments are coming out unarmed. Can anything beat this?'[7]

Britain's French allies were also supplied with the Minié rifle and this combined with the fact that the Enfield rifle fired the Minié bullet led to some confusion in contemporary accounts as to the rifles carried by the British forces. Accounts, in both newspapers and from serving troops, as well as the writing of some modern historians, frequently refer to the Minié rifle when in truth the Enfield was being used. What is clear is that as the Crimean War ground on so more and more British troops arrived armed with the new Enfield rifle, although there is also evidence that some production difficulties at the Enfield works did result in delays.

Writing home on 5 April 1854 from Fort Veilderla on the island of Malta, whilst waiting for transport to the Crimea, R.T. Farren of the 47th Regiment, wrote:

> We have just received 164 volunteers from four of the Regts in Garrision and have been very busy in distributing them amongst the different companies. We are now up to 825 rank and file and shall have 41 more volunteers as soon as the 14th Regt arrives. We have got 100 more Minie Rifles, and, if there were more of these arms in store, every man would get one of them, but as it is we have only 200 Rifles, and the rest are the percussion smooth bore flintlock. 'Tis astonishing the quantity of things to be done to get a Regiment efficient and equipped for the field.[8]

What is equally clear is that both the troops and their officers had a reluctance to appreciate, or lack of understanding, of how potent their new rifles were. Viscount Hardinge oversaw the introduction of both the Minié and Enfield rifles into British service. So as to aid the troops to gain an understanding of the capabilities of these new rifles Hardinge established a School of Musketry at Hythe in Kent. Here there was sufficient space to ensure that the Minie's and Enfield's greatly improved range and accuracy were properly understood and applied to the infantry's shooting skill and knowledge. The newly promoted Lieutenant Garnet Wolseley (1833–1913), later to become the Commander-in-Chief of the British Army, recalled:

> In the early spring of 1854 the new Minié rifle was given to us [90th Perthshire Light Infantry]. Months were spent in teaching the men how to aim with it, and we were ordered to send an officer to one of the newly opened schools of musketry [at Hythe] to learn the theory and practice of rifle shooting. No one cared much about going there, and it was thought an excellent joke when a one-armed officer was selected for that purpose . . . We were all so thoroughly ignorant of war and of tactics to comprehend the complete change the rifle was soon to make in the fate of battles, and even in our mode of fighting.[9]

Charles Ashe Windham saw, firsthand, the troops lack of training and wrote, 'The Enfield Rifle . . . should be the aim for the Infantry and they should be a hundred times more practised in its use than they are . . .'.[10] Some attempts were made to provide rifle training when the troops arrived first in Bulgaria and then the Crimea.

However, on occasion, these opportunities again illustrated the lack of understanding of the capabilities of the new rifles. For example, Colonel Bell, commander of the 1st Royals and a veteran of the Peninsular War, recalled in his autobiography, *Rough Notes by an Old Soldier*, his first, almost deadly encounter, with the Enfield rifle.

Hastily improvised ranges were set up wherever they could be sited, so as to at least give the troops the experience of firing a few rounds from their new rifles. Bell tells how he inadvertently stumbled into the vicinity of one of these impromptu ranges and had to gallop for his life as Minié bullets whizzed past him, even though he was more than half a mile from the firers.[11]

Such was the ignorance and lack of appreciation of the range and accuracy of both the Enfield and Minié rifles that it would take active service in the great battles of the Crimean War to finally demonstrate what new powerful weapons the troops now possessed. These weapons would revolutionise the battlefield and gave both the British and French troops a huge advantage over their Russian foes. The Russians carried a muzzle-loading, smooth-bored, percussion ignition musket.

Many of these weapons were poorly made at the Tula arms factory. Some Russian reservists, who fought in the conflict, were issued with flintlocks made during the Napoleonic Wars, or even earlier. The calibre varied from .700 and .720in and had a range of 100–200yd and was hopelessly inaccurate.

Just a week after landing, virtually unopposed, in the Crimea at Calamita Bay, the armies clashed at the Battle of the Alma (20 September 1854). The Russian, commander, Prince Menshikov (1787–1869), decided upon a defence on the heights above the south bank of the River Alma, which was the last natural barrier to the Allied armies on the march to their objective of the port of Sevastopol. Although outnumbered, the strength of the Russian position, centred on the heights and manmade redoubts, along with close to 100 artillery pieces, meant that the battle would be a very bloody affair.

The initial Allied plan of attack saw the French forces, led by General Bousquet's (1810–61) Division, attack the Russian flank. It was hoped that this would divert Russian attention from a British advance in the centre and on the left. However, when the British attacked, the nature of the rough terrain, and the vagueness of the orders from the British Commander, Lord Raglan (1788–1855), meant that it was extremely difficult to maintain the cohesion of the advancing formations and regiments became disorganised and in places the attack faltered and stalled under a hail of Russian artillery shot. Despite this confusion there remains a considerable amount of firsthand anecdotal evidence from the Battle of the Alma as to the effectiveness of the new British Enfield and Minié rifles.

At a crucial moment in the battle, when the Russians were organising themselves to launch a counterattack, a Private Kirwin saw a mounted Russian officer urging his men on:

> He was waving his sword for the men to come on. I said to Michael McNearney, John Tuckford and two other men of the Regiment, 'Do you see that big bugger waving his sword? Let us have a slap at him.' We raised our slides to 600 yards and took deliberate aim on the knee, five comrades together, and fired. I happened to look up after the shot. 'Mick,' said I, he is down. He will never wave his sword again.'[12]

At another critical point, the Guards Brigade (composed of the Grenadiers, Scots Fusiliers and Coldstream Guards) was given the order to advance. Sir Colin Campbell (1792–1863), the commander of the Highland Brigade, frustrated with the slow pace, spurred the troops on and ordered them not to fire their rifles until 'within a yard of the Russians'. In the confusion of advancing over difficult ground, whilst under constant enemy fire the Scots Fusiliers lost cohesion and it was left to the Coldstream Guards and the Grenadiers, 2,000 men, to stop the Russians as they attacked down the hill towards them. Ignoring Campbell's orders, these Guards formed into line and fired fourteen consecutive volleys into the enemy infantry. Nearly 30,000 Minié bullets tore into the massed Russian columns stopping their advance in its tracks, and those that fell were left in heaps. Shattered, the remaining enemy withdrew back up the hill. Captain Wilson served with the Coldstream Guards and described the effect of the British volleys, 'Every soldier takes deliberate aim; the distance does not exceed sixty paces; hence the Minié has easy game and works miracles.'[13]

The Guards had shown their understanding of the capabilities of their new rifles and had clearly demonstrated the long-range effectiveness of the firepower of modern weapons.

The Guards were soon joined by men of the 2nd Division and together the troops directed their rifle fire on the exposed gunners of three Russian batteries. Many of the enemy fell unaware from where the deadly British fire was coming from; such was the range of the new rifles. With the Russian artillery fire neutralised the British troops were able to advance. Although their officers might not have realised it, the Enfield and Minié rifles had transformed the battlefield in their first serious engagement. The correspondent of *The Times* wrote that Enfield rifle had 'smote the enemy like a destroying angel'.[14]

The Battle of the Alma was not the defining and decisive battle of the war which many had hoped for. Both a reluctance and timidity were the features of the Allied advance upon the retreating Russian troops, who were able to flee the battlefield and seek refuge behind the fortifications of Sevastopol. The war now became one of siege, apart from two significant engagements when the Russians attempted to lift that siege. The first was the Battle of Balaklava (25 October 1854) which is best known for the infamous 'Charge of the Light Brigade' in which a misinterpreted order from Lord Raglan led to the ill-fated charge in which over 270 men of the British light cavalry were either killed or wounded. However, in terms of British arms, it is the so-called 'Thin Red Line' which is of greater significance.

British and French forces jointly besieged Sevastopol with the British positioned in and around the southern port of Balaklava. From this location the British were, by default, committed to the defence of the right flank of the Allied siege operations. It was a worry to Raglan that he had insufficient troops to both pursue the siege and protect this rather exposed flank. The Russian General Liprandi (1796–1864) was also aware of this weakness and determined upon an attack on the defences in and around Balaklava. At the very least Liprandi hoped that the Russian attack would disrupt, or even cut, the supply chain of the British troops and would force the abandonment of the siege.

The Russians began the battle with a heavy artillery barrage, followed by an infantry assault upon Balaklava's first line of defence, which was held by Ottoman Turkish forces. The Turks were overwhelmed by the Russians and forced to retreat from their redoubts. This allowed the Russian cavalry to charge towards the second defensive line which was again held by Turkish troops and a small force of British soldiers, the 93rd Highland Regiment. At the Battle of the Alma, General Buller (1802–84), at the approach of Russian cavalry had deployed the 88th Regiment from line formation into a square bristling with bayonets. The Russians fully appreciated the message that the British were displaying and refrained from attacking the strong square. Thus General Buller had resorted to Napoleonic tactics to deter the enemy, unaware of the effectiveness of the Enfield rifle. At the Battle of the Balaklava the Highlanders were, once more, commanded by Sir Colin Campbell who had witnessed firsthand the killing power of the new British rifles at the Battle of Alma. So instead of resorting to the square Campbell put his trust in the bravery and resolute behaviour of the men under his command, as well as the effectiveness of the Enfield rifle.

Four squadrons of Russian cavalry, some 400 men, descended upon the Highlanders from the Causeway Heights, with the Scots the last and only defence between the charging enemy and Balaklava itself. Campbell certainly understood the predicament and responsibility that he and his men now faced. He formed his troops into two thin lines, rather than the normal three so as to allow for a long enough front to meet the enemy, and was reported as shouting, as he rode up and down the lines, 'Men, remember there is no retreat from here. You must die where you stand.'[15] Lieutenant Colonel Sterling, of the 93rd, was certainly one who thought 'he [Campbell] looked as if he meant it'.[16]

With confidence in both their commander and their rifle, the men of the 93rd did indeed stand firm as the Russians raced towards them. From the hills above, *The Times* correspondent, William Russell (1820–1907), had a grandstand view and described the Highlanders as 'that thin red streak topped with steel', which Tennyson later described as the 'thin red line'.[17] Campbell ordered the first volley to be fired at the advancing Russians at a range of about 600yd. When the smoke from the rifles cleared there seemed little effect on the charging cavalry who showed no sign of slowing their attack or even being diminished in numbers. At a distance of 150yd a second volley rang out which did cause confusion and forced the enemy to swerve to the right of the 93rd. A further volley, at much closer range, caught the Russians in the flank, which caused them to ride sharply to their left and ride back to the safety of their own army.

Although the fire of the Enfield rifles, for this was indeed the rifle that the 93rd were armed with (as clearly seen in Robert Gibb's famous painting entitled *The Thin Red Line*), had beaten back the Russian cavalry there was some surprise and comment amongst contemporaries that so few of the advancing enemy were flung from their mounts. However, two years after the end of the war a Sergeant Munro of the 93rd, who had been present on that fateful day, chanced upon a Russian Hussar officer, with a severe limp, who had been part of the Russian charge. Munro reported that the officer's limp was attributed to a Minié bullet breaking his thigh. The officer also claimed that many of the Russians had been severely or mortally wounded by the fire of the 93rd but had had sufficient strength to retain their seats in the saddle long enough to ride back to their comrades.[18]

Although the Highlanders had successfully repulsed the first Russian attack, the main body of Hussars, more than 2,000 strong and flanked by Cossack outriders, now descended from the Causeway Heights towards the 93rd. Seeing the danger, the 700 men of the British Heavy Brigade galloped into the Russians and after a brief, but brutal melee, the Russians gave way first and retreated back to the North valley, where they received covering fire from the Russian artillery. What followed next were delays in orders, confusion and misunderstanding which all ultimately resulted in the brave but foolhardy charge of the Light Brigade. After this moment of horror, the Russians withdrew from the battlefield, claiming victory, whilst the British centred their blame on their Turkish allies for the loss of the redoubts on the Causeway Heights, but optimistically comforted themselves that the enemy had been scattered.

Again there occurred another important moment the day after the Battle of Balaklava, the significance of which has perhaps been overlooked in the controversy that surrounded 'The Charge'. For although British riflemen had silenced Russian guns at the Battle of the Alma with long-range fire from their Enfields, at Balaklava their acts were recorded in Lord Raglan's official reporting of the battle and its aftermath. Thus this action was one of the first recorded incidences in the history of warfare where the infantry, armed with a standard issue rifle, could outreach and outgun the enemy's artillery. In this particular example, Lieutenant Godfrey, of the 1st Battalion Rifle Brigade, led a handful of his men close to the Heights recently occupied by Russian artillery. Godfrey was recorded as saying that using the cover of a ridge, the Riflemen got to within 600yd of the Russian artillery and from there, firing prone to avoid being seen, 'got the credit of silencing them [the guns]'.[19] The position of artillery, once the dominant firepower on the battlefield, was being usurped by infantry armed with a long-range rifle that was rapidly becoming a revolutionary weapon.

With the Heights in their hands, the Russians had a commanding position from which to launch an attack on the British supply lines between Balaklava and the Sevastopol heights. The very next day, 26 October 1854, the Russians launched a sortie on the right flank of the British Army on the Inkerman Heights. The engagement, which was later to be given the name of 'Little Inkerman', was dominated by the range of the Enfield for picquets and men of Lieutenant General De Lacy Evans' (1787–1870) 2nd Division were able to delay and break the momentum of the Russian attack by their fire. Over the next days the Russians launched a series of reconnaissances in force to probe the British position on the heights of Inkerman, and for the next week the adversaries restricted themselves to sniping and the occasional exchange of artillery shells. During this period Lieutenant Mark Walker, of the 30th East Lancashire Regiment, was to relate further evidence of the superior range of the Enfield. Writing from the British camp before Sevastopol on 27 October 1854, Walker said:

> The Enfield rifle is in order, and a first rate weapon it is. I have seen a Ball from it astonish a Cossack when fired from a distance of upwards of a 1,000 yards, and it struck the ground close to the hoofs of his horse and he waited not for a second but galloped away at the top of his horse's speed.[20]

Unbeknown to the Allies, the Russians had gradually and secretly been sending reinforcements to the Crimea from Odessa, giving them around 120,000 troops in and around Sevastopol. Confident in their superiority in numbers, and with pressure upon them from the Tsar for a more aggressive act, the Russian commanders devised a plan in which the garrison of Sevastopol, around 19,000 infantry under the command of Prince Soimonov, would sally forth to join the 22,000 men of Prince Gorchakov's (1793–1861) army north of Balaklava to make feint attacks against the Allied armies on the Chersonese uplands. A further 16,000 infantry under General Paulov would descend from the Mackenzie Heights and attack across the River Chernaya, whilst the main attack would be delivered by General Dannenberg (1792–1872) with 40,000 troops who would attack over the same ground as 'Little Inkerman'. Facing this main thrust were just 3,300 troops of the 2nd Division, along with 12 artillery pieces.

At daybreak on 5 November 1854, the Russian infantry, dressed in their long peppery grey coats, with cloth caps, circled with red bands, upon their heads, began their attack upon the lightly held British position. The Russian battalions advanced with 3 companies in line, each 25 paces apart, with 1 in reserve, some 25 paces to the rear. Each battalion presented a frontage of around 140 paces. To the British picquets, the Russians appeared as a grey mass through the fog, moving slowly and inexorably forward. These massed ranks showed a clear target for the deadly Minié bullets which were soon tearing holes in the Russian advance. The penetration of the British fire was such that two or even three of the enemy would be hit by the same bullet.[21] The British troops could hardly believe that the Russians would attack in such massed columns, as described by Sergeant Andrew Munro:

> I want to tell you about the strange way in which the Russians here [Inkerman] advanced under fire in close column and how thus they were easily decimated. I remember upon that early morning, seeing dense columns of Russian troops advancing before it was properly daylight. Our picquets held their ground, keeping these columns at bay as long as possible, to enable our troops to advance before the enemy could take possession of the ground upon which these picquets stood. This they did splendidly.[22]

At first the British resistance was weakened by the fact that the fog and constant drizzle had soaked the percussion charges, as recorded by Captain Hugh Rowlands who was amongst the picquets, 'When we retired the Russians came on with the most fiendish yells you can imagine. We commenced firing. To my dismay I found that half the fire locks misfired, which dispirited the men...'[23] This problem affected most of the British units that were engaged at the start of the battle and served to neutralise, for some moments, the advantage that the Enfield provided.

Once the percussion caps had dried out, the Enfield fire again restored the British advantage in the fire-fights. Despite the poor visibility, which reduced the Enfield's range advantage, it was a more accurate weapon, which greater penetration, than those muskets used by the Russians, as described by Major Fordyce, of the 5th Company of the 47th Regiment:

> The foremost Russians made haste to be plying their muskets, but they did our people no harm, for the force being gathered in column and firing with an inferior weapon at a range of eighty yards and from a narrow front, stood under conditions which made its energy vain. On the other hand, the men, whilst remaining untracked themselves, were all of them carefully file-firing from a widely extended front; and since each of them with a good rifle in his hands, and with ample space round him could shoot at his ease, they soon began to work havoc in the mass which served for their target. After enduring a few rounds the column broke in confusion, and began to fall back with all the speed that the heaviness of its formation and the nature of the ground would allow.[24]

Although taken by surprise, and initially hampered by their damp, misfiring rifles, the British picquets reacted admirably, and the Russians met a stiff resistance. General Sir John Pennefather (1798–1872), now commander of the 2nd Division in the absence of the injured de Lacy Evans, realised that his force was massively inferior. So he decided to fight as far forward as possible, gradually feeding more and more skirmishes forward to support the picquets as they fell back. The morning fog and smoke of battle greatly assisted Pennefather in cloaking the actual size of his available force from the Russians. Eventually, sheer weight of numbers and a few mistakes by British commanders such as the Duke of Cambridge, who advanced too far with the Guards, and Sir George Cathcart (1794–1854), whose mistake cost him his life, meant that the Allies were in real danger of defeat.

Fortunately, Russian Commanders also proved themselves open to numerous mistakes, and they were hindered by the poor visibility and lack of maps.

Furthermore, many of the Russian troops were not only poorly armed, but also poorly trained and many showed a reluctance to advance against the determined resistance of the Allies. Inkerman has become known as 'The Soldier's Battle' for the confused nature of the command orders, the lack of knowledge of the terrain and the poor visibility meant that the battle developed into a mass of smaller engagements. The Russian superiority in artillery did, at one point, look as if it might be decisive, and yet again the Enfield had a role in nullifying its impact.

After the battle Lieutenant Colonel Nathaniel Steevens of the 88th Regiment, The Connaught Rangers compiled a series of statements from officers of the Regiment present during the battle. These accounts not only give a picture of the confused and deadly nature of the fighting, but also reflect the killing power that the range of the Enfield now gave the infantry:

> The companies halted, and, lying down in the brushwood, fired occasional shots at the Russian Infantry and Artillery in their front until they had expended all their caps, and therefore could no longer maintain this desultory firing – The four Companies now continued to retain their position – without being able to fire a shot – and anxiously awaited the arrival of ammunition.

Quartermaster Moose, who is described as a 'brave old Soldier', acted on his own initiative to re-supply the men with ammunition:

> The pouches being now replenished, Colonel Jeffreys at once ordered the men to extend in skirmishing order – to lie down among the brushwood and, sighting their rifles for 800 yards, to keep up an incessant fire upon the Russian batteries on the opposite hill.

The Russians use of grapeshot forced the Rangers to retire about 20 paces from where they continued to pour fire at the Russian batteries:

> The fighting reputation of the old regiment was nobly maintained by this mere handful of brave fellows, who kept-up

such a steady withering fire upon the enemy Artillery – almost every Artillery Man in the batteries on Cossack's Hill was either killed or wounded and the Rangers can claim the credit of having nearly silenced these batteries.[25]

After nearly 4 hours of confused and bitter fighting, the appearance of two heavy 18prs, ordered up by Lord Raglan himself, seemed to have been the decisive moment. Their fire upon the Russian batteries cited on Shell Hill forced the enemy to withdraw and with that the Russian Commander Dannenberg decided to call for a general retreat, which soon became a rout. The Russians left nearly 12,000 men upon the field. The British listed 2,610 casualties, the French 1,726. As Orlando Figes has pointed out, this was a rate of loss on par with the Battle of the Somme.[26] When the French Commander, Bosquet, saw the results of the carnage at the Sandbag Battery, in the middle of the battlefield, where the broken bodies of British, French and Russians were piled on top of each other, he was heard to comment, 'Quel abattoir!'[27]

An editorial in *The Times* of 6 December 1854 clearly places the Allied success at Inkerman down to the Minié and Enfield rifles as well as demonstrating that there was a contemporary debate between the merits of percussion rifled muskets and smooth-bore flintlock muskets. The editorial stated:

> The value of the Minié [Enfield rifle] is now placed beyond any question, and nothing remains but to put it into the hands of every soldier in the army. This weapon it was which, as our correspondent observes 'did our work' at Inkermann, and so fearfully did it tell on the advancing columns of the enemy that they 'rushed upon us with the bayonet to get out of its scope'. In the very same engagement the inferiority of the old musket was plainly shown, and it deserves to be noticed that the circumstances of the battle precisely those under which, according to some theories, the advantages of the common flintlock should have been greatest. It was not an interchange of musket-shots, in which the longest range and the deadliest bullet would naturally tell with the most fatal effect; it was a close hand-to-hand fight, where no ball it might be fancied could fail of hitting its mark. Yet, while the regiments of the Fourth Division and the Marines were armed with old and much beloved Brown Bess, could do nothing with their thin

line of fire against the massive multitudes of the Muscovite infantry, the volleys of the Minié [Enfield] cleft them like 'the hand of the Destroying Angel' and they fell 'like leaves in autumn before them'.

The historian Andrew Lambert considers that the Allied victories at both the Alma and Inkerman was due to the 'allied superiority in infantry fire-power'.[28] The Russians recognised the importance of the new rifled weapons possessed by the British and French. Reflecting on the impact of the Minié and Enfield rifles, the Russian military engineer Eduard Totleben (1818–84) wrote in his history of the Crimean War:

> The British . . . were full of confidence once they found out the accuracy and immense range of their weapon . . . Our infantry with their muskets could not reach the enemy at greater than 300 paces, while they fired on us at 1,200. The enemy, perfectly convinced of the superiority of his small arms, avoided close combat; every time our battalions charged, he retired for some distance, and began a murderous fusillade. Our columns, in pressing the attack, only succeed in suffering terrible losses, and finding it impossible to pass through the hail of bullets which overwhelmed them, were obliged to fall back before reaching the enemy.[29]

The Russian defeat at Inkerman led to the abandonment of any further attempts to dislodge the Allied forces. The Allies now concentrated their efforts on besieging the enemy behind the walls of Sevastopol. In was in this period, particularly after the Great Storm of 14 November 1854 in which a tremendous amount of damage was done to army camps and shelters, that the inadequacies of the supply situation exposed the troops to great hardship, exposure, malnutrition, disease and death.

By the spring of 1855, with the support of business, industry and private initiative, Britain at last seemed to have gained a fresh understanding of what modern warfare required. For example, the architect of the Crystal Palace, Sir Joseph Paxton (1803–65), organised 2,000 navvies into the Army Works Corps to build an all-weather road from the British military port at Balaklava Bay to Sevastopol. The engineer and businessman Isambard Kingdom Brunel (1806–59) sent out a prefabricated hospital, with air conditioning and drainage, for 1,000 patients. Alexis Soyer (1810–58), the former chef de cuisine at the Reform Club, travelled at his own expense to the Crimea to teach the army how to cook and supply the troops with his pioneering field stove. The first military railway was built by the firm of Peto, Brassey & Betts. The Grand Crimean Central Railway brought supplies up to the British forces besieging Sevastopol and took the wounded back down.

In addition, modern communication came to the battlefield. The company responsible for the Channel Cable of 1851, R.S. Newall & Co., laid a 310-mile-long submarine telegraph on the bed of the Black Sea from the British military headquarters at Balaklava to Varna in Bulgaria. From here the British submarine cable met the French landline to Bucharest, the outpost of the European telegraph network. Such connections meant that Whitehall was separated from the front line by a mere day. All these initiatives and schemes, many of which originated from ideas or products first conceived at or for the Great Exhibition, illustrated, as *The Times* said, the arts of peace had been translated into the science of war.[30]

It was also during the siege that the Allies, now alive to the capabilities of the Enfield and Minié, were able to adapt their new, long-range rifles to a fresh and more specialised task, that of sniping. The exceptional distances covered by the fire of the French and British weapons was utilised, in the hands of marksmen, to good and deadly effect. Using the cover provided by rifle pits, or hastily constructed 'nests', which gave the advantage of both protection and concealment, British riflemen, or snipers, targeted Russian gunners behind gun emplacements or enemy sharpshooters concealed in their own rifle pits, placed in advance of the Russian Redoubts of Mamelon and Malakov. Lieutenant Colonel Davidson of the 1st City of Edinburgh Rifle Volunteers, who would later invent a telescopic sight for the Enfield rifle, wrote in the *Army and Navy Journal* of August 1864 about how a sniper and the newly developed role of 'spotter' would work together:

> One soldier was observed lying with his rifle carefully pointed at a distant embrasure, and with his finger on the trigger ready to pull, while by his side lay another with a telescope directed at the same object. He with the telescope was anxiously watching the movement when the [Russian] gunner should show himself, in order that he may give the signal to the other to fire.[31]

Similarly, the *Illustrated London News* of December 1854 reported that:

> The latest accounts from the English camp inform us that our riflemen in the trenches continue to pick off the Russian gunners in the most astonishing manner. One rifleman is said to have killed no less than fourteen in one battery, so we need not be surprised at their [the Russians] bad gunnery. Never was the superiority of skill and science in war so plainly demonstrated . . .[32]

Lieutenant Vaughan of the 21st Fusiliers, a keen and practised shot, wrote to his father on 27 November to describe how a few days earlier, 'I was on a working party . . . down at the trenches, and I took one of the Minie [Enfield] rifles and went to the front and I picked off three men at about eight hundred yards in about 30 shots . . .'.[33]

In a rather macabre fashion Major Henry Clifford, VC (1826–83), of the Rifle Brigade, related the following in a letter home:

> I could not help laughing the other day I was in the advance trench. I saw groups of six or seven men with their rifles full cock and sights up watching anxiously over the parapet. 'What are you on the look out for' I said. 'Oh sure Sir' said the old soldier 'We're waiting for the Russians to go to the rear.' About six hundred yards off was the quarry in which the Russians had lodged a strong party of men, but not having provided them with a patent water-closet the enemy are obliged to go a distance of about fifteen yards for that purpose. Our men watch out for them, and when one makes his appearance they all fire at him. One ran out as I was looking on. The bullets went all round him but he got off safe. My friend the Irishman remarked that at any rate it would be as good as a dose of opening medicine to him. On the return of the poor devil a second volley was fired and he came over like a rabbit, as dead as a stone, and was hailed with a merry shout by our men.[34]

Sniping was not restricted to the British and French for both suffered from fire from Russian sharpshooters. The Russians had quickly learnt, from deadly experience, just how effective the long-range fire of the Enfield was. Using, presumably, captured rifles they were able to disrupt and pin down the Allied artillerymen besieging Sevastopol. Hedley Vicars wrote of the results of Russian sniping:

> We were obliged to walk about to keep ourselves warm, regardless of the bullets which kept flying about our ears like bees. A marine was mortally hit in the breast... and I saw the fellow carried past on a stretcher. He died in less than half an hour. As one of my men was walking up and down close to the rampart, a Minie ball hit him behind the ear. He fell on his side and died without a groan. I buried him at dusk outside the trench.[35]

Writing in 1856, Major Alfred Mordecai (1804–87) of the United States Army who had been tasked with reporting lessons from the Crimean conflict, stated:

> The protracted siege of Sevastopol served to develop the importance of these arms of long range, as an auxiliary, in both attack and defense of places ... it is only necessary to refer to the extraordinary means used by the besiegers and the besieged to protect their gunners from rifle shots, which could be fired with sufficient precision to enter an embrasure at 500 or 600 yards, and which were effective at much greater distances.[36]

Such reports clearly illustrate that the Enfield rifle, and with it the new science of sniping, had opened up additional areas of the front line to ever more deadly fire. Troops at distances of 1,000yd, or more, away from the enemy's front line now had to consider the dangers of both bullet and artillery shot.

On 8 September 1855 the long siege of Sevastopol finally came to an end. From early October 1854 to its conclusion, the Allied troops had flung over 45,000 tons of shot into and over the Russian defences and both sides had faced privations and death. As the defeated Russians withdrew, the remains of the fortifications were blown up by the defenders and the Allied troops entered a devastated city and a harbour littered with sunken and damaged vessels. Britain and France could claim victory.

By the end of the conflict most regiments in the British Army had been supplied with the Enfield rifle. Its arrival in India was to cause huge controversy amongst the Bengal regiments of the East India Company, who were the first to receive it. Hostility, verging on outrage, centred on the belief that the paper cartridge containing the bullet had been lubricated with grease which was a combination of beef and pork tallow. The Enfield was loaded by the rifleman placing the paper cartridge in his mouth so as to tear the paper and then pouring the powder and bullet down the barrel. With the cow sacred to Hindus and pork considered unclean by Muslims, the cartridge managed to offend huge numbers within the army of the East India Company. Whilst it cannot be said that the greasing of the cartridge was the main reason for the outbreak of the Indian Mutiny in May 1857, it was another factor which added to the sense of injustice and persecution felt by the mutineers. The rebellion by Indian troops was bloody and extremely violent, but the retribution and vengeance enforced by the British was even more so.

In the sieges and battles that featured in the Mutiny the Enfield rifle gave the British a distinct advantage. By rejecting the new cartridge and with it the rifle, the rebels denied themselves a potent weapon. Armed with only their old smooth-bore muskets the mutineers were outgunned. Arthur Moffat Lang kept a journal of the siege of Jalalabad and of the attacks upon the city. He wrote:

> Masses of infantry with scaling ladders came on . . . but they could not stand the penetration of our bullets, which would kill two men one behind the other. Those [Enfields] do give us a wonderful advantage over Pandy [a contemporary phrase used by the British for the rebels], and he finds it very disagreeable to find the conical bullets dropping in at 1500 yards into his column. He can hardly ever get the pluck up to venture within range of his own muskets . . . must now mourn the folly of rejecting these same cartridges which play such mischiefs with him.[37]

Indeed it is clear that if the rebels had accepted the Enfield rifle and then mutinied after, then the British forces would have found the difficulties in suppressing the revolt enormously increased.

The Indian Mutiny was a huge shock to the British and resulted in great changes in how India was governed. The political and military power of the East Indian Company was removed and transferred to a firmly British administration, centred on a Governor or Viceroy and a strong British military presence. Significant strides were made to improve the coverage of both the railways and telegraph networks. This enhanced communication and the speed of movement of troops, as well as having the additional advantage of improving economic growth and penetration. The British were determined that if there was to be any future uprisings then their forces would maintain a superiority in weaponry. To this end, although Indian forces were issued with the Enfield rifle they were the Pattern 1858 and Pattern 1859 muskets for native infantry. Although outwardly very similar to the standard British Enfield, and manufactured to the very high standard as the British rifles, these Indian Service Enfields were predominantly smooth bore and not rifled like the British versions. This meant that these Patterns were less accurate, especially at distances and the range of these weapons was significantly less, thus ensuring that in any possible future conflict British forces would have superior weapons than their potential foes.

Whilst the 1853 Pattern Enfield rifle is strongly associated with both the Crimean War and Indian Mutiny, its use in the American Civil War (1861–5) was on a much larger scale than in these earlier conflicts. The geographical area of the Civil War was close to the combined size of Europe and India and around 620,000 soldiers died in that conflict. The rifle was used to devastating effect by both the Union and Confederate forces. Around 1 million Enfields were exported in more or less equal measure to the two participants by private munitions traders in both London and Birmingham. Many had been discarded and sold off by the British government as worn, damaged or obsolete or they had parts declared as unserviceable. Refurbished by expert gunsmiths in Britain, these rifles found their way to the battlefields of America. Politically this is a crucial point for the British government despite extreme pressures to intervene or take sides directly in the Civil War did not do so and it could firmly say that the Enfield rifles supplied from England were done so from private gunsmiths.

There remain few documented accounts of Enfield rifles being used in specific battles, but with around a million issued their use must have been widespread. However, some specific examples are worth quoting. For example, at the Battle of Shiloh (6–7 April 1862), Union Colonel Morgan Smith (1822–74) reported capturing fourteen Confederate Enfield muskets with the 1861 Tower of London Stamp on their barrels. Similarly, after the Battle of Fair Oaks (31 May 1862) General Dan Sickles (1819–1914) claimed that the field was strewn with Confederate Enfield rifles.[38]

As in the previous conflicts, there are examples of the effectiveness of the Enfield rifle in nullifying artillery fire as well as its use as a sniper rifle. At the Battle of Thorough Gap (28 August 1862) Colonel Henry Benning deployed the 2nd and 17th Georgia regiments, armed with Enfields, so as to fire on an Union artillery battery. At a range of 500–600yd, Benning reported, 'Under our stinging fire, the battery was driven off despite the commanding position of those field guns.'[39] Snipers on both sides of the conflict favoured the long range of the Enfield rifle and certainly in the Confederate forces new Enfields were generally assigned to the sharpshooters in each regiment. Indeed, there are numerous examples of snipers utilising the range and accuracy of the Enfield rifle to claim lives, whether it be at the sieges of Vicksburg and Petersburg or more specific examples, such as the shooting of Union General John Reynolds (1820–63) on the first day of the Battle of Gettysburg (1 July 1863) by a Confederate marksman.

Many of the great battles of the American Civil War, such as Gettysburg (1–3 July 1863), Antietam (17 September 1862), Fredericksburg (13 December 1862) and Shiloh (6–7 April 1862), had specific moments, often more than one, which involved infantry forces attacking en masse across open ground against forces armed with the long-range, and accurate, Enfield rifle. The results, even if the attacking forces through sheer weight of numbers gained some success, were predictable with huge casualties inflicted upon the attacking troops. Today these attacks seem almost suicidal in their execution and perhaps they foretold of the slaughter of First World War where men were sent in a similar fashion to their deaths. Whether it was 1862 or 1916 the troops faced death from the latest scientific advances. Yet, from reinforcing defence the introduction of first the Minié rifle and then the Enfield revolutionised the battlefield in attack too. As Alastair Massie has written:

> The ordinary infantry now possessed a weapon long-ranged and accurate enough to enable him to operate independently. He need no longer manoeuvre in line and fire in volleys to compensate for the inaccuracy of his musket. To that extent the thick skirmishing line into which the Light Division dissolved at the Battle of the Alma during its attack on the Great Redoubt, far from being an aberration, foreshadowed the tactics which, out of necessity, came to be adopted on the even more lethal battlefields of the Franco-Prussian War sixteen years later.[40]

The historian Ben Wilson has written that technology was the symbol of nineteenth-century civilisation and that the weapons devised and produced by the Western powers battered down all resistance. Wilson states, ' The trusty Enfield rifle was the new imperial enforcer, its range and accuracy giving those armed with it advantages over numerically superior forces.'[41] Yet, within just a year of the conclusion of the American Civil War large armies were again fighting in Europe with the next, even more deadly, development of the rifle. Here the next stage in the advancement of the rifle was the breech loader. Like the Enfield, the breech-loading rifle was once again to revolutionise the way armies fought and dramatically alter the landscape of the battlefield, for this time it was not just the rifle's range but also the ease, and thus increased rapidity of fire, that would decide the outcome of the battlefield.

Chapter 3

Breech-loading Rifles – Amoaful, 31 January 1874

> Every man of the right column feels that this is a critical moment, and that he must roll back the tide of the attack, or be driven to flight, and so he plies his faithful Snider with the nervous rapidity born of necessity.
>
> Henry Morton Stanley,
> Coomassie and Magdala

The second half of the nineteenth century witnessed crucial advancements in military technology. Howard Bailes has concluded that the thirty year period from 1855 to 1885 was characterised by rifled ordnance, range finding, the use of electric telegraph and railways for military purposes and, significantly, the adoption of breech-loading rifles by all the main military powers.[1] This weapon became the focus of an arms race amongst the major European armies for the lessons of conflict in the 1860s was that the army which possessed a breech-loading rifle, with a considerable range, would command the battlefield.

The innovation from muzzle-loaders to breech-loaders in the 1860s was, according to Daniel Headrick, no ordinary technical improvement. For it dramatically widened the power gap between Europeans and non-Western peoples and, as Headrick has claimed, led directly to the outburst of imperialism at the end of the century.[2] The concept behind the breech-loading rifle was a simple one: if a gun could be opened at the breech then it could be reloaded quickly and from a prone position. Furthermore, a tighter and harder bullet could be used, making the rifling much more effective and increasing the range and accuracy.

Breech-loading rifles had a long genesis. The concept had been first adopted for cannon as early as the fourteenth century and the manufacture of a breech-loading rifle was first seen in France in 1758. However, technical problems, such as fouling and the escape of gases, could not be overcome by the rifle's inventor, Bordier, who, in despair and frustration, committed suicide.[3] In the 1770s, a British Army Captain, Patrick Ferguson (1744–80), produced an improved weapon, which saw successful service during the War of American Independence, but this initiative was lost after Ferguson's death at the Battle of King's Mountain (7 October 1780). Although the American Army adopted a breech-loading rifle in 1819, from a design conceived by John Hall (1781–1841), the weapon was not widely used due to technical limitations.

The Prussian Dreyse Zundnadelgewehr, or 'needle' rifle, named after its needle-shaped firing pin, first saw action in 1849 against German revolutionaries in Baden and Hesse. Prussia was not a combatant in the 1850s and thus the early design faults, such as a brittle firing pin, a bolt action that was liable to jam, and a weak gas seal around the breech were not immediately resolved. This meant that the full potential of the weapon was not developed for a further fifteen years. However, despite these faults the ease of loading of the Dreyse rifle allowed a rate of fire of four to seven times a minute and could be safely loaded lying down, thus the soldier operating the gun presented less of a target on the battlefield. By the 1860s, although the problems of escaping gases had still to be overcome, the Dreyse was displaying impressive results. Not only was the volume of fire significantly increased, but accuracy had also improved: at a distance of 300ft accuracy was in the region of 65 per cent and at 700ft the rate was an acceptable 43 per cent.[4]

The benefits of the Dreyse breech-loading rifle were readily demonstrated in two European wars of the 1860s. In the war with Denmark in 1864 and again in the war with Austria in 1866, the Dreyse needle gun gave the Prussians two great advantages. Not only could Prussian troops fire three times faster than their enemies, but they could do so laying down or kneeling, thus significantly reducing casualties. The Danes, still reliant on muzzle-loaders, were simply outgunned as the Dreyse rifles were faster to load and had a greater range. The merits of each weapon were clearly demonstrated at the Battle of Lundby (3 July 1864) where Prussian volley fire stopped the Danish assault and inflicted 70 per cent casualties, whilst the Prussians, firing from behind an earth dyke, suffered only 2.4 per cent casualties. Similarly, during the Austro-Prussian War of 1866, or the Seven Weeks War, Prussian infantry fire devastated successive Austrian advances at the battles of Burkersdorf, Rudersdorf and Skalice. At the Battle of Trautenau (27 June 1866) firepower from the Prussian Dreyse rifles inflicted casualties in a ratio of 4:1.[5] At the decisive and final battle of the war, Sadowa (3 July 1866), the Austrians, despite holding a strong defensive position and having superior artillery, then the Prussians were defeated by a combination of irresolution by the Austrian commander, Ludwig August von Benedek (1804–81), flexible Prussian troop movements, at both a company and corps level, and the greater range of the Dreyse rifle, as compared with the Austrian muzzle-loading Lorenz rifle.

The superiority of the breech-loading rifle, so adeptly demonstrated by the Prussians, was clearly understood across the European powers, as well as in America. An arms race was triggered with the French entering the competition first with the adoption of the Chassepot rifle. With an effective range of 650yd, as compared with Dreyse's 350yd, and a rate of fire of six rounds a minute the Chassepot was a superior weapon, as demonstrated at the Battle of Gravelotte (18 August 1870), where the majority of the 20,000 Prussian casualties were as a result of Chassepot fire. However, French superiority in infantry arms did not result in military victory during the Franco-Prussian War (1870–1). During this conflict, a combination of inept and timid French command decisions and the skilled use of troop movements and inspired tactics from the Prussians resulted in crushing victories, for example at the Battle of Sedan (1–2 September 1870).

Following the lead of other major powers, the British also realised that the muzzle-loading rifle was now obsolete and somewhat conservatively the government appointed a Select Committee in 1864 to consider the various options to convert the British Army to breech-loaders. Although the Committee decision was recognised at the time as something of a stopgap, in the circumstances of the urgent need to produce a breech-loader in large quantities it was undoubtedly a correct one. With the British armed with a first-rate rifle in the muzzle-loading Enfield, and possessing tens of thousands of these weapons, the Committee recommended converting the Enfields into breech-loading rifles.

On 23 August 1864, the War Office published a memorandum requesting gun makers to forward their designs for the conversion of the Enfield Pattern 1853 rifle to a breech-loading system. The War Office only insisted upon two broad conditions: the cost of converting the Enfield rifle should not exceed £1 and that the accuracy of the converted weapon should not be in any way inferior to the Enfield. The initial response was rapid and encouraging with forty-five individuals submitting their designs. Of these, six designs of the converted rifles were submitted for trials and tests at the Hythe shooting range. The favoured conversion was one created by Jacob Snider (1811–66) of New York. Although the Snider design was not the most accurate rifle in the trial, it was favoured by the Committee for the ease of the conversion as well as the simplicity of loading and unloading the composite bullet.

The conversion was effected by removing 2½in of the barrel at the breech end, and fitting a 'shoe' or receiver which carried the new breech block. The block was hinged on an axis pin mounted on the right side of the action body, with the pin also incorporating the claw extractor and block return spring. The extractor partially pulled the new centre-fire cartridge case out of the open breech, which was discarded by turning the rifle upside down. The Snider Pattern I was, like the Enfield, chambered for a .577 bullet, as, of course, the barrel remained the same. The army began to be equipped with this Snider–Enfield rifle in 1865 and the first breech-loader to be adopted as the standard weapon for British infantry was officially approved on 18 September 1866.[6]

Like other early military breech-loaders, the Snider fouled quickly and leaked hot gases out of the breech and the more they fouled the more they leaked, until soldiers, due to the obnoxious fumes, and resulting heating of the breech mechanism, had to hold the rifle at arm's length to fire. Apart from being incredibly uncomfortable, holding the Snider in this manner dramatically reduced accuracy.

The Royal Laboratory at Woolwich, which conducted extensive tests on breech-loaders, realised that the weakness was with the paper cartridges. It was concluded that a metal cartridge would solve the problem. In 1866–7 Colonel Edward Boxer (1822–98) of Woolwich developed, from an initial design by George Henry Daw, a brass cartridge that held the bullet, powder and cap together, that was sturdy and waterproof and, best of all, sealed the breech during the explosion, allowing accurate aim. The bullet could now be made harder and tighter and the grooves shallower than before, without fear of gas leakage. As a result the bullet had a longer and flatter trajectory. The Snider's range was extraordinary; whilst the Dreyse needle gun was accurate to 350yd and the Chassepot to 650yd, the Snider–Enfield could fire accurately to 1,000yd.[7] In addition, the Snider mechanism allowed the infantry to rapidly load and reload the new Boxer cartridge and rates of fire of eight to nine aimed rounds a minute were now possible, even in battlefield conditions.

By the end of 1868 the supply of Enfields suitable for conversion had been exhausted. Many of the rifles, having seen hard service in the Crimea and India, were deemed not worthy of conversion so the manufacture of new Sniders, known as the Mark III began. The Snider was later produced as a cavalry carbine and a short-barrelled rifle of 27in was produced for the Royal Irish Constabulary. By the end of 1871 over 650,000 Sniders, whether new manufactures or conversions, had been issued to Regular Forces, Militia and Reserves and colonial governments, with a further 225,000 rifles in store. Such enormous figures indicate the size of Britain's imperial obligations at the time and the huge undertaking to convert the existing Enfields.[8]

Despite the occasional rumblings, between Britain and such military powers as America and France, which might have led to war, British troops were not engaged against a continental enemy from the end of the Crimea War to the beginning of the First World War in August 1914. Indeed, apart from a brief campaign in Egypt in 1882, where the enemy was armed with Remington rifles, British soldiers were not to face an enemy armed with modern breech-loading rifles until the Boer Wars of 1881 and 1899–1902. Britain's nineteenth-century foes were to be primarily indigenous forces found in Africa, the Indian Sub-Continent and New Zealand. These adversaries were either armed with obsolete muzzle-loading rifles or traditional spears, swords or clubs. Thus, against such enemies the British troops were equipped with vastly superior and technologically advanced weapons. Such 'Colonial' campaigns led to British commanders adopting and adapting their tactics to take full advantage of their technological superiority and the terrain conditions in which they fought. Thus, although in many cases the British found themselves greatly outnumbered, the battlefield advantages given to them by advanced breech-loading rifles and the use of defensive formations, such as the square, saw the British repeatedly achieve crushing victories against overwhelming numbers.

The first colonial campaign in which the Snider–Enfield rifle was to demonstrate its effectiveness was the Abyssinian campaign of 1867–8. British and Indian forces, under the command of Sir Robert Napier (1810–90), veteran of the Sikh Wars, the Indian Mutiny and of the taking of the Taku Forts outside of Peking in 1860, were involved in an expedition to free European hostages. The British government had been forced to act against Emperor Tewodros II of Abyssinia (1818–68), who had taken a number of European missionaries and two British envoys hostage for what the mentally unstable Tewodros viewed as a slight to his personal prestige. Patient negotiations by the British came to nothing and with public pressure demanding action the government decided, in August 1867, to despatch an expedition. With the proximity of Bombay the bulk of the forces under Napier's command came from India, where he was then Commander-in-Chief. In all the force would consist of 4,000 European troops, 9,000 Indian troops and a further 7,000 camp followers, and 25,000 head of cattle. Whilst the Indian troops were armed with either smooth-bore Enfields or obsolete muzzle-loading muskets, the British regiments, which included the 4th (King's Own Royal) Regiment of Foot and the 33rd (Duke of Wellington's Regiment) were issued with the Snider–Enfield.

To march the 400 miles from the East African coast to Tewodros' fortress of Magdala, where the hostages were being held, was an enormous logistical challenge and one that Napier relished and rose to. Forty-four elephants were required to carry the heavy components of the four Armstrong artillery pieces and two mortars across high mountainous terrain. In addition, the force was supplied with nearly 1,000 bullocks, 1,800 camels and almost 5,000 mules and ponies. All water and food supplies had to be carried along with the new metal cartridges for the Snider rifles, which were packed in 70lb boxes for the mules to carry. As well as the difficult terrain and harsh climatic conditions, which varied from scorching daytime heat to freezing night-time temperatures, Napier had to use all his diplomatic skills to negotiate safe passage through the numerous tribal areas for his force. Fortunately, Napier was aided by the fact that Tewodros had, by his erratic and autocratic behaviour, managed to upset and alienate many of his followers and many of them wished to see the end of the Emperor's rule.

By 10 April 1868, after nearly three months of arduous marching, Napier's force had reached its goal of the Aroge plain, below the Magdala citadel. The British force comprised an advance 'flying column' of around 5,000 men with the remaining men strung out along the line of advance. To face his adversaries Tewodros had 7,000 fanatical warriors behind the walls of his fortress. These men were generally armed with long curved swords, stabbing spears and had some protection in the form of round, leather shields, 3ft or more in diameter. Around 2,000 were armed with ancient muskets, flintlocks and matchlocks, whilst some 1,000 men carried a double-barrelled percussion weapon, which had been imported from Europe.[9] All these weapons required that Tewodros' men engage with the enemy at close quarters, something Napier was very keen to avoid.

However, as Napier's advanced forced reached the Aroge plain, 1,000ft below the fortress of Magdala, the commander quickly perceived that he had inadvertently given Tewodros an opportunity to launch a potentially catastrophic attack. By taking an easier route than the main body, the mule train and baggage column had arrived in advance of their supporting cavalry and infantry, with only the 23rd Punjab Pioneers in position to protect this vulnerable force. Napier riding ahead realised the danger immediately and despatched his ADC, Captain Scott, at full gallop back down the difficult mountain pass to spur on the men of the 4th who were wearily toiling some distance behind. From his lofty position Tewodros saw his opportunity to attack the prize of the expedition's baggage whilst it was so exposed. At 4pm on the afternoon of 10 April 1868, the first artillery volleys from the seven modern cannon atop of the Fallah Mountain began to fall disconcertingly near to the troops of the 23rd Punjab regiment and Napier and his staff officers. Although the British were aware that Tewodros did possess a sizeable number of artillery pieces, the accuracy of the firing caused some surprise and alarm. Fortunately these first, well-calculated volleys were followed by less accurate ones from the Abyssinian gunners, and the majority of shells now passed harmlessly over the heads of the deploying troops.

After some worrying moments, the 1st Battalion of the 4th King's Own Regiment arrived exhausted. The men were given just a few minutes to recover themselves, before Major General Sir Charles Staveley (1817–96) bellowed, 'Fourth to the Front!'[10] This was met with a rousing, if hoarse, cheer, from the parched throats of the men of the 4th. Just as the 300 men of the 4th advanced so Tewodros unleashed his main attack and around 6,500 warriors descended the slope from Magdala in a rush of screams onto the Aroge plain. The Snider was now to see its first action.

During the trials of the Snider one of the minor disadvantages that had been highlighted was the relatively poor penetrative capacity of the bullet. A plate of wrought iron, a mere quarter of an inch thick, would stop the bullet at just 100yd, as would 6in of sandbag. It was concluded that this poor performance was a result of the hollow nature of the front of the bullet which would allow it to collapse very easily on impact. Yet, in battlefield conditions, as discovered by the troops of the 4th on the Aroge plain, the collapsing nature of the bullet effectively transformed it into a lethal dum-dum-like bullet which produced small entry holes, but horrific exit wounds, increasing the lethal nature of the Snider.

Tewodros delegated command of the assault to one of his most-trusted chieftains, Fitaurari Gabri, who rather conspicuously wore a scarlet robe. Along with the foot soldiers, Gabri also had some 500 chiefs, or principal men, mounted upon either mules or sure-footed Galla ponies, which seemed to fly over the precipitous drop to the plains below. With a thunderstorm as a dramatic backdrop, Gabri led the mile-wide crescent of screaming warriors from the front. As the mass approached the baggage train, hopeful of easy pickings, they were confronted by the 300 men of the 4th in skirmishing order. The small, thin line of khaki-clad infantry waited patiently, and resolutely, for the order to fire. The Commanding Officer of this small band of men was the experienced Colonel Cameron, who watched intently, calculating in his mind the range and speed of movement of the approaching enemy. Although both he and his men knew that the Snider was effective at ranges in excess of 500yd, he waited and waited for the right moment to unleash the rifle's devastating firepower. Many of Cameron's men must have shifted nervously as they waited for the decisive order. Finally, as the warriors approached to within 250yd of the British skirmish line, Cameron calmly gave the order for volley fire.

Simultaneously, 300 rifles were raised to shoulders. Hammers clicked back to full cock and suddenly, and violently, the first volley erupted. As the smoke cleared a wide gap could be seen in the centre of the Abyssinian line, but still the warriors charged on, their pace seemingly unchecked. Gabri fell in this first volley, along with hundreds of his men. The remaining warriors discharged their obsolete muskets in an ineffective salvo and prepared to reload. The British, now firing independently, gave these men no time to do so, as the British fire was continuous. As one man fired, another had rapidly reloaded his Snider. With the men of the 4th easily able to fire between six to eight rounds a minute the line was producing between thirty to forty well-aimed shots every second.[11] The effect of this rate of fire upon the mass of warriors was totally devastating and its intensity seemed to have even taken the men of the 4th by surprise. With a steady breeze blowing the black gunpowder smoke away, the British riflemen had an uninterrupted view of their unfortunate targets.

As Lieutenant Scott was to later describe in a letter home, the Abyssinians 'did catch it!'[12] Tewodros' warriors fell in their hundreds until the line, smashed beyond endurance, wavered and fled. A group of around fifty to sixty managed to get within a hundred yards of the British line before they were reduced to a twitching pile of humanity. The 4th now began a steady advance, firing slowly as targets presented themselves. Some of the Abyssinians, still defiant, stopped to fire their ineffectual muskets only to meet death as dozens of Sniders fired back to riddle their bodies. The retreat was not a rout, despite the firing of rockets from the Naval Brigade, under Captain Fellows, which added shrillness amongst the thunder. Napier was only too aware that he should not allow his troops to advance too far and called a halt. The heavens now opened and the exhausted and desperately thirsty men of the 4th were able to halt and drink their fill.

Despite some flanking movements by the Abyssinians upon the baggage train which had to be beaten back by troops of the Sikh pioneers in fierce hand-to-hand fighting, the battle was effectively won. It had lasted 3 hours and in that time some 2,000 of Tewodros' men had fallen, with around 700 confirmed as dead. His army had been crippled in the first demonstration by the British of the superiority of the breech-loading rifle over the muzzle-loader. British casualties amounted to just twenty wounded of whom two subsequently died.[13]

Although defeated in open battle, Tewodros and 500 of his most loyal supporters remained defiantly behind the walls of the Magdala citadel. Napier knew that an assault would likely be costly and tried to persuade the Emperor to surrender unconditionally, releasing all his hostages at the same time. Tewodros' paranoid and deluded mind did not allow him to see reason and he refused all overtones. Napier steeled his men for the assault, which began in the early morning of 13 April 1868, led by men of the 33rd Regiment. Despite Napier's fears, the assault proved easier than expected and its success owed much to the firepower of the Snider. As men of the 33rd rushed towards the gates of the citadel they were assailed with musket fire. Yet, rapid fire from the Snider kept the defenders heads down. Every puff of smoke from the loopholes was met by a devastating and incessant rattle of the Sniders from the support companies. This allowed a small party of men from the 33rd, including Drummer Magner and Private Bergin, to haul themselves over the outer wall and begin to fire down on the defenders. Both men were to receive the Victoria Cross for their bravery.[14] Tewodros, with his last remaining followers, retreated to the inner wall. Here he released these men from their obligations to him, although many continued to offer resistance. Finally, as the men of the 33rd approached nearer, Tewodros drew a pistol, ironically presented to him as a gift from Queen Victoria, placed its barrel in his mouth and ended his own personal suffering. With his death all further resistance ceased. Forty-five corpses lay around, once more demonstrating the effective firepower of the Snider.

The Snider was to remain in front-line British service for a further nine years, after which it was heavily utilised by troops of the Indian Army. In this period the rifle was to see action in the Ashanti campaign of 1873–4, when its ability to be rapidly loaded and fired in a prone position greatly aided the British in their ultimate success over the West African foes. The warlike Ashanti people, under their ruler King Coffee Calcalli (reigned 1867–74), had been playing a skilful game for a number of years against the British, and the various Governors of the West African Settlements, in which they espoused complacence to a peaceful like existence, whilst pursing their warlike ambitions against neighbouring tribes. When their aggressive intentions turned upon the British protectorate and the numerous forts, and trading posts held by Britain along the coast, including the strategically important fort of Elmina, the British finally awoke to the threat presented by the Ashanti. A small detachment of Royal Marines, and a number of West Indian troops, fought off an early incursion against Elmina in June 1873 and the warlike behaviour of the Ashanti, along with the capture of two German missionaries who were held in the Ashanti capital of Kumasi, finally shocked the British government from its lethargy. A further 200 Marines were urgently despatched, whilst Sir Garnet Wolseley was appointed, on 13 August 1873, to the position of Administrator and Commander-in-Chief on the Gold Coast, with a brief of planning an expedition to West Africa with the aim of both freeing the missionaries and teaching the Ashanti a hard lesson.

In 1870, Wolseley led a bloodless and successful expedition to the Red River to quell a Metis rebellion against Canadian sovereignty over the Northwest Territories and Manitoba. The revolt, led by Louis Riel (1844–85), was focused at Fort Garry (now modern day Winnipeg). As a result of this success, Wolseley was riding high in the War Office's esteem. Indeed, apart from the obvious climatic differences, the logistical difficulties of the Red River and Ashanti expeditions were similar. In 1870, Wolseley led his men through a network of lakes and rivers which extended over 600 miles to reach their goal of Fort Garry. On many occasions his men had to manhandle their boats out of the water concourses and across land to reach another lake or tributary, whilst at the same time they had to worry about how the Native Americans would view their presence. If the British were to reach the Ashanti capital, Kumasi, nearly 150 miles from the coast and deep in the jungle, they would have to cut their way through forest and ford rivers and streams, building boats and bridges on route. Wolseley was the obvious choice to lead such a logistically difficult and physically challenging expedition.

However, initially Wolseley was frustrated by the British government's reluctance to use British regiments for the task in hand. Recognising the demands of the climate and terrain, Wolseley informed the government that he wished to take two battalions, composed of hand-picked men, to Ashanti. Aware of the need to economise, and fearful of the toil the climate make take upon British troops, the government declined and instead instructed Wolseley to take thirty-five special service officers, as well as the West Indian troops already in place, and with these men train up local friendly natives to advance upon Kumasi. Amongst these men, who were later to be christened 'The Ashanti Ring', were such future senior officers as Evelyn Wood (1838–1919), Redvers Buller (1839–1908), George Colley (1835–81), Henry Brackenbury (1837–1914) and Archibald Alison (1826–1907). Yet, even with such talent on offer the task facing them of assembling a local force was to prove impossible.

At first Wolseley and his officers, particularly Evelyn Wood, focused on the local coastal tribe, the Fantis, as their primary source of foot soldiers. Yet, it soon became apparent that the Fantis were not natural soldiers and Wolseley was forced to despatch Major Baker Russell (1837–1911) along the coast to the Gambia and Sierra Leone to recruit more warlike troops. Wolseley discovered that a number of the Ashanti who had previously attacked the fort at Elmina were still close by at the village of Essaman, where they were enjoying the hospitality of the local chief.

Wolseley felt that, despite the inferior nature of the troops he had at his disposal, he should send a force to Essaman, under the command of Wood. Although this small expedition was a success, capturing the Ashanti completely by surprise and forcing their retreat, neither the locally recruited troops, nor the West Indian soldiers, covered themselves in glory. Both demonstrated a lack of discipline, firing wildly whilst showing a distinct reluctance to close with the enemy. Wolseley learnt much from this sortie, especially about the nature of the advance through thick jungle. At one point Wood's men had taken 3 hours to advance just 4 miles. Men fell behind through exhaustion and although the troops had carried as much water as possible, it proved insufficient. Clearly the march on Kumasi would require the most-detailed planning.

Yet, it was the poor performance of the troops that was of huge concern to Wolseley and he used their example to persuade the government of the need to despatch the two battalions of infantry, with artillery and engineers, which he had originally sought. In addition, Wolseley realised that he would require more special service officers for the nature of the jungle, the density of the foliage which reduced visibility significantly, meant that a larger than usual ratio of officers to men would be needed to maintain order and cohesion. Later engagements were to prove that this was to be a very wise precaution.

Wolseley received news from the War Office that his requests would be met and that the 2nd Battalion, The Rifle Brigade, Royal Welch Fusiliers (23rd Regiment of Foot) and the 42nd Royal Highland (The Black Watch) Regiment, all armed with the Snider rifle, would arrive on the Gold Coast in early December 1873. The Black Watch was brought up to the stipulated strength of 650 men with a draft of 170 men from the 79th Highland Regiment. Wolseley and his officers used the intervening weeks to concentrate on gathering intelligence on the enemy's whereabouts and intentions and for planning the advance. Having proved themselves of limited military ability, Wood's Regiment of local men were used by Wolseley primarily to begin construction of a road way from the coast, through the jungle to the Prah River, the natural border into Ashanti territory proper. To ensure that the British regiments would arrive at the operational assembly area by the Prah River dry-shod, Major Home, the Commander of the Royal Engineers, not only had to construct the road, but also to build nearly 240 bridges to cross the many rivers and streams on the route, as well as numerous causeways across areas of swamp.

Before the British regiments could join the expedition, Wolseley's irregular troops were involved in two clashes with the Ashanti, under the command of their most successful and fearsome commander, Amanquatia. On 7 November 1873, Wood and his irregular forces were ordered by Wolseley to support an attack upon the village of Abrakampa which was held by a sizeable Ashanti force. The attack was something of a farce with the new recruits simply refusing to advance upon the village. Despite 'encouragement' from the special service officers, one of whom broke his umbrella over the back of one of the Hausas, the men lay down and refused to move. Fortunately, Amanquatia considered it prudent to withdraw. The casualties were restricted to 'friendly fire' when twenty Hausas were killed when their companions began firing in panic at the Ashanti rearguard. This caused the remainder of the coastal men to flee the 20 miles back home. Wolseley later wrote of their actions that, 'Their duplicity and cowardice surpasses all description.'[15]

The next, equally disastrous, engagement took place on 27 November at another Ashanti-held village, Faysowah. The main Ashanti force was aiming to retreat back across the Prah River, just as Wolseley's men continued to hack their way through the jungle. Amanquatia decided, on this occasion, to make a stand in a strong defensive position. Initially the attack by the Hausa and Sierra Leone troops against the enemy's rearguard went well. However, the main Ashanti body adopted their usual tactic of trying to outflank the advance. Realising that his men were in some danger, Wood gave the command for an orderly withdrawal, which quickly became a rout as the irregular troops dropped their guns, ammunition and baggage and fled in panic. The situation was only saved by a group of the special service officers, including Wood and Lieutenants Eyre and Woodgate, who formed a sufficiently strong fighting rearguard action which allowed all the troops to extract themselves from a dangerous position. The Snider's ease of loading and reloading proved a significant advantage in this challenging and dangerous situation. Clearly the British regiments could not arrive soon enough.

Wolseley and his officers had managed to achieve something of a small miracle in constructing a pathway from the coast to the banks of the Prah River, battling both the climate, the harsh terrain and the constant threat from the Ashanti. The path was 12ft wide, clear of roots, allowing the British regiments to march four abreast to various staging camps along the route, in which the troops would spend the night. Each of these camps was designed to house 400 men and their officers in huts constructed of wattle with palm-leaf-thatched roofs. There was fresh meat and bakeries and the perimeter was cleared to a distance of at least 100yd to deny cover to an attacking force.

Now work on a base camp, on the edge of the river bank, began which it was intended would be sufficient to accommodate all the men of the British battalions as they arrived. From here Wolseley could launch his final assault upon Kumasi. It was here on Boxing Day 1873 that Wood received ambassadors from the Ashanti king who arrived to discuss possible peace terms. With Wolseley still at the coast, awaiting the arrival of the British troops, Wood was in no position to negotiate so instead he decided to demonstrate the destructive firepower of the latest addition to the armoury of the British Army, the Gatling gun. Although the Gatling would become an important weapon in the future conflicts of the 1880s, it was not used in combat by the British until 1879. Yet, its deadly potential was amply shown to the Ashanti delegation, one of whom, in his despair, promptly blew his head off with his own antique blunderbuss.[16]

Wolseley traded numerous letters with the Ashanti king in an attempt to secure the release of hostages held in Kumasi as well as trying to negotiate possible peace terms. These letters became more frequent as British troops began to arrive at the coast. Whilst the British government was keen to see a peaceful resolution, which secured the release of hostages, Wolseley deduced that the king's letters were being used as a stalling tactic. King Calcalli began to release his missionary hostages from 12 January 1874, in the face of the British advance, but Wolseley was becoming exasperated by the king's letters of petition and platitudes. He announced in a letter to the king on 24 January, when just 30 miles from the capital, that, 'I intend to go to Coomassie [Kumasi]. It is for your Majesty to decide whether I go there as your friend or your enemy.'[17] Wolseley also announced that he would require Ashanti hostages, which included the queen mother and the king's heir, as a gesture of the king's peaceful sincerity. Whether Wolseley realised it or not, such terms would have been politically impossible for Calcalli to accept and thus the king must have now realised that further conflict was inevitable.

Wolseley used the next week to accumulate supplies of both food and ammunition and to bring up the last of the British troops. Two hundred men of the Welch Fusiliers advanced from the coast to replace those troops that had succumbed to sickness. His force now numbered 1,509 European and 708 native troops. Available intelligence put the Ashanti Army at in excess of 10,000 men. Wolseley was fully aware of the Ashanti's battlefield tactic of using the dense jungle foliage as cover to close on their foes unseen, whilst a large part of the available force would try to outflank their enemy's position. Such tactics were eloquently explained by Evelyn Wood on his return to England when he was invited to speak to the Royal United Services Institution:

> The study of previous battles, and the experience gained in the minor actions of the previous four months, showed plainly that the Ashanti tactics are ever the same. The centre is refused, while sweeping turning movements are made on the flanks.

There is for naked and hardy warriors in thick forests, little of the danger which in Europe would be incurred by such tactics; for unclothed, without baggage, they can always retreat on their hands and knees through the tangled underwood, and re-form, almost unmolested by Europeans.[18]

Wolseley devised two specific tactics to overcome this approach, both of which relied heavily on the firepower of the Snider. The first of these was the sensible and practical decision to subdivide his force into small interlocking sections as they advanced through the thick jungle. It was soon discovered that the men could often only maintain contact with those either side of them in the bush, such was the density of the foliage. Control at company level was simply impossible. Thus, delegation was given to sectional commanders, junior officers and NCOs, who had total responsibility during the advance for a small detachment of four to six men. Contact could be maintained and orders and directions given and just as importantly fire discipline and control was established so that the rapid and devastating fire of the Snider could be used to its best advantage.

Wolseley's second innovation, to overcome both the jungle and the Ashanti's flanking tactics, was to advance into battle in a square formation. It was thought that not only would this nullify the threat to the formation's flanks but it would also maintain cohesion and maximise the effect of concentrated Snider rifle fire. Whilst the battle at Amoaful was to highlight the difficulty of maintaining a square formation during an advance through jungle terrain, the square did allow Wolseley to hold on to the essences of his command and he was able to direct the battle effectively.

As the British force advanced towards the Ashanti capital, clashes between troops and enemy scouts became more frequent. On one noteworthy occasion, Sergeant Armstrong of the Rifle Brigade was leading a patrol when it collided with a party of Ashanti warriors. Calling upon his comrades to lie down, he killed one of the enemy at close range with his Snider rifle, then a second with his sword bayonet and was then able to reload his Snider quickly to kill a third. The rest of the Ashanti scouts fled. Armstrong, who was, in 1878, to win the Queen's Medal as the best shot in the British Army, had ably demonstrated that, with a cool head, the rapid reloading ability of the Snider made the rifle a very lethal weapon.

Throughout the campaign, Buller worked tirelessly in his role of intelligence officer to gather as much information about both the movements and intentions of the Ashanti. Spies and patrols were sent forward of the British advance and from the details received from these sources it soon became clear that King Calcalli was preparing to make a stand on rising ground a mile outside the village of Amoaful. Here the Ashanti forces, under the command of Amanquatia, began to mass. Wolseley was concerned to hear this intelligence for two reasons. First, he understood how strong the Ashanti position was to be and second by forcing a battle at Amoaful, King Calcalli had given his army an opportunity to resist the British advance a second time if Wolseley and his men could not be stopped at Amoaful. Wolseley had very much hoped the war could be won with one decisive battle, thus minimising British losses and reducing the huge logistical demands on the expedition. He described his thoughts in his autobiography, *The Story of a Soldier's Life*:

> I was anxious to finish the war with one big fight: but the King's determination to fight at Amoaful made it tolerably certain I should have two battles, which was a disappointment. Throughout this war my one longing was to end it with all possible speed, as every extra day it lasted, meant more deaths from fever. This thought was never absent from my mind.[19]

On the night of 30 January, with it clear to Wolseley that battle would be faced the following morning, the British commander called together his senior officers to carefully explain his plans for the British advance upon the Ashanti position. Wolseley informed his officers that he believed that the British would be attacked in force and that the Amanquatia would attempt to use his numerical advantage to try and outflank the British. Wolseley issued the following order:

> The troops will advance to-morrow . . . in the following order: 42nd Highlanders, Rait's guns, Naval Brigade, Rait's rockets, 23rd R.W. Fusiliers, Rifle Brigade. Wood's and Russell's Regiments [of irregulars; native troops], which are now in advance, will be drawn up on the side of the road, and will, on the above column reaching them, strike in between the 23rd R.W. Fusiliers and Rifle Brigade.[20]

Wolseley clarified to his commanders that as the enemy's picquets were approached the troops were to deploy in a square formation, of approximately 600yd in width, with the front commanded by Brigadier

General Sir Archibald Alison, leading his Highlanders, the left flank by Colonel M'Leod, the right by Lieutenant Colonel Wood and the rear by Lieutenant Colonel Warren, with the Rifle Brigade. The reserve of ammunition was to be held inside this square and here was to be found Wolseley, his aides, surgeons, a company of Fusiliers and the special correspondents of the national newspapers. The Royal Engineers were given the task of trying to clear a path for the advancing Highlanders, a task that was soon to prove impossible. The briefing was concluded with a reminder to the troops that when meeting the enemy, 'Be cool; fire low, fire slow, and charge home. . .'.[21]

After a disturbed night's sleep, which had been punctuated by the sounds of defiant drumming from the Ashanti force in front of them, the British began to break camp at dawn on 31 January 1874. Following an early breakfast, the British force assembled and scouts, forty in number, under the command of Lord Gifford advanced ahead of the main British formation. On approaching the village of Egginassie, at around 8am, Gifford's men were fired upon, although a rush by the scouts saw the enemy hastily withdraw. However, as the British ventured further forward it became clear that a sizeable Ashanti force awaited them. Gifford informed Alison who began to bring forward the Highlanders. It was not long before three companies were heavily engaged and Alison quickly realised that the Ashantees were attempting to turn his left flank. Orders were quickly despatched to bring up reserves.

The battle quickly developed and intensified. Alison fed in company after company of his Highlanders in skirmish order, whilst the Naval Brigade and the irregular forces of Wood and Russell attempted to defend the flanks. The Royal Engineers under Major Buckle tried to clear a path for 300yd from the jungle path so as to ease the passage of the troops forward. However, despite the tremendous efforts of the Royal Engineers, and their Sierra Leone labourers, the men suffered from continuous heavy fire from the invisible Ashanti warriors and when Buckle was mortally wounded the progress stalled.

Winwood Reade (1838–75), the special correspondent of *The Times*, had forsaken the relative safety of the centre of the square and had advanced, with a Snider in his arms, with the Black Watch and had thus been able to observe the battle from the start. Reade recalled that the Highlanders had advanced about 200yd from the village of Egginassie when the Ashanti, lying quietly and invisible in the undergrowth, opened up with a wall of fire. Reade dived and sought refuge behind a tree. He later wrote, 'A hundred yards ahead the forest was filled with smoke, and seemed to roar. Tongues of flame shot forth, and these alone served as a mark, for not a man was to be seen.'[22]

The fire from the enemy was so intense that no single shot could be distinguished. Fortunately for the British, the Ashanti were armed with flintlock smooth-bore muskets, old if not antique and poorly serviced. However, more importantly the gunpowder used was very inferior and this combined with the lack of proper bullets meant that the Ashanti fire produced a great deal of smoke and noise, but little penetration. The Ashanti resorted to using a varied collection of projectiles, ranging from pebbles to rusty nails, and thus whilst British casualties were high, fatal wounds were not.

Wolseley had centred the square in Egginassie and initially his only idea of the progress of the battle was the distinctive sound of Snider volley fire and the dull roar from the Ashanti muskets. The seriousness of the situation soon became apparent with the return of the first wounded Highland officer bearing a report to Wolseley from Alison. It stated that the 42nd were heavily engaged and that 'our loss in wounded is pretty severe' and requested further troop support and surgeons to be sent forward. Alison's message also made clear that he only had one company in reserve and 'that the enemy is holding his ground stoutly and some relief to my men would be advantageous'.[23] This message was followed by a steady stream of wounded Scotsmen returning from the front. The Ashanti, so skilled in the use of the jungle cover, were able to lay in wait as the Highlanders advanced and fire at them at near point-blank range. Lying flat on the ground, naked and without accoutrements, the Ashanti would fire then crawl away backwards on their stomachs unseen by the British. One section of the 42nd killed an Ashanti a mere 4yd from their position, never spotting their foe until he fired at them. Initially, the only British response was to follow Wolseley's advice and fire low and fire slow and rely on the killing power of the Snider.

Alison later graphically described the nature, and confusion, of the jungle battle. The Highlanders were forced to descend into a ravine and up on the other side was the main Ashanti force. As the troops pressed on they disappeared into the undergrowth, with only the sound of the Snider and the bagpipes giving any indication as to their location. Furthermore, Ashanti skirmishers caused additional confusion by infiltrating between the British companies and firing at each. Frequently the British found it difficult to know where the incoming fire was coming from and, on occasion, they found themselves firing upon other British units. At least one wounded officer had a Snider bullet extracted from him. Alison wrote, 'The Ashantis stood admirably and kept up one of the heaviest fires I was ever under [Alison had previously fought in China, the Crimea and in India]. While opposing our front attack with immensely superior numbers, they kept enveloping our left with a series of well-directed flank attacks.'[24]

Private Ferguson, of the 42nd Highlanders, recalled, 'The Ashantees were swarming in advance on our flanks in thousands . . . We were fighting in sections, every man in his place, and doing his best. Seldom we got a right shot at a black fellow, they kept so well under cover, but they did keeping popping at us! And so close it was too!'[25]

Wolseley's hoped for mutual support from the square formation began to disintegrate as both the troops on the left and right flanks were stalled either by the intensity of the Ashanti fire or the impenetrable nature of the jungle. Indeed, on the right flank the square could not be properly formed due to the density of the jungle foliage. Since there was nothing to be gained by surprise, Wolseley tried to regain some control by ordering the bugles to keep sounding the regimental calls to inform the units of each other's location.

Just as the British casualties in the centre and front of the advance were reaching a critical level the situation was saved by the hard work and commitment of Captain Rait and Lieutenant Saunders of the Royal Artillery, who, with their Hausa gunners, managed to manoeuvre one of the 7lb cannon to the front of the advance. With the sweating and exhausted Fante ammunition bearers following behind, Rait was able to position his gun, which soon became a rallying point for the Highlanders. Each time the gun fired, the men of the 42nd roared encouragement to each other and flung themselves forward a few yards and Rait's men rolled their weapon forward to. Gradually in this fashion the Ashanti were pushed back.

Winwood Reade wrote:

> Up went the gun; every five minutes there was a halt; the gun was fired two or three times; the Highlanders crept into the bush on the right and the left. Then I heard a clear cheery voice cry out 'Advance!' and the 42nd gave a cheer, and the Hausas cheered, and the Fantes cheered and the gun was wheeled

along for fifteen or twenty yards . . . yet still the slugs sang over us and savagely slashed the boughs above our heads.[26]

The work of Rait's gun began to have the desired effect and after nearly 3½ hours of continuous fighting the resistance in front of the Highlanders began to slacken. Several Snider volleys deadened the last of the Ashanti fire and with the pipers playing 'The Campbells are coming', the Black Watch, with a stumbling charge, carried the village of Amoaful. Wolseley learnt of the success when he heard the cheers of the Scotsmen and noticed that the casualties were now not Highlanders, but Welshmen, Riflemen and men of the Naval Brigade. In a letter to his wife, Louisa, written the day after the battle, Wolseley wrote, 'Our loss was heavy and my heart was sick as I stood on the road behind the fighting and each wounded man went past me. Every doctor looked like a butcher his hands and clothes covered with blood . . .'[27]

The objective may have been captured but the battle was far from won. As the Rifles and the Welsh Fusiliers advanced to support the success of the Highlanders they were met with Ashanti resistance from the same ground that the Scotsmen had just passed over! The Ashanti might have melted away in front of the Highlanders advance, but had clearly used the cover of the undergrowth to once more infiltrate the British line. Lieutenant Maurice Fitzgerald, serving with the Rifles, described his experiences of being under fire during the battle, 'The slugs were dropping thick and fast, and there was a moment or two when the men's nerves were certainly a very ticklish condition. There is something very unpleasant about shots that come suddenly out – sometimes singly, sometimes in loud and continuously repeated bursts, from places that a moment before gave no indication of human life.'[28]

In a letter home, one of Fitzgerald's colleagues, Rifleman Gilham, wrote of his first encounter of fighting in the jungle,

> We cut our way right and left into the jungle . . . lying down in the underwood, standing behind trees for cover, pegging in where we could, and forming a semi-circle to the front; but the foliage was so dense that it was like being in a net, and the farther we went the thicker it seemed to get, so that I don't believe we advanced a hundred yards during the whole fight.[29]

Battle of Sobroan, 10 February 1846. British and Gurkha troops enter the Sikh defences. (*National Army Museum*)

The Grenadier Guards, with Enfield rifles, at the Battle of Inkerman, 5 November 1854.

Men of the 77th Regiment in the Crimea. Their Enfield rifles are clearly on display.

Snider Action (open)

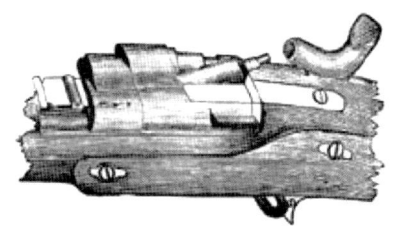

Snider Action (closed)

Loading the Snider rifle – the mechanism designed by Jacob Snider to adapt the Enfield rifle into a breech-loading weapon is clearly seen.

The fighting in Ashanti, 1874, from a painting by Orlando Norie. British troops, wearing their specially designed jungle uniforms, advance in skirmish order with the Snider rifle.

The Martini–Henry breech-loading system.

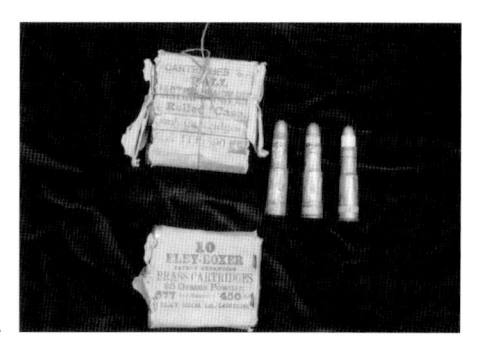

Martini–Henry Boxer cartridges.

The Battle of Gingindlovu. Men of the Naval Brigade (HMS *Shah*) with the Martini–Henry rifle.

The British square at the Battle of Abu Klea.

The Lee–Metford Mark I.

The 11th Hussars, part of the Light Camel Regiment, during the Gordon Relief Expedition of 1884–5, with Martini–Henry rifles.

Troops of the 1st Lincolnshire Battalion waiting between the two dervish attacks at the Battle of Omdurman, 2 September 1898. Their Lee–Metford rifles are clearly seen.

A .47in naval gun mounted for land operations during the Boer War.

A Maxim gun, used as both a defensive and offensive weapon during Buller's attempts to relieve Ladysmith.

A .47in naval gun positioned on top of Monte Cristo which targeted the Boer position on Pieter's Hill.

Troops of the Royal Lancashire Regiment carrying Pieter's Hill following the barrage assault.

In addition, the enemy's resistance on both the right and left flank was as strong as ever.

Captain Luxmore, RN, part of the Naval Brigade detachment was supporting the advance of Wood's Irregulars on the right who soon were stalled by heavy fire from the Ashanti warriors. Luxmore's right wing was ordered by Wood to clear a path 300yd eastwards into the jungle before turning north and advancing parallel to the road. However, the intensity of the enemy's fire was such that this move was pinned down after only a hundred yards. Luxmore described the battle:

> My men lying down to escape the enemy's storm of bullets and slugs, and there we had to remain for over four hours without being able to advance . . . the bush was so dense that one could scarcely see one's own men . . . The whole day I only saw one living Ashantee about 50 yards from me, and as I was in the act of going to snatch a rifle out of a man's hand, he saw my movement and hid.[30]

Wood's command had been pinned down for nearly 4 hours and were forced to make a clearing in the undergrowth and defend this perimeter against constant Ashanti attacks. Repeated volleys of Snider fire held the enemy en masse at bay, but individual warriors were able to use the jungle cover to good effect. Wood himself was hit by a rusted nail, which penetrated his chest just above his heart. He was forced to hand over command to Luxmore and return to the centre of the square to seek medical assistance. Wolseley despatched men of the Rifles to link up with the right flank and with the troops of the left flank finally forcing their way through the undergrowth it seemed that the battle was finally won. The Ashanti fire slackened further and Gifford's scouts reported that the Ashanti forces in front of Amoaful had retired. Yet, the enemy now moved again to the flanks and launched an attack on the centre of the square. Ashanti bullets were flying, once more, thick and many of the already wounded were hit again, as well as some of the headquarter staff, including Lieutenant Maurice. One of the newspaper correspondents, a certain Henry Morton Stanley (1841–1904), who was later to acquire worldwide fame as the man who located Dr Livingstone, was forced, like other correspondents, to reach for a Snider which he fired, in his own words, 'with the nervous rapidity born of necessity'.[31]

Wolseley, realising that at this crucial moment many of his men were looking to him, was determined to display confidence and indifference and walked around the square, puffing on one of his favourite cigars. Eventually men of the Welch Fusiliers and Rifles, following the example of Commodore Hewitt who led them into the bush waving his naval cutlass over his head, managed to force the Ashanti back with volleys of Snider fire.

After continuous fighting from 8.30am to after 2pm, the battle seemed to be finally won. Stanley ventured from the centre of the square and moved through the battlefield to Amoaful. Along the route he was able to witness the results of the Snider fire:

> Around their camp the Ashantees were thickly lying, with most frightful wounds, proving that Snider rifles have terrible force and penetration. If other evidences were needed to establish this fact, the wreck of the bush, and the deep rugged rents of great trees, seen all around, did so. Those who undervalue this gun make a great mistake. Its rapidity and ease of manipulation is such that a regiment has to be kept constantly supplied from the reserve ammunition, while the perfect construction of the Boxer cartridge and its excellent materials leaves nothing to be desired in the shape of an efficient small arm for any service.[32]

The battle had been bloody. The Ashanti, firing their mostly Dane-gun smooth-bore muskets had peppered the British, inflicting 25 per cent casualties on the Highlanders. Captain Buckle of the Royal Engineers and 2 privates from the 42nd were killed, whilst 21 officers and 173 men were wounded of whom 3, including Major Baird, were to die of their wounds.[33] Colonel Wood was to live to the ripe old age of 81 and he reached the rank of Field Marshal, after a distinguished career. The Ashanti nail in his chest, however, could not be extracted and he carried it forever.

As Wood said in his report to the Royal United Services Institution, 'It is difficult to compute the enemy's loss. 163 bodies were found in one trench on the plateau of Amoaful and the next morning several rows of dead bodies were laid out in a dell on the flank – clearly waiting to be buried'.[34] Yet, it seems very likely that the real number of Ashanti killed was between 2,000 and 3,000 for it was the Ashanti custom to remove their fallen from the field even at the height of battle. One of the staff officers, Brackenbury, reported that as he ventured from the centre of the square to the Highlanders' forward position with a message from Wolseley he had passed a dead Ashanti chief propped up against a hut. On his return the body had been removed.[35] What is known for sure is that Amanquatia had been killed by a private in the Black Watch and several other important chiefs had also died. The British success owned much to Rait's gun as well as the determination and bravery of the British troops. Yet, the Snider had more than proved its worth in such trying conditions. The ease of loading and reloading had been crucial in breaking up Ashanti attacks. Whilst the enemy had been able to snipe at the British, the effective Snider volleys had deterred the enemy from massing and from charging in overwhelming force. Yet, even Wolseley was not slow to admit that the battle had been close and he later wrote, 'The enemy fought well under the terrific fire we poured into them, and had they been armed with Snider rifles we must have been destroyed.'[36]

Yet, the Ashanti had one last surprise in that a force now turned its attention on the supply line up from the village of Quarman. Here a large force attacked the supply base at around 3pm and were held at bay by a small group of West Indian troops, until a relief unit of Rifles managed to reach the base an hour later. Colonel Colley received a nasty surprise when, towards evening, he was at the head of a main baggage column, some 5 miles in length, that was approaching Quarman. Suddenly the column was attacked along its length. Many of the porters fled in panic and Colley was swept in the rush back down to Insafu. The next morning Colley returned along the same route, which was now lined by nine companies of Rifle men and Highlanders. Unfortunately, a great deal of Wolseley's limited supplies was lost to the enemy and the British commander was faced with a critical decision. He knew it was very likely that a further advance towards Kumasi, now just 15 miles away, would result in another pitch battle. Yet, with supplies dwindling, and 12 per cent of his force wounded, he knew he had to risk one last advance on the Ashanti capital.

Wolseley thus resolved on a bold dash. With just four days' rations for a potential five-day operation to cover the 30 miles there and back to Kumasi, as well as probably having to fight yet another pitch battle, this was a risky plan and one Wolseley felt he needed to put to his troops. The decision was unanimously in favour of one last push and steps were made to entrench Amoaful and leave behind the heavy baggage, the weak and the wounded.

Carrying only their Sniders, grey coats, ammunition and rations, the flying column advanced on Kumasi in the early morning of 3 February.

With Gifford's scouts again leading the way, with support from Baker Russell's men and the Rifles, the British were soon under almost constant sniping. Their progress was slowed by such attacks and on numerous occasions a halt had to be called so that Snider volleys could crash into the jungle so as to deter the Ashantees. These volleys had the desired effect and for the last few hours, as the force reached the Ordah River, it moved unmolested. Here, the British entrenched once more, whilst engineers built one last bridge. The following morning, after a very wet night of continuous heavy rain which resulted in little sleep for the expeditionary force, Wolseley set the immediate objective of capturing the village of Ordashu, the last significant place before Kumasi itself. Again, Buller had been busy gathering intelligence so Wolseley was aware that the whole of the remaining Ashanti Army, up to 10,000 men, was immediately ahead of his force, and ready to oppose the advance on Kumasi.

Wood, who had recovered sufficiently to lead forward his force of Irregular troops, was the advanced guard. As Ordashu was approached Wood's men came under sustained fire. The men of the Bonny tribe, who had received little or no training on how to fire the Snider, became very reluctant to advance. At this critical time, the Ashantees once again infiltrated close to the British and Wood's loyal Lieutenant, Arthur Eyre, received a mortal wound from which he died 2 hours later. Wolseley sent forward the Rifle Brigade, with Lieutenant Saunders and one of the 7pdr field guns, and they passed through the Bonny men and the advance finally progressed, albeit slowly. Just as at the Battle of Amoaful, the gun fired and the infantry would then advance and gradually the Rifles pushed on to enter Ordashu. The Ashanti were not offering anywhere near the same resistance as they had previously. Generally, there was a reluctance to come to close quarter and the British received much more long-distance enemy fire, which, with their poor quality of arms and ammunition, meant that the Ashanti inflicted minimal casualties.

After 2 hours of fighting Ordashu had been secured, but at around 11am, under the gaze of the Ashanti king, who was seated on a stool to the rear of his army, his troops made one last determined effort to retake the village. Wolseley had moved up to Ordashu and established his command there. He later described the scene as a 'regular inferno'.[37] Rait's two guns were in action and there was a deafening roar of Ashanti musketry on all sides. The enemy now pressed close, so close indeed that Wolseley's Chief of Staff, Colonel Greaves, emptied his revolver amongst them.

Wolseley was even hit on his helmet by an Ashanti slug, which fortunately did not penetrate it. Again, it was the deadly volleys of the Snider rifles that finally silenced the enemy, for the Ashanti began to copy the tactics of the British and even formed line, as well as they could in the bush, to fire a volley, but as soon as they had fired they were mowed down by Snider fire. By noon Wolseley had been able to move all his supplies and men into Ordashu and had entrenched and fortified his position.

Many of the Ashanti moved on the now empty British bivouacs of the night before and this gave Wolseley the opportunity to order forward the men of the Black Watch with the task of making a dash on Kumasi. Ignoring and overcoming ambuscade after ambuscade on the route, the Highlanders penetrated all resistance as the Ashanti fled back to Kumasi. Within 3 miles of the capital the exhausted 42nd stopped at the village of Karsi and Alison called upon Wolseley for support.

Sir Garnet now advanced with his whole force to join the Scotsmen. After some rest the Black Watch marched into Kumasi, to find all opposition gone and only a long line of Ashanti resentfully staring at the strangely clad white men. Wolseley, and the remainder of the force, entered just as darkness was falling and the British hastily established a perimeter and made camp. Several of the irregular troops were caught looting during the night and one Fante was hanged by the British as an example to others. Wolseley had hoped that an intact capital would finally persuade the king himself to negotiate with the British. There was no possibility of the British marching further into the interior in search of the recalcitrant monarch and after a further night in Kumasi, during which the king's promised arrival never materialised, Wolseley recognised that he must march his force back to the coast, to tend to the wounded and sick and embark for home before any more of his troops succumbed. Thus, in the early morning of 6 February, after Buller, under Wolseley's instruction, had looted the Palace Treasury, the British force departed, leaving the Ashanti capital in flames.

Wolseley finally managed to secure a huge indemnity from the king as part of a peace deal, although this was never paid, but it did at least bring some finality to the conflict. Crucially, the Ashanti never threatened the coastal settlements again. With only forty-three fatalities, fourteen killed in battle, the rest dying of wounds or sickness, the expedition was considered a huge success. The bravery of the troops, Wolseley's expert planning to reduce the incidences of tropical illness and the devastating firepower, combined with the ease of loading, of the Snider had resulted in this being one of the most successful of the many campaigns of Victoria's reign.

Although the Ashanti expedition and the earlier Abyssinian campaign were the only two significant occasions in which front-line British troops used the Snider in battle, the rifle had a long and distinguished life as an arm for colonial forces. Its ease of maintenance and loading and its ability to operate in the most testing of climatic conditions meant that the Snider was to see service in Afghanistan, the North West Frontier, Burma, the Sudan and Egypt.

After the initial conversions from the existing stock of Enfield rifles, the Snider was produced and issued in several variants. There were four Marks of Artillery Carbine, including one for the Cadet Corps, and three Cavalry Carbines, the last of which was produced as late as 1885. In addition, there was a Short Snider Rifle, with a barrel length of 30.5in, as compared with the standard rifle which had a 36.5in barrel. A naval version also had the same barrel length as the Short Rifle, but could also take the cutlass bayonet. A Snider Carbine issued to the Royal Engineers was converted from the Lancaster Carbine and a small number of Enfield rifles were converted into a carbine for use by the Prison Service and these were given the official title of 'Carbine Snider, .577, Convict Civil Guard'. Over 13,000 Snider Carbines were produced specifically for the Irish Constabulary and were used to suppress the Fenian Rising of 1867. This particular carbine was issued with a sword bayonet with an 18in sawback blade.[38] The Irish Constabulary used the variant until the early 1900s and some units of Artillery Militia, Yeomanry and Cadet Corps for even longer. Therefore, to employ the word 'temporary' to the service of the Snider is undoubtedly incorrect. Indeed, in the hands of Indian troops the Snider was to have a distinguished service in front-line action as late as 1893, nearly twenty years after it began to be withdrawn from British regiments.

The shock of the Indian Mutiny (1857–8) had taught the British military many lessons and perhaps the most important one was that if the mutineers had had access to, or wished to use the superior range and firepower of, the Enfield rifle then many of the engagements, or even the Mutiny itself, could have had different outcomes. It was thus resolved that in future Indian Army forces would be armed with weapons that were inferior to those carried by British regiments so that the British would always have a battlefield advantage, at least in terms of rate and range of fire, in any possible future conflict. Thus, the Snider rifle, in the hands of Indian troops, was to remain in service long after it had been superseded by the Martini–Henry rifle as the front-line weapon for British troops. Throughout the Second Afghan War (1878–80), the Snider was carried by both Indian and Ghurkha Regiments. Two particular engagements in which the Snider distinguished itself were at the Siege of Sherpur (15–23 December 1879), just outside of Kabal, and the Battle of Ahmed Khel (19 April 1880).

The British commander, Lieutenant General Frederick Roberts (1832–1914), had retaken the city of Kabul after the assassination of the British envoy, Louis Cavagnari (1841–79), at the hands of an Afghan mob. Roberts and his men brutally sought revenge and many Afghans were publicly executed. The British obtained intelligence that a huge force of Afghans, under the overall command of Mohammed Jan, were assembling to retake the city and Roberts decided to entrench his force of 7,000 British and Indian Army troops to defend the 8,000yd perimeter of the Sherpur cantonment, whilst at the same time calling for reinforcements. The British were able to stockpile sufficient food, rations, ammunition and firewood to last a siege of many months if necessary. With news of the approach of a British relief force, Mohammed Jan resolved to use his overwhelming force of 60,000 men to attack the cantonment on the night of 23 December 1879. Roberts had fortified his position well, had a great superiority over the Afghans in both artillery and in the firepower of the Martini–Henry and Snider rifles, and, these factors, combined with the discipline of his troops and the unimaginative tactics of the Afghans, resulted in a stunning victory.

The initial Afghan attack against the eastern walls of the cantonment was spearheaded by Ghazis, religious fanatics who were prepared to lose their lives for their faith. The British artillery fired star shells to illuminate the attackers and the concentrated fire of Martini–Henry and Snider volleys, combined with the spasmodic rattle of Gatling gun fire, filled the air. Wave after wave of tribesmen threw themselves at this wall of fire, but few got within even 300yd of the defences. Whilst the men of the 92nd Highlanders and 67th Foot directed their Martini–Henry rifles at the attackers, the troops of the Guides, the 28th Bengal Native Infantry and the 3rd Sikhs, aimed their Sniders with deadly precision. In such a battle, against an enemy in overwhelming numbers, it was the ease of loading and thus the rapidity of the well-directed fire that won the day. Hour after hour the Afghans attacked. The barrels of the defenders' rifles glowed red-hot in the darkness and both British and Indian troops struggled to hold the burning metal of their weapons. Finally, after more than 12 hours of constant attack, the Afghans saw the futility of continuing the action and began to retreat.

This became something of a rout as Roberts sent his cavalry and then infantry out from behind the walls of the cantonment in pursuit.

Victory was total. For the loss of 5 killed and 28 wounded the British artillery, Martini–Henry and Snider rifle fire had killed in the region of 3,000 Afghans, with an unknown number of wounded fleeing or being carried from the battlefield.

At the Battle of Ahmed Khel (19 April 1880) the British, under the command of Lieutenant General Donald Stewart (1824–1900), were once again grateful for the fire from the Snider rifle. Leading a mixed column of British and Indian troops from Kandahar to Kabul, via Ghazni, Stewart's force of over 7,000 troops, 7,000 followers and more than 11,000 animals, both cavalry horses and baggage animals, was forced to live off the land for much of the journey through enemy controlled country. This became increasingly difficult as the Afghans adopted a 'scorched earth' policy of destroying crops and moving animals in front of the British column. The difficult terrain and lack of food naturally began to take a toll on Stewart and his men, yet despite this they covered 195 miles in three weeks and were only 25 miles from Ghazni when they were attacked.

On the morning of 19 April, Stewart's force had moved off at daybreak and within a few hours the column was strung out over a distance of 6 miles. The Headquarters staff halted for breakfast, which allowed the column to begin to concentrate. Advanced mounted troops galloped back to report that the road ahead was held by a large Afghan force. Stewart realised that a battle was likely, but hoped that by carrying the attack forward his force might disperse the enemy. He advanced his available troops to within 1,400yd of a spur behind which the Afghans were reported to be, but before the troops could be deployed a mass of the enemy charged down from behind the hill directly at Stewart's infantry. At the same moment large bodies of Afghan cavalry attacked the flanks, which were being protected by the Bengal Lancers. The impact of the attack was such that the Lancers were propelled into the deploying infantry who were struggling to form a firing line. Thousands of the Ghazi swordsmen, their long white robes flowing in the wind, charged towards the disorganised firing line. The situation was desperate but gradually some semblance of order was restored and the fire from Martini–Henry and Snider rifles began to inflict enormous casualties upon the attackers.

Yet, the danger was far from over. Stewart now made a tactical error in ordering the 59th Foot, which had occupied the centre of the makeshift firing line, up to a fresh position in front of it. The men of the 59th were hit by a tsunami of Afghan swordsmen and some had insufficient time to fix their bayonets before the enemy was upon them. The line began to give. The 3rd Gurkhas now directed well-aimed Snider fire in support of the 59th, who in turn were able to regain their cohesion. Now together both units focused their deadly fire upon the Afghans. Support fire from the 19th Bengal Native Infantry added to the butchery and when the 2nd Punjab Cavalry and the reformed Bengal Lancers routed the Afghan cavalry on the flanks, then victory was assured.

Although the battle had been a close one, eventual victory was overwhelming, thanks to the rapidity of fire of both the Snider and Martini–Henry rifles. Of the 2,800 British and Indian troops involved, 17 were killed and a further 124 wounded. The Afghan force of 15,000 tribesmen left 1,200 bodies on the battlefield and it is estimated that a further 1,800 died of their wounds.[39] Whilst there are many examples during the Victorian period of the technological superiority of British arms over their indigenous foes, the Battle of Ahmed Khel illustrates, very effectively, how the use of modern, easy loading rifles could command and win a close-run engagement.

Similarly, at the Battle of Tofrek (22 March 1885), fought 5 miles inland from the port of Suakin on the Red Sea coast of Sudan, the British and Indian force was surprised by the sudden advance of the Mahdist forces under the command of Osman Digna. This battle was the last, and the most costly in terms of lives lost, of the two eastern Sudanese campaigns. The British commander, Major General McNeill (1831–1904), had ordered his troops to construct a stockade, known as a zariba, made of the local thorn bush into which his force would camp for the night, and which would offer them some protection from a surprise attack.

As men of the Royal Engineers and the Madras Sappers were busy constructing the zariba, advanced scouts rushed back to the position with news that the enemy were advancing in large numbers. McNeill immediately ordered all work parties to retreat behind the partly finished zariba and take up arms and at the same time the outlying cavalry scouts raced back with the enemy hot on their heels. Many of the troops were unable to reach the half-built sanctuary and the enemy force initially overwhelmed the first firing line composed of the 17th Bengal Infantry and half a battalion of the Berkshire Regiment. The enemy then descended upon the Royal Marine contingent, and again caught them unable to organise a defensive line. Fortunately, the 28th Bombay Infantry and the 15th Sikhs, in the north-west of the incomplete zariba had time to raise their Sniders and delivered effective devastating fire. The battle lasted a mere 20 minutes, but it was a very bloody encounter. Over 130 British and Indian soldiers and a further 150 drivers had been killed whilst British firepower had claimed the lives over 1,000 tribesmen.[40] Again, British and Indian troops had achieved an unlikely victory and their success can be largely attributed to their technologically superior weapons.

The interim introduction of the Snider enabled the British to join the global race for an effective breech-loading rifle. Although the Snider's service with front-line British forces was relatively brief, the virtues of the rifle, primarily its ease of loading and rapidity of fire, ensured that it would remain in use around for the world for decades to come. Whilst perhaps not as iconic as the Martini–Henry rifle, which was the Snider's replacement, there is no doubt the Snider has earned its rightful place in British imperial history as a very deadly tool of Empire.

Chapter 4

The Martini–Henry Rifle – Gingindlovu, 2 April 1879

At Ginghilovo our Martini-Henrys swept away the Zulus like a broom.

'Breechloaders and Sabres at Ginghilovo',
Perthshire Advertiser, 28 April 1879

The Snider rifle proved to be both a military success and a cost-effective means by which the British Army was able to introduce a breech-loading rifle into its arsenal. However, at the time the Snider was always considered no more than an interim solution.[1] As early as 1869 the British were trailing a brand-new model, the Martini–Henry.[2] The name 'Martini–Henry' is derived from the names of its two inventors; the Hungarian-Swiss inventor Friedrich von Martini (1833–97) and the Scot Alexander Henry (1818–94). Their single-shot rifle was first patented in 1868 and it soon became associated with Britain's colonial campaigns of the late 1870s and throughout the 1880s, in particular the Anglo-Zulu War of 1879.[3]

The need to replace the Snider was recognised in 1865, when, on 22 October, the War Office issued an invitation to all 'Gunmakers and Others' requesting that proposals be submitted 'for breech-loading rifles, either repeating or not repeating, which may replace the present service rifles in future manufacture'.[4] The War Office provided a comprehensive list of criteria and technical specifications to be met and these included a weight limit of 9lb 5oz, without bayonet and length to be no more than 51in, as well as specific limits for recoil, fouling, accuracy and penetration. The decision as to calibre and rifling were left to the individual manufacturer.

A total of 104 rifles were submitted to the War Office for its consideration, with every inventor invited to explain their design and fire the weapon.[5] A process of assessment and rejection continued throughout 1866–7 until of the original submissions only nine remained. These included the rifles of Samuel Remington, Fosbery, Peabody, Freidrich von Martini and Alexander Henry. All nine were subjected to strenuous tests, including that of exposure in which 100 rounds were fired on 4 consecutive days, with the rifles being kept dirty and exposed to the elements throughout. They were then left un-cleaned for a further fourteen days and nights and then fired again. Finally, each was disassembled and examined.[6]

The trials highlighted a number of problems with eight of the rifles. For example, the Remington's breech block frequently jammed and the Martini could only be fired once after the fortnight's exposure. However, the Henry's breech mechanism 'worked well throughout'.[7] Furthermore, both the Martini and Remington rifles were eliminated from the 'Rapidity of fire' test due to faulty cartridges. This test was jointly won by the Peabody and Henry rifles which demonstrated an impressive possible fire of sixteen rounds per minute. The War Office declared the Henry rifle to be the best of the weapons submitted, and duly awarded its inventor £600 for producing the rifle with the best breech mechanism. The Martini, along with the Peabody, Remington Fosbery and Joslyn rifles, was not considered satisfactory, although the Trials Committee did concede that the Martini's failings could be largely attributed to faults with its cartridges.

Although it had won the trial, the Trials Committee, concerned with the lack of accuracy displayed by the rifle, failed to recommend the adoption of the Henry rifle, or any of the other eight weapons, for general issue. Indeed, the Committee concluded that the present service rifle, the Snider, 'performed well during several of the trials to which it was subjected, and proved itself in many respects an efficient military weapon'. In addition, the Committee expressed the hope that future trials would enable them to recommend the introduction of a new rifle that 'shall be more accurate and have a flatter trajectory than the present Snider rifle'.

Clearly the prize competition, from the point of view of producing an acceptable breech-loading rifle for British service, had been a failure and there was some criticism at the time that the Trials Committee had imposed too strict criteria, which had eliminated several promising designs at too early a stage in the procedure. It was felt that to be able to effectively assess the accuracy of each rifle the Committee would need to lay down the barrel length, at 35in, the weight, at 4lb 6oz, and the calibre, at 0.45in, so as to be able to obtain a fair assessment of each entry. The cartridge to be used in the new trials was decreed to be the government Boxer cartridge, with a weight of 480 grains of bullet and 85 grains of charge. As the Henry rifle's breech mechanism had been considered superior in the first trial, manufacturers were instructed to fit their barrels to the Henry breech arrangements and this new trial began in the spring of 1868. The firms initially invited to submit a new design were Henry, Whitworth, Westley Richards, Lancaster, Rigby and Metford, although the latter company declined to enter.[8]

Tests were conducted throughout 1868 and into 1869 and, rather surprisingly, the Henry barrel showed a marked superiority in terms of accuracy and fouling over its rivals. Clearly the adoption of the barrel's rifling and calibre had transformed the accuracy of the Henry barrel. The Trials Committee could confidently proclaim 'that the Henry barrel, 0.45 inch bore, is that most suitable in all respects for the requirements of the service'.

With the issue of the new rifle's barrel now resolved, trials now focused on the breech mechanism. Again rigorous tests were imposed upon a number of manufacturers' mechanisms, including those of Henry, Peabody, Martini and Remington. Rapidity of fire, and the ability to withstand mistreatment, such as sand thrown into the mechanism and exposure to the elements, were amongst several tests. Although the Henry mechanism again shone, it was the Martini breech mechanism which 'worked well during the trial, and when stripped the breech mechanism was in perfect order, free from rust or dust'. It seemed clear that the Martini's failings in the earlier trials had been due to defective ammunition. The final recommendations of the Small Arms Committee was that the rifle selected was to be a hybrid of the Martini-designed breech block and a .45in rifled barrel of seven shallow grooves designed by Henry. After the adoption of a bottle-necked rolled brass cartridge with a bullet of 480 grains, the specifications to govern the manufacture of the new Martini–Henry rifle were issued to private contractors at the end of 1871.

Service trials continued throughout 1872 and in 1873, and these highlighted various defects, mostly concerning the trigger, block axis pin, sights and striker. These issues led to even more extended trials and the manufacture of three separate patterns of Mark I rifle before the final modification of the troublesome trigger mechanism, which had a tendency to discharge without warning. In November 1875 this final alteration again underwent a number of trials with 1,000 modified rifles sent to various regimental stations. The eventual result was that the new trigger mechanism was adopted to produce the Mark II

Martini–Henry rifle. The aim, or objective, of this modification was so as to obtain 'a more regular pull off of the trigger, and of removing a liability to accidental discharge, caused by dirt becoming deposited between the trigger guard of the action'.

Despite the delays, the extended trials and the inherent problems with the Mark I, the overwhelming view of the soldiers who used this new rifle was one of delight for this single-shot weapon offered them simplicity. The trigger guard was the actuating lever, which, once depressed, allowed the breech block, hinged as it was at the rear, to drop down away from the breech face. As this happened, an ejector forced the spent cartridge out of the breech. A new cartridge could then be hand loaded into the breech. Lifting the trigger guard closed the breech and the weapon was ready to fire.

By the time the Mark II was approved for service, in November 1877, considerable numbers of Mark I rifles, in excess of 250,000, had been manufactured and some had been issued to colonial governments. These weapons were not modified for some years, if at all, and have become great collector's items. The remaining numbers underwent a modification to become Mark IIs throughout the period 1877–9, with the result that few original Mark II rifles were produced in these years.

The Martini–Henry rifle was not without its faults or its critics. The rifle possessed a dreadful recoil when fired, especially once the bore was fouled, and in sustained combat severe bruising and even dislocation of shoulders and nose bleeds were likely. Once fouling occurred, after as little as ten or twelve shots, and with it a corresponding increase in the recoil, there was a tendency for the user to flinch before firing with the anticipation of the painful recoil. This natural reaction would reduce the accuracy of the firing. However, a quick use of the ramrod, even in battlefield conditions, could remove the fouling and reduce the recoil. The rifle had no safety mechanism of any sort and was prone to discharge if grit or sand entered the trigger mechanism. As mentioned, this fault was particularly noticeable in the Mark I version and troops were ordered never to carry the rifle loaded. The weapon could jam, for the extractor grip might tear through the soft brass of the cartridge, or sand could enter the mechanism and cause a similar jam.[9] This was a particular problem during the Egyptian campaign of 1882.[10] The barrel became intensely hot when fired and although, from the Mark II design onwards, a wooden forestock was added to give some protection, the barrel would frequently become too hot to touch.

British troops in South Africa soon learnt to wrap cowhide around the barrel to ease their discomfort.

Indeed, the introduction of the Martini–Henry rifle was met with 'a torrent of adverse criticism'.[11] Writing in the journal *Engineering*, W.P.P. Marshal went so far as to suggest that 'to adopt such a rifle [Martini–Henry] would not be a mechanical credit to the country'.[12] Yet, for all the criticism, both inside and outside Parliament, H.P. Miller, assistant musketry instructor to the National Rifle Association, was able to conclude, in 1881, that the 'regulation Martini–Henry Rifle is a sound, reliable, and accurate military arm. This is certainly my experience.'[13]

Despite its many inherent faults, the Martini–Henry Rifle Mark II was to serve the British Army well. The weapon certainly possessed the necessary 'stopping power' that the British Army required against the 'savage foes' of colonial warfare. The seven grooved barrel, and 83 grains of black powder in the .45in Boxer type cartridge, allowed the hardened lead bullet of 480 grains to emerge with a muzzle velocity of 1,350ft per second, rising in a curved trajectory of 8.1ft at a range of 500yd. This compared to a trajectory of 11.9ft for the Snider and 15ft for the Enfield over the same range. Thus, the accuracy of the Martini–Henry was much improved over the two former rifle stalwarts of the British Army.[14] The Martini–Henry was sighted to a thousand yards and, in the hands of a trained marksman could maintain a reasonable degree of accuracy at that range. Battalion volley fire against massed targets frequently opened at 600 to 800yd, and even an average rifleman could score a high percentage of hits at 300 to 400yd, where volley fire could be particularly devastating.[15] The lead bullet could stop a charging warrior in his tracks; the slug would flatten on impact with bone and cartilage, smashing anything in its path, inflicting small entry holes with horrific exit wounds. In experienced hands ten to twelve 'aimed' volleys could be fired per minute into the charging ranks of a massed enemy.[16]

The Martini–Henry Mark II was far superior to any fire-arm previously issued to the British Army. Its small bore allowed soldiers to carry more ammunition.[17] Greater accuracy, lower trajectory, ease of operation and reloading with consequent rapidity of firing, as well as its robustness, all combined to make the Martini–Henry a solid, if not always completely dependable, weapon. Daniel Headrick, in his 1981 work *The Tools of Empire*, described the Martini–Henry as 'the first really satisfactory rifle of the new generation'.[18] Even Rudyard Kipling

(1865–1936), the ultimate literary chronicler of the Victorian soldier, extolled the merits of the Martini–Henry in a stanza from his poem entitled 'The Young British Soldier':

> When 'arf of your bullets fly wide in the ditch,
> Don't call your Martini a cross-eyed old bitch; She's human
>   as you are – you treat her as sich,
> An' she'll fight for the young British soldier.
> Fight, fight, fight for the soldier . . .[19]

The Martini–Henry rifle first saw active service with the British Army during the Perak campaign of 1875–6 (in what is now modern day Malaysia). It was carried throughout this campaign by men of the 80th (Staffs) and 3rd (Buffs) but it was not until 1878 that the rifle was to see more widespread use, both in Afghanistan and in the Eastern Cape, during the Ninth Cape Frontier War. Here, at the Battle of Nyumaxa, in January 1878, the new rifle proved its worth. The British Commander, Sir Arthur Cunynghame (1812–84), was very impressed by the performance of the Martini–Henry in the hands of British regulars, the 1/24th Regiment, and wrote, 'At no time had the power of the Martini Henry been more conspicuously shown; indeed, it was perhaps the first occasion when it had been fairly used by the British army.'[20]

Cunynghame and his troops were again to be thankful for the devastating stopping power of the Martini–Henry at the Battle of Centane on 7 February 1878, when 450 British troops, armed with the new rifle, defeated 4,000 Gcaleka warriors under the command of the rebellious chief, Sandile.

Supported by native allies, the Mfengu, and locally recruited men of the Frontier Light Horse (FLH), the troops of the 1/24th awaited the onslaught of the Gcaleka from concealed trenches. At a range of 900yd the muzzle-loaders of the Mfengu and the carbines of the FLH opened fire upon the charging mass. It was quickly apparent that these weapons lacked the stopping power to thwart the advancing warriors and if anything the fire seemed to spur them on.

As the advance reached a watercourse at the foot of the British position, the helmets of the 1/24th appeared atop of the hidden trenches and a disciplined volley of Martini–Henry fire crashed out. Warriors smashed to the ground. One Gcaleka survivor later recalled the moment as 'a sudden blaze' and 'our men fell like grass'.[21] The British troops fired slowly and deliberately but still managed five aimed rounds a minute. The ground was soon littered with hundreds of fallen figures.

Amazingly, under such devastating fire, the Gcaleka held their ground, although further advance was impossible. Cover was sought behind every rock, bush and anthill. An early morning mist descended and this, combined with the smoke emitted from the Martini–Henry's black powder cartridges, threw a brief veil over the battlefield. This allowed the Gcaleka to continue their attack and some were able to creep to within 100yd of the British trenches before the mist cleared. At this range the Martini–Henry fire was devastating; for F and G Companies of the 1/24th it was little more than rifle practice, with their former musketry instructor, Lieutenant Carrington, shouting encouragement. Soon even the brave Gcalekas could stand no more and the survivors broke and fled. It was a complete victory.

Over 260 warriors were found dead near the British position and, it is thought, a similar number died in the bush of their wounds. The British lost not one man. Cunynghame was delighted by the performance of both the 1/24th and the Martini–Henry. He wrote of the troops' 'high state of drill and discipline and instruction' which had made such a decisive victory possible. The Governor of the Cape, Sir Bartle Frere (1815–84), wrote to the Colonial Secretary, Lord Carnarvon (1831–90), that the '24th are old, steady shots whose every bullet told'.[22] Frere was also most complimentary about the performance of the Martini–Henry at Centane and, again in the same letter to Carnarvon, stressed the rifle's destructive power: 'They [Gcaleka] came on in four divisions very steadily and in the days of the Brown Bess would certainly have closed, and being eight or ten to one would possibly have overwhelmed our people. They held on after several shells had burst among their advanced masses, but they could not live under the fire of the Martini-Henry.'[23]

The rebellious warriors would never meet the British in a pitch battle again, yet none of rebellion's leaders, including Sandile, had been killed or captured at Centane and the conflict now descended into a guerrilla war. Cunynghame, whose brisk manner had upset both his subordinates and the local politicians, was replaced by Major General Sir Frederic Thesiger (1827–1905), soon to become, on the death of his father, the second baron Lord Chelmsford. Seeking refuge in the Amatola Mountains, between Grahamstown and King William's Town, Sandile and the remaining rebels defied Thesiger's attempts to corner and defeat them for three long and arduous months. Eventually, by the continued reduction of the areas available to the rebels, the British were finally able to bring the Ninth Frontier War to a successful conclusion.

It is clear that Thesiger found his first independent command difficult. He was frustrated that the Gcaleka refused to stand and fight, and by their ability to slip through the cordons that the British tried to establish. Thesiger considered the enemy's actions as pure cowardice and he viewed the Gcalekas with undisguised racial contempt. Furthermore, Thesiger showed a deep reluctance to listen to the advice of the local white settlers, who had years of experience in this form of bush warfare. It was only when Thesiger swallowed his pride and adopted the colonial plan of dividing the Amatola Mountains into eleven separate districts that the British achieved their final success.[24]

Although the final campaign was prolonged, it was still successful, with relatively few losses. According to historian John Laband, Thesiger's experiences in the Eastern Cape led him to over-confidence. At the start of the Zulu campaign, in January 1879, Thesiger, now Lord Chelmsford, and many of his command, presumed that the Zulus would be an adversary only slightly superior to those the British had fought in the Eastern Cape.[25] As such the Zulus would be no more than 'kafirs [a nineteenth-century racially derogatory term], who are only to be hunted'.[26] The renowned war artist Melton Prior (1845–1910) recorded a meeting that Chelmsford held towards the end of the Ninth Cape Frontier War with many of the Burghers and Boers that had fought alongside the British. When the subject of a possible war with the Zulus was discussed, it is clear that Chelmsford was disdainful of the advice that the British must laager, or entrench, every position once they had crossed into Zulu territory, to avoid the danger of a surprise attack. The locals also stressed the mobility of the Zulu Army and that in this regard the British should consider the Zulus as almost a cavalry force and deploy accordingly. Prior noted that Chelmsford responded to the Boers' pleading with the words, 'Oh, British troops are all right; we do not need to laager . . .' and that the General 'smiled at the notion'.[27]

The Boers had many years of experience fighting the mobile Zulu forces. Their success at the Battle of Blood River on 16 December 1838 has become part of Boer folklore. From behind laagered wagons, less than 500 Boers held off repeated attacks from several thousand Zulus. Over 500 warriors were later found dead and hundreds more were killed in the subsequent flight and pursuit, for only 3 wounded Boer casualties. To the Boers, it was clear that sustained accurate fire from behind a defensive position was the tactic to defeat the enveloping attack of the Zulu Army.[28]

Before the British invasion of Zululand Chelmsford demonstrated, in December 1878, that he had taken some note of the Boer warnings. He issued Regulations for Field Services South Africa 1878, which provided some useful intelligence for his officers on Zulu tactics and their mobility, and stressed the need for defensive preparation against such attacks. Guidelines were also provided on how to treat the civilian Zulu population.[29] However, once the invasion began, much of the information provided in the Regulations was either forgotten or ignored.

Bred from his experience in the Ninth Cape Frontier War, Chelmsford's initial concern was that it would be difficult to bring the Zulu Army to battle. Again, Chelmsford showed his reluctance to listen to local advice. John Dunn (1834–95), a frontier settler who had lived in Zululand and had enjoyed some influence in the Zulu court of King Cetewayo (1826–84), advised Chelmsford to divide his available force into two columns, each strong enough to defeat the Zulu Army if engaged separately. According to Dunn, Lord Chelmsford laughed at this idea, and said, 'The Only thing I am afraid of is that I won't get Cetywayo to fight.'[30]

Chelmsford resolved to use the 17,000 troops at his disposal to invade Zululand in three separate columns, with a fourth and fifth held back to bolster the defences of the boundary between Natal and Zululand and supply reinforcements if required. The three advancing columns would converge on the Zulu capital at Ulundi. Chelmsford hoped that at least one column would be able to meet the Zulu Army in a pitch battle as Cetewayo sought to defend his capital. Furthermore, Chelmsford placed a high emphasis on the proven killing power of the Martini–Henry. Writing to one of his more enlightened officers, Colonel Wood, Chelmsford stated, 'I am inclined to think that the first experience of the power of the Martini-Henrys will be such a surprise to the Zulus that they will not be formidable after the first effort.'[31]

The success of the Martini–Henry at the Battle of Centane had bred on over-confidence in the British command that the Zulus would likewise be stopped by the rifle's punishing firepower. The British invaded Zululand on 11 January 1879 and, on the following day, the central column first engaged the enemy in a successful attack on Prince Sihayo's stronghold, which was subsequently burnt. The pace of the advance was now driven by the ponderous speed of the oxen wagon train that accompanied the British and it was not until 20 January that the British column finally formed a camp at the base of a hill named Isandlwana. The rocky nature of the ground made the digging of defensive trenches impractical and the marshalling of the oxen to form a laager was considered but rejected as being too time consuming and difficult for what was going to be a temporary camp. On the evening of 21 January, Chelmsford received reports of a concentration of Zulus in the Mangeni gorge, 12 miles east of the camp. He resolved to lead a reconnaissance in force and, at 4am on 22 January, he left Isandlwana with six companies of the 2/24th Regiment, four Royal Artillery 7pdr guns and a detachment of mounted infantry. The camp was left under the command of Lieutenant Colonel H. Pulleine (1838–79), who had at his disposal five companies of the 1/24th, one of the 2/24th, two 7pdr guns and more than a hundred mounted infantry. Before departing, Chelmsford ordered Number 2 Column, commanded by Lieutenant Colonel A. Durnford (1830–79), with units of the Natal Native Horse and the Natal Native Contingent, to move from Rorke's Drift to the Isandlwana camp. If attacked, Pulleine was instructed by Chelmsford to keep his cavalry, vedettes, or mounted patrols, advanced, draw in his line of outposts and defend the camp. With Durnford's force, Pulleine had a total of 67 officers and 1,707 men at his disposal.[32]

The mobility and speed of advance with which the Zulu Army was so renowned was demonstrated during the march to face British troops of the central column. Leaving Ulundi on 17 January, the main Zulu Army had arrived, completely undetected, in the Ngwebeni valley, just a few miles north of Isandlwana, on 21 January. Whilst Chelmsford led half his force away from the Zulu Army, the warriors rested and prepared for an attack on the camp at Isandlwana on 23 January.

However, a cavalry patrol from the British position discovered the sheltering enemy by chance, and this triggered the events that followed. As the British galloped back to report the presence of a large Zulu army to the north of the camp, the enemy quickly moved into regimental formations and boldly advanced on Isandlwana.

The Zulu Army rapidly formed into its usual battle formation of 'chests and horns' as it moved on the British camp. Whilst those regiments that formed the 'chest', supported by the tactical reserve that formed the 'loins', made a frontal attack, the warriors of the two 'horns' would swing round the hill of Isandlwana, unseen by the defending British, and envelop the position, surrounding and cutting-off any possible retreat. One of the few British survivors of the subsequent Battle of Isandlwana, Lieutenant Henry Curling, Royal Artillery, later wrote of the complacency in the camp at the sight of the advancing Zulus:

> We congratulated ourselves on the chance of our being attacked and hoped that our small numbers might induce the

Zulus to come on . . . I suppose that not more than half the men in the camp took part in its defence as it was not considered necessary . . . The 1/24th had been in the last war and had often seen large bodies of Caffirs before. Not one of us dreamt that there was the least danger and all we hoped for was the fight might come off before the General returned . . . All the time we were idle in the camp, the Zulus were surrounding us with a huge circle several miles in circumference and hidden by hills from our sight. We none of us felt the least anxious as to the result for, although they came on in immense numbers, we felt it was impossible they could force a way through.[33]

Pulleine, in his first and last engagement, followed his orders to defend the camp to the letter and his initial disposition reflected Chelmsford's wishes. The companies of the 24th fell in in columns in front of the British tents and the two 7pdr guns were placed out to the left front of the camp. Durnford's arrival complicated the defence, for as senior officer he seems to have decided to act independently and took his horsemen out roughly a mile to the right of the camp to engage the Zulus. It might have been that Durnford felt there was a danger that the Zulus might simply bypass the camp and attack Chelmsford's column in the rear. Whatever his thinking, Durnford's troops were soon engaged with the Zulu advance. The defence of the camp was far from concentrated and much would depend on the killing power of the Martini–Henry rifle.

Initially, the British defences remained strong. The troops in the firing line remained steady as their Martini–Henry rifles checked the Zulu advance. Captain Edward Essex, one of only five imperial officers to survive, later wrote, 'I was surprised how relaxed the men in the ranks were despite the climactic tension of the battle. Loading as fast as they could and firing into the dense black masses that pressed in on them, the men were laughing and chatting, and obviously thought they were giving the Zulus an awful hammering.'[34]

Despite Essex's assertion that the troops were 'loading as fast as they could', this would have gone against the training that the men would have received. The last Musketry Instruction Manual had been published in 1874 with the result that the troops fighting in 1879 had been trained according to principles which had been learnt from the use of the Snider rifle.[35] The 1874 manual emphasised slow, controlled and accurate fire and further evidence seems to suggest that this is how the men of the 24th fired at Isandlwana. With the smaller bore of the

Martini–Henry allowing the men to carry around seventy cartridges, the myth that the British firing line collapsed due to lack of ammunition seems implausible.

This view is supported by evidence from the subsequent battles of Gingindlovu and Khambula. In the latter, the British commander, Evelyn Wood, noted that the British troops 'expended in four hours an average of 33 rounds a man'.[36] There seems little reason to conclude that the 'old steady shots of the 1/24th', as Frere had earlier described them, would have been any different. Indeed, as described, the musketry training of the day, for good reason, stressed slow, controlled fire. Rapid fire would have resulted in troops not taking careful aim, and the target would soon have been obscured by dense clouds of smoke from the black powder cartridge. Slow fire allowed the men to carefully select their targets and officers could more easily direct their fire as the targets moved or altered. Volley fire, by section or company, could be carefully controlled and, in the heat of battle, the psychological effect of being at the receiving end could be just as discouraging as the casualties it inflicted. In such a battle as Isandlwana, and in subsequent engagements throughout the war, there would have been 'long pauses when some companies did not fire at all, either to allow the smoke to clear, or because they had no targets, the enemy having changed position or gone to ground'.[37]

At the receiving end of this slow controlled fire from the Martini–Henry rifles, the attacking Zulus were suffering dreadful casualties. The British bullets tore through the hide shields of the Zulus and into the flesh of the warriors. Many were sent tumbling backwards by the impact of the bullets. Limbs were shattered or heads 'blown open like pumpkins'.[38] Fifty years after the battle, one Zulu veteran could still recall the shock of his first exposure to the British fire, 'Some of our men had their arms torn right off . . . The battle was so fierce that we had to wipe the blood and the brains of the killed and wounded from our heads, faces, arms, legs and shields after the fighting . . .'.[39]

As the iNgobamakhosi regiment advanced to support the first Zulu attack, the warriors rushed forward in short bursts, throwing themselves down to try to avoid the volley fire. One Zulu, named Mehlokazulu, explained to the missionary Revd A.W. Lee how he had advanced with twenty comrades only to be caught by volley fire. Only he was left standing.[40] Mlamula Matebula, also of the iNgobamakhosi regiment, described how the warriors tried to avoid the crippling fire:

> I with many others, adopted the style of crouching as we advanced in order to avoid the bullets as our shields could not stop them. While crouching I received a wound on my back, the bullet entered over the shoulder blade and came out lower down . . . We fell down by hundreds, but we still advanced, although we were dying by hundreds we could not retreat because we had encircled them.[41]

Horace Smith-Dorrien, another of the five imperial officers who was to survive the battle, supplied the firing line with ammunition and commented that the 24th were: 'Possessed of a splendid discipline and sure of success, they lay on their position making every round tell.'[42] Of course, this was a wild exaggeration. In tense, battlefield conditions, with smoke obscuring the targets and the enemy doing everything in their power to avoid being hit, it took a surprisingly high number of rounds to kill or incapacitate a single enemy. Ian Knight has estimated a figure in the region of forty or fifty rounds fired for every hit.[43] Although the men of the 24th were above average shots, there is no reason to suggest that these figures would have been significantly lower. However, there is no doubt such sustained fire deterred any further Zulu advance, which became stalled 300–400yd from the British firing line, at a range when fire from the Martini–Henry was at its most effective and accurate. A Zulu veteran, named uMhoti, described how: 'The soldiers . . . in front of the camp poured volley after volley into the impi [regiment] – we crouched down and dare not advance'.[44] The Martini–Henry, the psychological effect of being under sustained volley fire and the steadiness of the British troops had checked the Zulu attack.

The sequence of events during the final stages of the Battle of Isandlwana is hard to establish. Not only were there few survivors, but many things happened either simultaneously or in quick succession. What seems clear is that Durnford's isolated command on the right flank of the British position was forced to retire to the camp as it was in danger of becoming outflanked and running low on ammunition, having left the camp with only around forty to fifty rounds per man. This movement isolated Pope's G Company of the 24th, which had been sent forward by Pulleine to support Durnford. These infantrymen were quickly overwhelmed by the advancing

Zulus and killed to a man. The remaining British firing line, seeing its right flank exposed, retreated towards the tent line, so as to concentrate its position and fire. The lull in the firing whilst this movement happened allowed the Zulus, just 300–400yd away, to seize their chance and charge at the British. The suddenness of the advance sparked fear in members of a detachment of the lightly armed Natal Native Contingent, who promptly discarded their weapons and fled for their lives. This resulted in a collapse of the firing line and, before the British could reform, the Zulus were upon them, stabbing and killing with their short assegai spears. Furthermore, the 'horns' swung around from behind the Isandlwana hill, cutting off any possible retreat. Only a very few mounted men managed to successfully flee the carnage. Of the over 1,700 men who had been in the British camp, only 60 white and around 400 black troops survived. Zulu losses are difficult to evaluate for there was never an accurate count, but it is clear that they were numerous. The Martini–Henry rifle had claimed at least 2,000 warriors, and scores, with terrible wounds, must have dragged themselves from the battlefield to die miles away. When the news of the Zulu victory and his nation's losses reached Cetewayo, he was heard to say: 'An assegai has been thrust into the belly of the nation . . . There are not enough tears to mourn for the dead.'[45]

Elsewhere, on 22 January 1879, the Martini–Henry rifle was claiming further Zulu victims. The British invasion force to the south, Number 1 Column, was under the command of Colonel Charles Pearson (1834–1909), who had been given the objective of crossing the Lower Drift of the Thukela River. His force, consisting of two British infantry battalions, the 2/3rd Regiment, the Buffs, the 99th and nearly 300 sailors of the Naval Brigade, complete with rocket tubes and Gatling gun, was then to march the 30 miles to the mission station at Eshowe, where he was to establish a base from which he could coordinate a further advance towards Ulundi. Like the Central Column, progress was painfully slow. By the morning of 22 January, Pearson was still some miles short of Eshowe, with his force split crossing over the Nyezane River. Waiting to ambush the British column were 6,000 Zulus, under the command of an inDuna named Umatyiya, concealed around the base of the Majia Hill. Fortunately for Pearson and his men, a reconnaissance patrol of the Natal Native Contingent stumbled across the hidden Zulus and the trap was sprung prematurely.

The British reacted quickly and decisively; a firing line was rapidly formed, the artillery and rocket tubes brought into action and, for the first time in British military history, the Gatling gun fired in anger, a short burst, which had the desired effect of dispersing a formation of Zulus. Unlike at Isandlwana, the Zulu regiments failed to coordinate successfully, and, in particular, the attack of the 'horns' was not pressed home.

Again, the Martini–Henry rifle proved its worth, stopping the advance of the Zulu 'chest' in its tracks, as was later testified by Zulu survivors of the battle. 'The whites shot us down in numbers, in some places our dead and wounded covered the ground, we lost heavily, especially from the small guns [Martini–Henrys] . . .' .[46] The Zulus, armed largely with antiquated firearms, many of them flintlocks, were unable to respond to the devastating British fire. 'We went forward packed close together like a lot of bees. We were still far away from them when the white men began to throw their bullets at us, but we could not shoot at them because our rifles would not shoot so far . . .'[47]

The British, too, recognised the superiority of the Martini–Henry. Lieutenant Hart wrote that, 'The Zulus fought well, showing judgement and courage quite equal to their enemy, but although they outnumbered us greatly, they could not hold their ground against our artillery and superior rifles. We had the best rifles in the world; they, for the most part, merely muskets, weapons of the past.'[48]

The British victory of arms and discipline was complete. For the loss of just fourteen killed and fifteen wounded, the British fire at Nyezane had inflicted well over 500 Zulu casualties. The British were to call upon the Martini–Henry again later in the day, when a Zulu army, 4,000 strong, fresh from its victory at Isandlwana, descended upon the British supply station at Rorke's Drift, defended by just 100 men of the 2/24th. From behind defences, the British were able to not only hold back numerous attacks, but the firepower of the Martini–Henry claimed around 400 Zulu lives. As at the Battle of Amoaful, five years earlier, the British were again fortunate that the enemy possessed inferior weapons. If the Zulu fire from the Shiyane terrace, 300–400m above the defences of Rorke's Drift, had been from Martini–Henry rifles, or even Sniders, then the British position would have soon become untenable. As it was the defenders faced largely ineffectual fire from elderly muskets, many of which did not even have the range to reach the British barricades.[49]

Several soldiers, including Corporals Hitch and Allen, were hit by Zulu bullets, yet survived wounds that would have certainly proved fatal if they had been inflicted by more modern rifles. In contrast, the British fire upon terraces claimed several victims, as testified by Corporal Allen, 'We fired many shots, and I said to my comrade, "They are falling fast over there", and he said "Yes, we are giving it to them." I saw many Zulus killed on the hill [Shiyane terrace].'[50]

However, the engagement at Rorke's Drift also demonstrated some of the inherent problems associated with the Martini–Henry. Private Hook, one of the defenders of the hospital who was to receive a Victoria Cross for his heroism, complained that, 'we did so much firing that [the rifles] became hot, and the brass of the cartridges softened, the result being that the barrels got very foul and the cartridge-chamber jammed. My own rifle was jammed several times . . .'.[51]

Similarly, after prolonged use the rifle barrels became so hot that soldiers were forced to fire them away from their faces, thus reducing their accuracy. Indeed, after the several hours of virtually constant fire endured by the defenders, it is hard to imagine how anyone could fire the rifle efficiently. Despite these drawbacks, the Martini–Henry rifle allowed the British to decisively defeat their foe and inflict horrific wounds upon them. Lieutenant Chard was impressed by the extraordinary wounds inflicted on the Zulus, 'One man's head was split open, exactly as if done with an axe. Another had been hit just between the eyes, the bullet carrying away the whole of the back of the head, leaving his face perfect, as though it were a mask, only disfigured by the small hole made by the bullet passing through.'[52]

After the devastating defeat of Isandlwana and the morale-boosting victories of Nyezane and Rorke's Drift the British High Command, and in particular Chelmsford himself, had much to ponder. The news of Isandlwana seriously affected Chelmsford's health and left him on the edge of a nervous breakdown for many days. Colonel Clery, who was on the General's staff, perceptively wrote: 'I feel greatly for the poor general . . . I fear there have been some sad miscalculations about the whole business and the enemy has been altogether underestimated'.[53] The formidable Martini–Henry rifle, with its tremendous 'stopping power', had added to the complacency that surrounded the High Command and allowed the British to place far too much emphasis on its tactical use to stop the charge of a determined enemy.

It is no doubt true that Isandlwana blighted Chelmsford's career and left him with a legacy that he was never to dispel. Personal criticism began almost immediately, both in the British press and from his subordinates. Colonels Evelyn Wood and Redvers Buller privately informed Sir Garnet Wolseley that they both felt Chelmsford was 'not fit to be a corporal'.[54] The editorial of the *Daily News* was typical of the comment surrounding the British loss, 'upon the face of Lord Chelmsford's despatch nothing can be clearer than that it ought not to have happened. The fact seems to be that our troops expected a walk over to Cetywayo's capital and advanced with corresponding negligence. They underestimated the strength and skill of their enemy and have paid a terrible price for their over confidence.'[55]

The British government agreed to Chelmsford's urgent request for reinforcements and dispatched six battalions, two cavalry regiments and two artillery batteries to South Africa. On their arrival in March, Chelmsford felt strong enough to renew his offensive and, in particular, relieve Colonel Pearson and his men, who were besieged at the mission station of Eshowe. What tactical approach was Chelmsford going to take now? The lessons of Isandlwana, Nyezane and Rorke's Drift were many; the Zulu Army was mobile and more determined, with greater tactical awareness, than the British had first considered. If allowed, the flanking movements of the Zulu 'horn' could be deadly to a static British firing line. Yet, the 'stopping power' of the Martini–Henry had been evident throughout the campaign and Rorke's Drift had clearly demonstrated that from behind prepared defensive positions the British could defeat the numerically superior Zulu Army. Further events served to clarify Chelmsford's thinking. In the early morning of 12 March 1879 a British force, which had failed to entrench their overnight camp at Intombi Drift, was surprised and overwhelmed by a Zulu attack, losing over eighty men. However, a fighting retreat by the British survivors successfully held the Zulus at bay with accurate and controlled fire from the Martini–Henry.

There has long been a tendency in the historiography of the Zulu war to blame Chelmsford for his many faults and oversights but not to recognise his achievements. Such an approach has been criticised by Howard Bailes, who has claimed that the traditional view of the British High Command as 'die-hard traditionalists' who possessed an inability to learn, change and accept is incorrect.[56] Certainly, Chelmsford, a man who had earlier displayed a higher degree of arrogance and a reluctance to accept advice, particularly from the Boers, now showed that he was capable of altering his tactics against the mobile flanking attacks of the Zulus. He decided upon the use of the 'square formation' which had been long associated with the Napoleonic Wars, during which infantry squares were commonly employed to deter and repel enemy cavalry attacks. The paintings of Henri Felix Emmanuel Philippoteaux, *The Charge of the French Cuirassiers at Waterloo*, and Elizabeth Thompson, *The 28th Regiment at Quatre Bras*, were exhibited at the Royal Academy in London in 1875. Both paintings remain with us today and illustrate the historic success of the square. Chelmsford now resorted to the infantry square which would provide several critical tactical advantages. It would allow the British to concentrate the firepower of the Martini–Henry, provide cohesion and mutual support and, crucially, nullify the Zulu's attempts to outflank the British firing line. The use of the square was also recognition that the mobile Zulus would now be viewed as disciplined 'cavalry', rather than ill-disciplined savages.

Chelmsford was not the only British commander to have learnt from the early engagements. The Number 4 Column, under Colonel Wood, operated as the northern advance column. Following the news of Isandlwana, Wood had entrenched a position upon raised ground at Khambula. Wood seems to have had a real affinity with the local Boers and was the only British commander to entice a contingent of Boers to fight alongside the British. Furthermore, Wood did not dismiss their advice and the entrenched British position was well constructed, with the use of wagons as barricade defences. When a Zulu army, 20,000 strong, attacked on 29 March 1879, these defences were tested, but were not found wanting. This is especially significant as a number of the Zulus fired captured Martini–Henrys at the British, who were able to withstand the fire from behind the safety provided by the wagons. In return, the British were able to inflict over 2,000 casualties upon the charging Zulus with Martini–Henry and artillery fire. The British were able to provoke a premature attack by the right 'horn', thus hampering any Zulu attempts to coordinate their advance. Khambula was, undoubtedly, a crushing victory for the British which shattered Zulu morale.[57] For John Laband, the Battle of Khambula had many parallels with the Battle of Blood River, 'though some forty years separated the two battles, they followed precisely the same pattern, the only difference being the improved firepower of the whites'.[58]

Three days after Wood's victory, on 2 April, Chelmsford was also to enjoy success over the Zulus at the Battle of Gingindlovu. Determined to avoid the previous mistakes, Chelmsford led his Eshowe relief force of 5,670 men into Zululand on 29 March. The men travelled light, with no tents or baggage, and the march was careful and considered. Forward reconnaissance was effective and thorough. Overnight camps were painstakingly laagered, with wagons packed into a tight square, and entrenched. Local advice and intelligence, particularly from John Dunn, was listened to and heeded. By midday on 1 April, Chelmsford and his men neared the vicinity of Nyezane. Scouts had reported the growing presence of larger groups of Zulus, and Pearson had, using a heliograph, been able to inform Chelmsford that a large Zulu army, in the region of 12,000 warriors, was, according to his own intelligence, being assembled to block the British advance on Eshowe. With the terrain and vegetation offering wonderful cover to the Zulus for a surprise attack, Chelmsford took no chances. John Dunn selected a position on the summit of a slight knoll to construct the British camp and later swam across the Nyezane River, under cover of darkness, to report to Chelmsford the presence of a large enemy force. Dunn informed Chelmsford that in all probability the British would be attacked at dawn.[59]

Writing in 1896, Colonel Callwell described the Battle of Gingindlovu as a 'tactical defensive' engagement in which the Zulus, as at Khambula, assumed the offensive.[60] Indeed, the British position was certainly a strong defensive one. The wagon laager was formed over 117m^2, giving sufficient room inside to accommodate 2,000 oxen, 300 horses and over 2,000 native troops. The 3,400 imperial troops were positioned in the enclosing shelter trench, which was 144m^2 and roughly 13m from the laagered wagons. The corners, the weakest point, were reinforced by placing the powerful 9pdr guns, the Gatling guns and rocket tubes close by. Although the British had worked tirelessly throughout the afternoon to prepare their strong defences, darkness and heavy rain, which was to soak the British throughout the night, meant it was not possible to cut back the high grasses and bush that encroached to within 100m of the defences.[61]

As the sun rose through the early morning mist, the British troops and their native allies stirred from a miserable, largely sleepless, night. The torrents of rain had finally stopped but both the floor of the laager and the shelter trenches had become a muddy quagmire. The Zulu force, commanded by Somopho, viewed the British position on the open plain as one that was ripe to be enveloped by the traditional tactics of the 'horns of the buffalo'. The shelter trenches concealed to Somopho and his followers the true strength of the British position. Chelmsford recorded that, 'our mounted men, as usual, were at earliest dawn scouting around. At 5.45 reports came in from them simultaneously with the picquets of the 60th and 99th Regiments, that the enemy were advancing to the attack.'[62] At almost 6am, the Zulus on the far side of the Nyezane River, to the west of the British position, came into general view. The troops in the shelter trenches were roused from their early morning lethargy and riflemen assumed positions on top of wagons, from where they could direct fire over the heads of the

British firing lines. The Zulus crossed the Nyezane in columns at two drifts, separated by a distance of a mile or so. As they advanced up the slope towards the British position, the Zulus deployed into the 'chest and horns' formation; one column veered off to the left to form the left 'horn', the other fanned out to create the 'chest'. Suddenly, from around a knoll on the British left, known as Misi Hill, appeared the right 'horn'. The British position had been enveloped in little over 15 minutes. As Lieutenant Julius Backhouse wrote, 'the laager was surrounded; we of course took up our positions in the shelter trenches, the men four deep, officers in rear of them. The ground sloped upwards towards the wagons in our rear so only the front two ranks of men were sheltered. The rest were exposed, and awaited their coming.'[63]

Corporal John Hargreaves of the 3/60th Rifles was on piquet duty when the Zulus were first spotted. The 3/60th had been hastily rushed out from England. To fill the battalion's roll, troops had been transferred in from other units and training reduced. Indeed, many of the men had not finished basic training and some had hardly ever fired a Martini–Henry in training and certainly not in battle. As Major Bindon Blood recalled, 'our battalions landed in Zululand full of incompletely trained men, a great proportion of whom had never fired a round of ball cartridge, while many had never fired a round of blank, before they embarked'.[64] This 'baptism of fire' was to prove a terrifying ordeal for these young, inexperienced recruits. As the first Zulu bullets whizzed over the heads of the British picquets, and the Zulus advanced, Hargreaves recorded that panic set in and, rather than the orderly retire back to the British trenches, some of the 'men commenced to run' and the Captain screamed for them to halt before stating that 'the first man who commences to run, I will shoot' and the officer drew his revolver. Hargreaves then reported that this statement had the men entering the trenches in an orderly fashion.[65]

Captain Hart wrote almost poetically of the Zulu advance and thought their approach:

> The most splendid piece of skirmishing the eye ever beheld. No whites ever did, or ever could skirmish in the magnificent perfection of the Zulus . . . they bounded forward towards us from all sides, rushing from cover to cover, gliding like snakes through the grass, and turning to account every bush, every mound, every particularly high patch of grass between us and them . . . if total concealment were possible, we should not have seen a Zulu till he reached our trench, but it was not

possible, and we could see them as they bounded from one point of concealment to another, always approaching.[66]

Similarly, Major Ashe recorded that the Zulus:

> White and coloured shields, the crests of leopard skin and feathers, and the wild oxtails dangling from their necks, gave them a terribly unearthly appearance. Every ten or fifteen yards their first line would halt, and a shot would be fired, and then, with an unearthly yell, they would again rush on with a sort of measured dance, while a humming and buzzing sound in time to their movement was kept up.[67]

At a distance of 800yd the petty officer of HMS *Boadicea*, in charge of one of the Gatling guns, begged Lord Chelmsford's permission to test the range of the weapon. Chelmsford nodded his ascent for a short burst, and at the turn of two handles, the gun fire was directed at the charging Zulus. Although a clear lane was cut through the body of warriors, the fire did not slow the Zulu advance in the slightest.[68] Within a few seconds the attackers had reached the 400yd distance markers that had been diligently placed out the night before. It would soon be the turn of the Martini–Henry to demonstrate its 'stopping power'. Charles Norris Newman, special correspondent of the *London Standard*, was inside the British position and recorded an accurate description of its formation:

> The 60th Rifles held the front face, with the Marines and a Gatling at their right-hand corner, and . . . two rocket tubes at the left angle. The 57th defended the right flank . . . having some of the Naval Brigade and a Gatling at their right-hand in the rear corner. At the left rear corner were the rest of the Naval Brigade with two 9-pounders; the 91st were aligned along the rear face of the laager, and the 99th and 3rd Buffs on the left flank. All the mounted men were assembled behind the regulars . . . while the N.N.C. [Natal Native Contingent] were located at the left rear angle, by the guns . . . all non-combatants who could obtain a rifle, placed themselves on top of the wagons, whence many an effective shot told on the on-coming Zulu ranks.[69]

With cries of 'they are encircled!' and '*uSuthu!*', the Zulu tried to close in on the British position.[70] The first Zulu assault was upon the north side of the position, manned by soldiers of the 3/60th Rifles. Regaled with gruesome stories of the slaughter of Isandlwana, the young, inexperienced soldiers were now confronted by hordes of fearless warriors. Lieutenant Hutton was not surprised that the first volley seemed so ineffectual for it 'could hardly be expected to have done much execution, since there were but a number of darting figures at irregular intervals and distances . . .' . Many troops simply froze or fired wildly. Officers, including Hutton, reacted quickly; some troops received a swift rap across the back from a parade ground stick, others the venom of their officer's tongue. As Hutton wrote, 'a smart rap with my stick soon helped a man recover his self-possession'.[71] Steadiness was restored and another round pushed into the breech of their Martini–Henrys.

The British, according to Lieutenant E.O.H. Wilkinson, were, at this early stage of the battle, 'volley-firing their rifles by sections', which would have facilitated greater control of the firing line, maintained a more constant fire and allowed battlefield smoke to clear between volleys.[72] Ian Knight has estimated that at long ranges of 700–1,400yd, volley fire was no more than 2 per cent effective in killing or wounding a charging adversary. At a medium range of between 300–700yd, Knight claims that the effective percentage rose only to 5 per cent and at close range of 100–300yd, volley fire was 15 per cent effective. Knight believes that even this figure might be optimistic, for a huge amount of smoke would have obscured targets and adrenaline would have reduced accuracy further.[73]

The reason for such low percentages can be explained by battlefield adrenaline combined with inexperience. Undoubtedly at Gingindlovu the inexperience of the troops, particularly the 3/60th Rifles, would have reduced the percentage of hits. John Dunn noted that the young soldiers were failing to adjust their rifle sights as the Zulus closed in on the British, with the result that many bullets would have sailed over the enemy's heads.[74]

Yet, for all the failings of British marksmanship, the young British soldiers, and the Martini–Henry, achieved a crushing victory. There is an important truth about the effectiveness of battlefield, particularly volley, fire in this. Again, as Knight has claimed:

> Killing the enemy was not the sole objective. Discouraging his attacks, breaking up his formations, and causing him to retire were the tactical necessities, and it was necessary to kill only a small proportion of the enemy involved to achieve

them. To withstand prolonged and accurate Martini-Henry fire was a terrifying experience that even the bravest warrior could not endure indefinitely.[75]

Lieutenant Hutton noted that the 3/60th, in their defence of the laager, fired less than seven rounds a man. Thus, approximately 4,000 rounds were fired by the 540 men of the 3/60th. After the battle sixty-one dead Zulus were found in the most destructive fire zone, opposite the Rifles' position. It follows that over sixty rounds were fired for every Zulu killed, although this does not take into account the numbers wounded.[76] Corporal Hargreaves wrote in his journal that, 'Aided by the cover of the long grass and small clumps of bushes, the enemy still managed to creep up to the edge of the cover and there lay for a long time, our firing being too hot to allow them a chance to make a rush any nearer.'[77] Effectively the Zulu attack stalled, not because of high numbers of casualties in the attack, but because British volley fire created an impression of impenetrability. This view is supported by John Guy, who states, 'we cannot deny the physical damage and the demoralisation caused by British firepower in Zululand . . .' .[78]

Colonel Callwell supports Hutton's claim for the number of rounds fired at Gingindlovu, 'Statistics show that a few rounds a man represents the amount in each fight . . . the expenditure was not over 10 rounds per man'.[79] Hargreaves recalled that, 'Lord Chelmsford was on foot going round the Laager with a red night cap on, and encouraging the men, directing their fire and advising them to fire low and steady.'[80] Such instructions were simply following the policy outlined by official training manuals, in which slow fire was considered effective fire. Such steady, controlled volley fire again explains the low number of shots fired per man.

Not all the British troops were indifferent shots. Lieutenant Wilkinson observed one marksman of the 60th drop 'four running Zulus at 400 yards with consecutive shots', whilst Hutton saw a group of ten to fifteen Zulus run for the cover of a clump of palm bushes only for all them to be killed by a directed volley.[81]

Taking cover in the long wet grass, the Zulus returned an ineffectual fire on the British square. Some of the warriors were armed with Martini–Henrys, plundered from the battlefield of Isandlwana, but, fortunately for the British, their fire was mostly high. Apparently, the Zulus also had difficulty in adjusting the range sights. Although the Zulu fire claimed some notable victims, including Lieutenant George

Johnson of the 99th and Colonel Northey of the 3/60th, the final British butcher's bill of thirteen killed and forty-eight wounded was, considering the intensity of the battle, remarkably light. Chelmsford's decision to prepare shelter trenches undoubtedly saved the lives of many riflemen.

As the Zulu advance ground to a halt, the warriors comprising the 'chest' began to edge to their right, past the corner of the square, and attempted to attack the men of the 99th on the left face. The left 'horn' had pushed forward to a point where they were able to make a determined attack upon the front right corner. It was here that one of the Gatling guns was placed and the 1,200 rounds it fired were sufficient to beat back the attackers, although it was claimed one Zulu warrior managed to get close enough to the Gatling to actually touch it before being cut down.[82] The Zulus moved further against the 99th. Their threat seemed so intense that even the special correspondent Norris Newman grabbed a Martini–Henry and claimed at least one Zulu victim. Again, as with the charge on the front face, the attack on the left stalled. At this point the right 'horn' appeared from Misi Hill and deployed to attack the rear face of the laager, defended by men of the 91st.

Although as inexperienced as their colleagues in the 60th, the men of the 91st equipped themselves well in their first engagement. Their sights were adjusted down from 500, 400, 300, 200 to 100yd and no Zulu got within 30yd of the shelter trenches. The Martini–Henry fire of the 91st was ably supported by fire from two 9pdrs and, at the other end of the line, a Gatling and rocket tubes. The British 'were able to put down a terrible barrier of fire around the square', which made the Zulu attack recoil from the rear face and roll round to attack the right face, desperate to find any place to break into the defences and engage the British in hand-to-hand combat.[83] Here defence was left to the seasoned veterans of the 57th, who met the Zulu charge with steady, well-directed volley fire. The battle had now been raging for an hour and, although stalled, the Zulus showed no sign of retreating, but clung on to the cover afforded by the long grass and continued their sniping at the British. Chelmsford considered it was time to unleash Captain Barrow's Mounted Infantry, who filed out of the square and launched themselves upon the warriors of the right 'horn'. A few warriors made a determined stand and sold their lives, but the majority of their comrades fell back rapidly.

Barrow later estimated that fifty to sixty Zulus fell in this mounted advance. Chelmsford then followed up this attack with the Natal

Native Contingent (NNC) which was instructed to clear the field, a task they completed with relish. Many a wounded Zulu was despatched by the marauding NNC, whose officers lost control of their men. As the surviving Zulus fled the battlefield, Chelmsford was able to claim a notable victory. Over 500 Zulu bodies were found close to the British square and a further 200 were discovered the following day. Total Zulu casualties were probably in excess of 1,200. The next day Chelmsford's column relieved Eshowe.

Lieutenant Hutton considered that the victory owed much to the Martini–Henry rifles, which he described as 'the most perfect weapons in the world'.[84] A colour sergeant of the 91st wrote that, 'Nothing in the world could stand our fire . . .'.[85] Whilst the *Perthshire Advertiser* printed a soldier's letter which claimed that, 'At Ginghilovo our Martini-Henrys swept away the Zulus like a broom.'[86] It seems clear that these firsthand accounts influenced the thinking of the editors of British newspapers, many of whom clearly felt that Chelmsford's victory was as a result of a superiority of firepower over the Zulus and the inability of the enemy to alter their tactics. The *Essex Standard*, for example, wrote:

> Our forces stood depending on their breechloaders entirely, to repel the assault. The Zulus on their part, true to their usual tactics, attempted another surprise, and early in the morning, in force it would appear about 11,000 strong, attempted to carry the British camp by storm, rushing down upon it in two separate bodies from the surrounding heights. The struggle lasted but for an hour or so, but was very desperate, the enemy, with a daring valour that it is impossible not to admire, sweeping onward in their assault amid the pitiless hail of rifle bullets which they had to face . . . Thus it will be seen, that it was the steady and well-directed fire of our Riflemen that repulsed the attack, and the experience of the battle shows that against this the soldiers of Cetewayo cannot stand.[87]

Similarly, the editor of the *Isle of Man News* wrote, 'We may suppose, then, that it will be claimed that we have scored a victory in Zululand, although, technically, it is simply a successful defence from a sudden and determined attack, due principally to our possession and skilful use of Martini-Henry rifles, Gatling guns, rocket tubes, and other ghastly apparatus of death.'[88]

Yet for all the emphasis placed upon the superiority of the Martini–Henry it was left to a letter in *The Times* to highlight an apparent weakness. An individual who signed himself 'IGNORAMUS' wrote:

> Sir, – I am surprised that so little notice has been taken of the comparatively small results obtained by our much vaunted arms of precision. At Gingihlova the loss of the enemy has been estimated at from 500 to 1,000. Taking the high number, and reckoning our troops at 5,000, it took five men firing away for an hour and a half to kill one Zulu. Even at Rorke's Drift, in a 12 hour combat, most of it at close quarters, 130 Englishmen slew 500 of the enemy, or about four-a-piece! What an amount of wild firing and enormous waste of ammunition does this suggest! The British soldier is a costly and valuable machine, and no pains should be spared to make him a cool and skilful marksman.[89]

It would seem clear that it was not the 'killing power' of the Martini–Henry that won the Battle of Gingindlovu for the British, but rather a combination of factors. Certainly, the rifle claimed many lives, but so did the Gatling and artillery fire and arguably it was the charge of the Mounted Infantry, and ruthlessness of the NNC, that claimed the most. Yet, the fire of the Martini–Henry presented a huge psychological barrier to the Zulu advance and this undoubtedly played an important role in halting the Zulu attack. The horrendous wounds the bullets could inflict and the certainty that any advance would be met by crushing volley fire meant that the Zulu attack stalled at a range of 300yd from the British square. Perhaps this was the ultimate test of the rifle's 'stopping power', if not 'killing power'. The biggest factor in the British success was Chelmsford's decision to alter his tactics and entrench his force behind a defensive square, so as to nullify the flanking attacks of the Zulus. The enemy obliged Chelmsford by not altering their tactics, which allowed him to direct the destructive British firepower in a concentrated manner.

Chelmsford repeated the tactics in the final battle of the Anglo-Zulu War at the Battle of Ulundi, on 4 July 1879. The Second Invasion was even more ponderous than the first. Over 15,000 troops were split between three formations: the 1st Division, which marched along the coast, the 2nd Division, which marched towards Ulundi from the north-west, and the newly christened 'Wood's Flying Column', which joined the 2nd Division on its march towards the Zulu capital. Again

Chelmsford was thorough; with the use of forward reconnaissance as well as entrenchment at night. Wood trained his troops to be able to form a laager from column in just 35 minutes.[90] Clearly the British were not going to be surprised again. Soon, however, even Chelmsford's subordinates were complaining about the slow progress towards Ulundi, to which Chelmsford responded in Italian, *'Chi va piano, va sano e va lontano'* ('Slow and steady wins the race').[91] On 17 June 1879, Chelmsford received news from London that he was to be superseded in command by General Sir Garnet Wolseley and it was this news that seemed to instil a greater degree of urgency in Chelmsford. He now seemed determined to defeat the Zulu Army once and for all and burn Cetewayo's capital.

Thus, on 4 July, the combined forces of the 2nd Division and Wood's Flying Column assembled in an infantry square, or more accurately a parallelogram formation upon the Mahlabathini plain and marched slowly on their target of Ulundi. Chelmsford was insistent that the Zulus be finally defeated in the open, rather than from behind a defensive laager, so as to demonstrate to the Zulus the superiority of the British soldier.[92] As Callwell wrote in *Small Wars*, 'the fact of troops being in a rigid formation under perfect control, ensures the maintenance of that fire discipline which is at the root of success when the conditions are critical. The compactness of the formation gives the troops confidence when facing a savage charge, and ensures that the line will not falter.'[93] Such a disposition risked higher casualties from Zulu rifle fire, but earlier battles had shown Zulu marksmanship to be poor and there was no reason to believe that it would pose any real threat.

As the British edged forward, the Zulu Army, of 15,000–20,000 warriors, was first seen approaching at around 8.30am. A screen of British cavalry on each flank ensured that the usual enemy tactical formation of the 'chest and the horns' could not be successfully deployed. Furthermore, accurate artillery fire smashed into any large congregating bodies of Zulus, again making a concerted attack difficult. The face of the advancing square was manned by men of the 80th Regiment, supported by Gatling and 7 and 9pdrs. Despite the disruptive artillery fire, the Zulus were able to approach to within range of the Martini–Henry rifles. The infantry, two front ranks kneeling, with two ranks standing behind, opened a fearful volley fire by sections. Corporal William Roe of the 58th wrote, 'They [Zulus] were falling down in heaps, as though they had been tipped off carts.'[94] The British fire ensured, as one corporal of the 90th claimed, that the Zulus went to ground and remained at 'a respectful distance'.[95] The Zulus now unleashed sniper fire upon the British square which the war artist Melton Prior described as 'very warm' and it was now that the majority of the British casualties occurred.[96] Grenadier Guards officer R. Wolride Gordon wrote of the Zulu fire as well as the power of the Martini–Henry:

> The battle began, and in a short time there was such a rain of bullets flying over our heads that it was, as one of the men remarked, 'for all the world like a hailstorm'. I remained standing, watching the battle through my field glasses. It was a curious sight, and one could plainly see men, when hit, throw up their arms and fall. The thud a bullet makes against a man's body is a most curious sound.[97]

As at Gingindlovu, the wall of fire surrounding the British square largely stalled the Zulu attack. Only at the rear corner of the square, where the 58th and 21st Regiments were deployed did a rush of Zulu warriors really threaten the British and here the attack got to within 30yd. Chelmsford was there at the critical moment and Melton Prior heard the General say to his troops, 'Men, fire faster, can't you fire faster?' Prior was rather disdainful of Chelmsford when he wrote in his autobiography, 'Now it is not my business to question the wisdom of this remark, but I cannot help contrasting it with Lord Wolseley's well-known order, "Fire, slow, fire slow!"'[98]

Once the threat had been repulsed, Chelmsford repeated his tactic at Gingindlovu and unleashed troopers from the 17th Lancers and Mounted Infantry to rout the enemy. The battle had lasted a mere half an hour. British casualties were ten dead and sixty-nine wounded. There is no accurate figure for the Zulu dead, but over a thousand bodies were found around the British square and along the path of the cavalry pursuit. Ulundi was burnt to the ground and Chelmsford had effectively brought the war to an end.

As at Gingindlovu, the expenditure of Martini–Henry ammunition was low, at an average of 6.4 rounds per man, despite Chelmsford's pleas for his men to fire faster at a critical moment.[99] For all the bravery of the Zulu nation, the British Army had decisively defeated their enemy, both from behind prepared defences and out on an open plain. The over confidence in the tactical superiority of the Martini–Henry at the start of the conflict had been found to be wanting and

Chelmsford had had the foresight to alter his tactical deployments so as to neutralise the tactics of the Zulu Army and best use the power of the Martini–Henry rifle.

Indeed, the Martini–Henry's famed 'stopping power' was proven during the war, even if it did not claim as many victims as the soldiers who fired it, and the historians who first wrote of the conflict, had first thought. It is worth recording that the majority of Martini–Henrys used by the British troops during the Anglo-Zulu war would have been the Mark I Third Pattern and this is particularly true of the men who fought in the First Invasion of January 1879, for converting the Mark Is to Mark IIs had only just begun at this time. The psychological effect of Martini–Henry volley fire is difficult to measure but it is clear that such fire repeatedly stalled attacks as the enemy faced a 'wall' of fire. The robustness, simplicity and 'stopping power' of the Martini–Henry were appreciated by the troops who used the weapon in anger in 1879, and this admiration would be carried over into the battles of the 1880s.

Chapter 5

A Wall of Bayonets and Fire – The Sudan Campaigns, 1884–5

'Strategic Offensive with a Tactical Defensive'
Our fellows soon realised that with the bayonet and Martini and coolness they had nothing to fear from the rudely armed and nearly naked savages.

Bennet Burleigh, Special Correspondent,
Daily Telegraph

Writing in the fourth edition of his *Soldiers' Pocket Book for Field Service*, Garnet Wolseley stated, 'The formation of Battalion Squares to resist cavalry may be almost regarded as a thing of the past, for with the long-ranging arms of the day, to put your battalions into such a formation would be to give it over to destruction.'[1] Clearly Wolseley's thinking had been influenced by the experiences of the Franco-Prussian War of 1870–1 and other Prussian victories against the Danes and the Austrians in which the devastating killing power of modern breech-loading rifles, and rifled artillery, was demonstrated against both advancing troops as well those in defensive positions. Yet, Britain had recently fought a bloody war against the Zulu nation in which the British had been forced, due to the mobility of the enemy, to resort to the square defensive formation. Indeed, troops under Wolseley's ultimate command would again turn to the square for protection against the determined attacks of Mahdist forces in the Sudan campaigns of the 1880s.

The early disasters of Isandlwana (22 January 1879) and Intombi Drift (12 March 1879) during the Anglo-Zulu conflict of 1879 had resulted in Lord Chelmsford amending and adopting both his tactics and battlefield formations so as to overcome the Zulus. Thus, as Howard Bailes has argued, the traditional view of Victorian commanders being slow to adapt to a rapidly changing military situation can be viewed as something of a myth.[2] Faced with an enemy that possessed an overwhelming superiority in numbers and who was also massively more mobile than the British columns, the British commanders in the Sudanese campaigns of 1884–5 had, like Lord Chelmsford, to resort to the square formation. Armed with advanced weaponry, such as the Martini–Henry rifle and early variants of the machine gun, the British possessed a huge technological advantage over their Mahdist enemies. Yet, unlike at the Battle of Ulundi where the Zulus displayed a reticence to attack the concentrated square, which may well have been as a result of the psychological scar left by the defeats of Khambula (29 March 1879) and Gingindlovu (2 April 1879), the Mahdists possessed a religious fanaticism that would propel them against the British defences and almost resulted in a British defeat on two separate occasions.

In the 1870s, a Muslim cleric named Muhammad Ahmed (1844–85) preached a combination of renewal of the faith alongside the liberation of the Sudan from Egyptian rule. He soon began to attract followers and early Egyptian attempts to quell this outright rebellion met with death and failure at the hands of Ahmed's fanatical supporters, first at the Battle of Aba and at subsequent ambushes, the most significant of which was the slaughter of 4,000 Egyptian troops under the command of Yusef Pasha on 7 June 1882.

With each bloody victory Muhammad Ahmed gained more fanatical followers, as well as modern weapons and ammunition. His decision to proclaim himself the Mahdi, or chosen one, the redeemer of the Islamic world, enhanced his position in the eyes of his supporters and gave him a self-proclaimed legitimacy. Now extremely concerned by the Mahdi's success the Egyptian government reacted by appointing William Hicks, a retired British Indian staff officer, to lead a force of nearly 10,000 Egyptian troops, armed with modern Remington rifles, artillery and machine guns. This sizeable, if poorly trained, force tracked the Mahdi, and his 40,000-strong army, towards the city of El Obied, which was under siege. Here faulty intelligence resulted in Hicks' force being surrounded by the Mahdists. Forming defensive square formations on a wooded plain called Sheikan, Hicks and his men held the enemy at bay for nearly two days until they were finally overwhelmed on 5 November 1883. Hicks and almost his whole command were killed.

This setback, which also saw the death of a number of European officers and journalists, caused a sensation in London, and the government of William Gladstone (1809–98) was placed under enormous pressure to avenge Hicks and relieve the Sudan. Furthermore, the Mahdi's continued military success encouraged and emboldened other tribal leaders, most notably Osman Digna (1840–1926), who led his tribe of Hadendowa warriors from their lands on the Red Sea coast. The British would soon learn to respect these fearsome tribesmen.

With both the British and Egyptian governments under increasing pressure to save Egyptian and foreign citizens still in the Sudan it was agreed that the region had to be evacuated of civilians and soldiers alike. The Egyptian government called upon Gladstone's government to provide a British officer to coordinate the evacuation of the various Egyptian garrisons at such places as Tokar, Sinkat and specifically Khartoum. The obvious choice for such a task was Charles Gordon (1833–85), a gifted engineer and soldier, who had previously been Governor of the Sudan and had achieved success in reducing the slave trade there. He was respected by both the Sudanese and Egyptians, although the British Consular General in Cairo, Sir Evelyn Baring (1841–1917), was opposed to Gordon's appointment as he viewed Gordon as insubordinate and likely to act in a fashion contrary to British interests. Yet, with the British public, and particularly the newspapers, calling for Gordon's appointment Gladstone had little alternative but to offer Gordon the job of coordinating the evacuation.

Gordon left England on 18 January 1884 and arrived in Khartoum, via Cairo, on 18 February 1884. He was shocked and surprised at how far the Mahdist forces had advanced and discovered that Khartoum was virtually surrounded, with only the Nile offering a means of access and escape. However, Gordon using his own initiative, as Baring had feared, decided rather than evacuate the Egyptians and Europeans and leave the Sudanese to their fate, he would instead stay and fortify Khartoum. Gordon hoped that he would be able to hold the city until a relief force of British troops could arrive from England. Very reluctantly, and again under enormous public pressure to relieve Khartoum and rescue Gordon, Gladstone gave the command of what became known as 'The Gordon Relief Expedition' to Sir Garnet Wolseley.

The British entered the Sudanese campaigns armed with both the Martini–Henry rifle and new variants of the machine gun, as well as the tactical awareness of how best to use their technological superiority so as to defeat their numerically superior foes. The first viable machine gun was developed in 1862 by an American, Dr Richard Gatling (1818–1903). In 1870, the British tested the Gatling gun and the French Montigny mitrailleuse breech-loader, and, after making improvements, the British adopted the Gatling the following year. It was first used in conflict by the British during the Zulu war at the Battle of Nyezane (22 January 1879) and it played a significant role in the subsequent British victories at Gingindlovu and Ulundi. It was the Royal Navy, and not the army, which advocated the use of the Gatling gun for it appears that there was much prejudice against it from the Headquarters of the Royal Artillery at Woolwich, where the Gatling was viewed as an inferior form of field gun. Indeed, both in South Africa and the Sudan it was men of the Naval Brigade that manned the various variants of machine gun used by the British. Lord Chelmsford was one of the earliest advocates of machine guns, yet he admitted, 'it is clear that development of the machine-gun has not, at present, received much encouragement from the military authorities'.[3]

Despite the Gatling guns, which had been placed in the corners of the British square at Ulundi, jamming several times during the action, Chelmsford was able to claim that they 'proved a very valuable addition to the strength of our defence on the flank'. As a result of his experiences in Zululand, Chelmsford emphasised that machine guns should be considered purely infantry weapons and should not be attached to the artillery. He reported that they would be of great value, 'if only they could be made reliable'.[4]

The Gatling gun consisted of a number of breech-loading rifled barrels (ten were preferred) grouped around and parallel to a shaft. The assistant gunner placed the ammunition in a hopper at the top of the gun, and the gunner turned a crank handle manually, with each barrel rotating and firing in succession, once in a revolution. The cartridges fell into the loading position by their own weight and were thus gravity fed. A stoppage, as witnessed by Chelmsford at Ulundi, could occur if a cartridge did not fall accurately in line with the chamber. In addition, the Boxer cartridges which were originally used did not have a solid-drawn metal case, but instead had one built up by rolling a thin brass plate round a mandril and attaching an iron base to it. As with the Martini–Henry rifle, it was by no means a rare occurrence to find that the exterior tore off this iron base which left the chamber of the barrel blocked up with the brass part of the cartridge. When working effectively, the Gatling could fire more than 600 rounds per minute. However, it was mounted on a fixed artillery carriage, which precluded the gun from traversing and limited its effectiveness.[5]

Two other variants of machine gun were adopted by the Naval Brigade. First the Nordenfelt in 1878 and then the Gardner in 1882, and it was these designs that saw service in the Sudan, rather than the Gatling gun. The Nordenfelt gun was a multiple-barrel organ gun that had a row of up to twelve barrels, although the variants adopted by the Royal Navy had three, five or ten barrels. The weapon was designed by a Swedish engineer, Helge Palmcrantz (1842–80), who created and patented a mechanism to load and fire the multiple-barrelled gun by simply moving a single lever backwards and forwards. A vertical frame between the barrels and the breech action carried the cartridges. The production of the weapon was financed by a Swedish steel producer, Thorsten Nordenfelt (1842–1920), who was living and working in London. Production of the Nordenfelt was centred in London along with a sales office.

During a sales demonstration at Portsmouth, a 10-barrelled version of the weapon fired 3,000 rounds of ammunition in 3 minutes without a stoppage or failure. Suitably impressed, the Royal Navy ordered the weapon, although insisting that the calibre of the ammunition to be used was 1in.[6]

The Gardner gun, which was superseded by and used alongside the Nordenfelt, was invented by William Gardner of Toledo, Ohio in 1874. Gardner sold his prototype to the Pratt and Witney company which developed and marketed the weapon to governments around the world. After successful trials and demonstrations in America, the Royal Navy became interested in the weapon and Gardner was invited to England to exhibit his invention. The Admiralty was suitably impressed and they purchased the rights to produce the gun in England, with Gardner remaining to supervise its construction and production. The first models of the Gardner gun had five barrels, all fed from a vertical magazine or hopper, and was operated by a crank. When this was turned a feed arm positioned a cartridge in the breech and the bolt closed and fired the weapon. Turning the crank further opened the breech block and extracted the spent case. This improved loading action made reloading so rapid that it permitted the number of barrels to be first reduced from five to two and then only one in the final Royal Navy variant.[7]

There has been a strong tendency amongst historians to focus on the negatives of the Sudanese campaign. Indeed, the ultimate objective of the relief of Khartoum and the rescue of Gordon failed. Throughout the campaign the advance of the British was slowed by the harsh desert conditions, the difficulties of navigation through the many cataracts on the River Nile and the strong resistance of the Mahdist forces. Brutal battles at such infamous sites as El Teb, Tamai and Abu Klea have left us with strong images of gallant and defiant defence in square formation as the Mahdist warriors threw themselves with fanatical bravery at the British positions. In the case of the battles of Tamai and Abu Klea, the British square was broken by the enemy and such actions became almost part of British folklore. The following extract from Rudyard Kipling's poem 'Fuzzy-Wuzzy' demonstrates this:

> We sloshed you with Martinis, an' it wasn't 'ardly fair;
> But for all the odds agin' you, Fuzzy-Wuz, you broke the square.
>
> . . .
>
> So 'ere's to you, Fuzzy-Wuzzy, at your 'ome in the Soudan; You're a pore benighted 'eathen but a first-class fightin' man;
> An' 'ere's to you, Fuzzy-Wuzzy, with your 'ayrick 'ead of 'air – You big black boundin' beggar – for you broke a British square!

Yet, for all the focus on the bravery of the Mahdists there is a danger of romanticising the incredible brutality of the warfare.

Fundamentally, and this seems to be forgotten in some writings, the British defeated the defiant Mahdist forces in every engagement in which they fought. Some may well have been close-run encounters, such as Abu Klea, but British technology, in the form of the Martini–Henry rifle and Gardner machine gun, along with determination, training and courage, and the defensive wall of fire and steel that the square provided, ensured that the British ultimately prevailed. This undeniable fact seems to have been overlooked by some writers.

As John Darwin has recently written:

> Forming a square was not the perfect solution. If the force's supplies and transport were kept safely inside, the square might swell to an indefensible size, with a herd of terrified oxen penned up in the midst. Left out, they might be an easy prize for the enemy, destroying the column's future mobility. By definition a square reduced available firepower on any one side, making it vulnerable to a heavy weight punch. A cool-headed opponent might aim at its corners where its cohesion was weakest. It was dangerous to use against serious enemy fire-power or guns.[8]

The latter point reinforces Wolseley's statement in his *Pocket Book* that the defensive square formation was extremely vulnerable to the firepower of modern weaponry. Yet, against the Mahdists this was one thing the British did not have to fear. The greatest concern, as experienced by Lord Chelmsford in the Zulu conflict, was to mitigate the danger caused by the numerical superiority and manoeuvrability of the enemy. To do this the British had little alternative but to resort to the square formation and rely on the discipline of the troops and the superiority of their weaponry. Although the Mahdists had captured modern rifles and artillery pieces, from Hicks' defeated army, these were largely used against the walls of Khartoum. Although the British did face modern Krupps artillery fire from Osman Digna forces in the coastal region of Sudan, again captured from the Egyptian Army, this fire was not effectively used and the British largely came up against spears and swords backed by a fanatical determination.

Despite Gordon's increasingly desperate besieged position in Khartoum, it was a further Egyptian disaster, this time in eastern coastal Sudan, that prompted the initial direct British intervention. Marching in an attempt to relieve an Egyptian garrison besieged in the town of Tokar, an Egyptian force of Gendarmerie, led by former British officer Valentine Baker (1827–87), was ambushed, on 4 February 1884, at a place called El Teb by a swift and ferocious dervish attack. Out of an original strength of nearly 4,000 men, roughly half were butchered or captured. Stung by this latest reversal and concerned to keep a toehold on the Red Sea coast, the British government acted in exasperation. Two brigades of British infantry along with the 19th Hussars, several companies of Mounted Infantry, Artillery, Marines and a Naval Machine Gun detachment were despatched, under the command of Major General Sir Gerald Graham VC (1831–99) to the Suakin coastal region. At the same time the 10th Hussars, en route to India, were diverted there. Combined, these troops were named the Suakin Field Force.

Graham, a good friend of Gordon, and a fellow Engineer, resolved very early on to use a square formation as a means to advance against the enemy whilst providing a defensive wall against a swift surprise attack. It was clear from Baker's earlier debacle that the dervishes relied on being able to engage in hand-to-hand combat to overwhelm their foe and Graham was keen to keep the enemy from closing, but if this was to be unavoidable then he would be able to rely on the cohesion of the square, the discipline of his troops and their skill with the bayonet.

The British, intent on confronting Osman Digna's forces as well as relieving Tokar, advanced with their infantry in one large square formation. On 29 February 1884, they were advancing over the same ground on which Baker's men had been recently slaughtered at El Teb. Osman's warriors must have been confident of another victory. Although reluctant to use the rifles captured from Baker's force,

Osman did order that the captured Krupps artillery pieces were fired at the British square.

However, the fire was inaccurate and was soon silenced by returning British fire. However, Sergeant William Danby of the Prince of Wales Own Royal Hussars wrote in a letter home that the British troops had to withstand over 15 minutes of fire before the battle commenced and this must surely have tested British nerves.[9] Finally, the dervish warriors, their impatience growing to charge at the square, were finally allowed to rise up from their prepared positions and were unleashed against their new enemy.

Unlike the Egyptian forces they had recently overwhelmed, this new enemy was different, for instead of abandoning both their position and their weaponry, the British stood firm. Calmly firing, reloading and firing again the British volley fire from the Martini–Henry rifles mowed down the charging tribesmen. Forewarned of the expected velocity of the dervish attack, many of the British infantrymen had nicked their bullets, effectively transforming them into even more deadly dum-dum bullets.[10] Yet, despite this precaution, and the intensity and accuracy of the volley fire, many dervish warriors reached the square where they were faced with the British bayonet.

The dervish swords and spears were razor sharp and could inflict horrific wounds, whilst the steel of the British bayonets, as well as some officer's swords, proved to be weak and defective for there are numerous reports of bayonets bending when hitting bone or swords shattering. Despite these weaknesses, their dogmatic training and discipline saw the British overcome the effectiveness of the dervish swords and spears.

With the initial assault beaten off, Graham advanced with his square towards the village of El Teb, which despite constant harassment was secured in the early afternoon. The only blot on an otherwise complete British victory was the behaviour of the supporting British cavalry which rather than attack the dervishes advancing on the square decided, under the leadership of Brigadier General Herbert Stewart (1843–85), to charge at a group of the enemy which had not yet engaged the infantry square. This act meant that the cavalry crossed disputed ground in which warriors were able to conceal themselves and attack the underbellies of the horses as they galloped past. The resulting 20 men killed and 48 wounded were a large, and totally unnecessary, percentage of the total British casualties of 35 killed and 155 wounded. Osman Digna's losses were estimated at over 2,000.

Despite the magnitude of the British victory at El Teb, neither Graham nor his troops were under any illusion about either the task that still faced them or the danger that the dervishes presented. In a letter written on 1 March 1884 to his cousin Adie, Sergeant William Danby of the 10th Hussars wrote:

> Without a doubt these Arabs are the most fierce, brave, daring and unmerciful race of men in the world they fear nothing, give and expect no mercy and they are indeed skilled with their knives, spears, swords and clubs. Our General [Graham] says that in all his experience of war he never saw such a hard fought battle, and in the face of all things so bravely won.[11]

The Special Correspondent of the *Daily Telegraph*, Bennett Burleigh (1840–1914), wrote of the dervish attack at El Teb, 'It was marvellous to see how they came on, heedless and fearless of death, shouting and brandishing their weapons. To the right and to the left they fell, but those left, even when wounded, rushed on. A few got within five or ten paces of the square, proving how many bullets it takes to kill a man.'[12] Similarly, the Special Correspondent of the *Standard* wrote, 'Every foot was contested by the enemy, who displayed a courage, a tenacity, and a contempt for death such as only steady troops could have withstood. There is no doubt that had General Graham's force consisted of Egyptians instead of British troops the former disaster would have been repeated here.'[13] Yet, within a few days Graham's troops were to face an even sterner test.

After the victory at El Teb, the British advanced, virtually unmolested to Tokar where 600 Egyptian men, women and children were evacuated. The town was now abandoned and Graham withdrew his force to Trinkitat and from there by ship to Suakin. The British troops were given little rest for intelligence sources warned Graham of a sizeable concentration of Osman Digna's forces at Tamai, just a few miles inland from Suakin. Graham clearly could not tolerate such a large enemy force so close to his position and he resolved to advance against it.

On 13 March 1884, at Tamai a battle took place which has passed into British military history as one of the bloodiest encounters ever against an indigenous foe. Although the battle is remembered, along with Abu Klea (17 January 1885), as one in which the enemy 'broke the British square', this, I believe, is too simplistic a view for in both battles the initial success of the Mahdist forces was partly as a result of British errors and again in both cases the British were ultimately victorious, a point that is sometimes overlooked in all the folklore which surrounds these two battles.

Marching out of Suakin on the evening of 11 March 1884, so as to avoid the worst of the heat, Graham and his men suffered two nights exposed to both enemy sniping fire and the harshness of the desert. On the morning of 13 March the British were in position to begin their advance upon Osman Digna's position at Tamai.

Graham decided to divide his force of two brigades, the first under the command of Brigadier General Sir Redvers Buller, VC (1839–1908) and the second led by Major General John Davis (1832–1901), into two separate squares which would mutually support each other and give covering fire.

Graham attached himself to the Second Brigade and it was this square which commenced the advance at around 8am. Buller was somewhat slow to form up his square and thus the gap between the two, at first about 1,000yd, although later it closed to half that distance, was greater than Graham had wanted or envisaged. The Second Brigade were first to encounter the enemy and both the scouts and a 9pdr battery, under a Major Holley, were soon heavily engaged. The first serious enemy attack was unleashed at around 9am. With the passing of time it has become impossible to categorically state the train of events that now followed but what is clear is that as the enemy charged, the men of the Black Watch, fronting the square of the Second Brigade, advanced to meet them. Unfortunately, those troops of the Yorks and Lancs failed to move with the Highlanders and a dangerous gap opened in the square, which the dervishes soon exploited. Whether an order was given to men of the Black Watch by Graham or their Colonel, or whether the Highlanders moved forward recklessly is not clear, but what is certain is that the Second Brigade's square was now very vulnerable.

The advance of the Black Watch initially achieved success and the enemy ahead of them were put to flight but then, almost magically, a much larger force which Osman Digna had held in reserve, rose out of a dry watercourse, or khor, and charged upon the right-hand corner of the square where the men of the Yorks and Lancs were desperately struggling to close the gap between them and the Highlanders, and into which the Naval Brigade had been bringing up its Gardner machine guns.

The enemy swarmed around the sailors who fought valiantly but were soon overwhelmed by the ferocity of the attack and ten lives and the guns were lost. Captain Ford and fifteen men of the York and Lancs stood their ground but they were all cut down or speared in moments and the rest of the regiment was pushed back into the Royal Marines at the rear of the square such was the weight of the enemy onslaught. The Black Watch who had advanced were surrounded by the dervishes and the battle quickly became one of brutal and confused hand-to-hand fighting in which every man struggled to survive.

The correspondent of the *Daily Telegraph*, Bennett Burleigh, was present in the square and wrote descriptively of the carnage and brutality that he saw, but also of the courage and discipline of the British troops at the critical moment:

> To their credit be it ever said many men disdained to run, but went back with their faces to the foe, firing and striking with the bayonet. The bulk of the regiment crowded in upon the Marines, throwing them into disorder, and back everybody was borne in a confused mass, men and regiments being inextricably mixed up. General Graham and his Staff tried their best to hold and rally the troops, and General Davis and all the officers laboured to get the men to stand their ground in an orderly way. . . . but here and there the Marines and Highlanders retired slowly, firing steadily at the rushing Arabs, whom they bowled over like ninepins, though, truth to tell, these were instantly replaced by others.[14]

Burleigh went onto describe the fanatical courage of the dervishes, or Hadendowa:

> As Arab after Arab was knocked over we laughed and cheered, shouting 'That's the way. Give it them, men!' Still on the enemy came, yelling and screaming with diabolic ferocity. The gaping wounds made by our almost explosive Martini-Henry bullets, scarcely checked the savages in their wild career. It was only when the lead shattered the bone of a leg, or pierced heart or brain, that their mad onrush was instantly stopped. I saw Arab after Arab, through whose bodies our bullets had ploughed their way, charging down on the square, with the blood spouting in pulsating streams from them at every heart-throb. Down they bore on us; some with two or three bullet wounds, reeling like frenzied, drunken

men, but still pressing onwards to throw themselves, without attempt to parrying, upon our bayonets, as the surest way to slay or cut one victim before Death's agony stiffened their limbs. Others there were, whose life-blood ebbed ere they reached our men, who fell within a pace or two of the soldiers. The last act of these poor warriors was invariably a despairing effort to hurl the weapon they carried at the moment in their hand-stick, spear, or sword – at their English foeman a savage gleam shone in their faces, defiant, unrelenting, hating, as they gathered all their strength, to thus make their last blow at us. Who but could admire and applaud such dauntless bravery? Those of us privileged to witness it, and the awful spectacle of those five minutes, can never forget it, or cease to remember the grand self-sacrificing courage of the brave Hadendowa.[15]

Despite the maelstrom in which the British found themselves, order and discipline was restored in a fighting withdrawal. The surviving men of the Second Brigade reformed 800yd further back from the initial clash and the troops of the First Brigade were now able to lay down steady volleys of covering crossfire.

Furthermore, men of the Mounted Infantry, under Stewart's command, who were out and to the side of the Second Brigade were now able to offer support firing into the mass of the charging dervishes. The immediate danger to the Second Brigade was now effectively over but as the First Brigade advanced it now became the target. However, the square formation was rigidly maintained and a steady fire from the Martini–Henry rifles kept the enemy at bay with not one of the dervishes getting to within 200yd of this second British square. The enemy soon began to head for the shelter of the distant mountains and the bloody battlefield was left to the British.

The battle over, Burleigh covered the ground in a 60yd radius of where the original right corner of the Second Brigade square had been when the enemy had rushed in. He counted a thousand dead dervishes and a hundred dead British soldiers. The sand, as Burleigh stated, was literally red with blood and all this carnage had occurred in just a 5-minute period.[16]

Despite Graham's two decisive victories strategically nothing had been achieved. Osman Digna had not been captured and his men still offered a formidable opposition so much so that all thought of trying to relieve Gordon along the Suakin–Berber line was abandoned. If

Gordon was to be saved the British would have to look to the Nile. At the disbandment of the Suakin Force General Graham issued the following notice to all ranks that had served under him:

> During the early days of the campaign the work thrown upon officers and men, in every rank and in every department was severe and unceasing. It was necessary to prepare for active operations required to overcome the power of a brave and fanatical foe, so as to clear the country for the special objects of the expedition. This work was performed under the harassing conditions of incessant night attacks by a cunning and resolute adversary, entailing constant vigilance and readiness on the part of the whole force. Whether engaged with the enemy, or in labouring under a burning sun in the deep sand of the desert, often with but scanty supply of water, the Suakin Field Force has displayed the true qualities of good soldiers.[17]

Unfortunately, against such a formidable determined foe, and fighting in extreme conditions, even the British soldier could not overcome the enemy.

Command, and the success of the Gordon Relief Column, now rested firmly in the hands of Wolseley and he set about the task with his usual gift for organisation. This time, however, unlike in the Red River campaign and the Ashanti expedition, the logistical and geographical obstacles were too much even for a man of Wolseley's obvious abilities. Preparations for the advance down the Nile were hindered by the need to stockpile sufficient supplies at Wadi Halfa as well as to transport the troops from Cairo to there and to ensure that the men were adequately acclimatised. In addition, the British had to master the use of camels as both pack animals and for transporting Mounted Infantry. They also had to build and then pilot transport vessels and the difficulty of negotiating men, suppliers and transports over and around the Nile cataracts proved to be harder than even the most pessimistic reports had suggested. All these factors, and many smaller ones, meant that much time was lost; time which the besieged Gordon could ill afford.

By Christmas Day 1884, Wolseley and his men had reached the outpost of Korti. Ahead of them lay three more difficult cataracts and many miles before Gordon could be reached. Realisation finally dawned that the main British force was still many weeks away from Khartoum and with the level of the Nile rapidly falling Gordon's last line of natural defence around the city was disappearing. After consulting his senior officers Wolseley resolved to form a desert camel column, commanded by Major General Herbert Stewart, which would cross the Bayuda Desert from Korti to Metemma on the Nile. Here it was hoped the force could rendezvous with steamers despatched by Gordon from Khartoum and from there return to reinforce the city. It was an enterprise full of risk. Not only was the Bayuda Desert a harsh environment, with few watering holes, it was strongly felt that the column would meet significant resistance from the Mahdist forces.

On 8 January 1885 Stewart led his command of 98 officers and 1,509 men, along with 2,228 camels and 155 horses into the Bayuda Desert. The columns first target was the water holes at Jakdul, a distance of 100 miles and slightly less than half way to their target of Metemma. Jakdul was reached in five days and on 14 January 1885 the column moved on towards the wells of Abu Klea. The Mahdi's spies had been aware of Wolseley's movements down the Nile for many months and the Mahdi himself had issued firm orders that Stewart's column should be opposed. A force commanded by Mus Wad Helu, comprising Jaalin, Dughein and Kenana tribesmen, estimated at between 8,000 and 14,000 men, were now ready to face the British in battle.

If such opposition was not enough, the camels on which the British depended were already suffering. Overwork, lack of fodder and mishandling took a toll and the sorry beasts began simply to collapse and die, forcing an even larger burden on the surviving animals and slowing the British. On 16 January a patrol of 19th Hussars led by Major John French (1852–1925) encountered a party of Mus Wad Helu's men guarding the pass to the Abu Klea wells. This information was soon passed to Stewart who resolved that the lateness of the day meant that he would not risk battle.

However, the condition of both men and camels meant that unless the wells were secured the following day many would die of dehydration and heat exhaustion. The British formed a defensive square behind a zariba made of thorny bush, and sat out the night. The men were kept awake by the occasional sniper fire and the dancing and drumming from an ever increasing enemy force. It must have been a terrifying experience for Stewart and his troops, for all must have known that unless they defeated the enemy in battle the following day then they would either succumb to the sword or thirst.

Dawn revealed that the enemy had used the cover of darkness to encroach on the British zariba and the accuracy and frequency of sniper fire increased, as did the British casualties. Stewart, under mounting pressure from the enemy and his officers who were looking for firm orders, dithered whilst more men fell. The British commander seemed to be waiting, and hoping, that the enemy would attack the defensive zariba but after suffering 2 hours of prolonged, and increasingly effective fire, it finally became apparent to Stewart that no attack would be forthcoming. Time was on the enemy's side for they could simply wait and watch the British die of thirst. The British would have to move towards the wells of Abu Klea knowing that they would be opposed by a ferocious and determined enemy.

Stewart finally gave the order for the men to move out of the zariba and form a defensive square, which had been carefully prearranged. The front was composed of the Mounted Infantry and the Guards Camel Regiment, with the Guards extending onto the right face. The left consisted of more Mounted Infantry and the Heavies whilst the rest was made up of the remaining Heavies, the Royal Sussex Regiment and the Naval Brigade with their Gardner guns. The square was constructed with two ranks of men who knew that if they came under attack that the front rank would kneel so as to allow the rear rank to fire over their heads. Stewart, his staff and the medical orderlies were placed in the centre and behind them were 120 camels and their handlers carrying what little was left of the water and the ammunition reserves. At 10am on 17 January 1885 the British square advanced.

Unfortunately for the British, the ground over which they were now travelling was exceedingly rough, littered with boulders and rocks from behind which the enemy could hide and direct fire, and it was extremely difficult to manoeuvre and maintain cohesion of the square. The camels soon fell behind and the square had to slow to a crawl so as not to disintegrate, which allowed the Mahdist snipers plenty of easy targets. Each time another man fell, the British would stop and deliver a withering volley from their Martini–Henrys to quell the enemy's fire. Stewart was forced to send out skirmishers to try and reduce the level of sniping. Then further danger was spotted as a squadron of enemy cavalry was seen rapidly approaching. Stewart ordered his artillerymen to run out their screw-guns from the sanctuary of the square and the second shot landed amongst the marauding cavalrymen killing forty-eight of the enemy outright. The rest fled.

After an hour of this tortuous march the British had covered only a mile-and-a-half and were still some distance from their goal. Looking up the slope towards where the wells were thought to be, a cluster of green and white banners could just be seen. As skirmishers from the square got within 400yd of the flags, the ground erupted with a swarm of hundreds of flags and thousands of the enemy who had concealed themselves in a hidden ravine.

The enemy rushed towards the British square, not in an uncontrolled fashion but in three arrowheads, each led by a mounted chief brandishing a banner. Although this sudden appearance of the enemy, and the manner in which their attack was coordinated, must have shocked the British, Stewart and his men were relieved that the expected and unavoidable battle was now to commence and they could rely on the formidable stopping power of the Martini–Henry. Stewart reacted quickly and confidently. He ordered the square to move 30yd on to a slight ridge for he did not want to be hit on low ground. There was a tense moment as the camel handlers struggled to get their charges inside the square, but with help from men of the Heavies this was achieved just in time to allow the sides of the square to blaze with Martini–Henry fire.

As the British had thought and trusted, their fire from the then most modern rifle in service brought down hundreds of the enemy. But to Stewart's amazement the enemy kept pouring towards the square and sheer weight of numbers seemed to be driving them on. At last, just 80yd from the square the British fire took its expected toll and, as at Ulundi and Gingindlovu, a wall of enemy dead began to form. The immediate crisis seemed to have passed. Yet, to the amazement of the British the Mahdist enemy wheeled to the right, almost as if the movement was preordained, and headed straight towards the bottom left corner of the square.

The resulting clash of arms lasted a mere 10 minutes, but like at Tamai, the resultant hand-to-hand fighting was extremely bloody. Again, as at Tamai, the fault for why the British square was 'broken' is not completely clear, but the likely culprit seems to have been Lord Charles Beresford (1846–1919) of the Naval Brigade who was in command of the Gardner guns. It seems that Stewart's short movement of the square to slightly higher ground had left a slight gap in the formation. Beresford, who was obsessed with demonstrating the effectiveness of the Gardner, decided to run it out through this gap so as it would gain an effective field of fire. It was at this moment that the enemy descended upon this exact spot, on the bottom left of the square.

Beresford looked up and quickly realised that the enemy was heading straight for him and the men of the Gardner. He later described the sound the dervishes made as 'like the roar of the sea'.[18] Seconds before the impact, the Gardner opened fire and Beresford had the satisfaction of witnessing the machine guns' bullets tear into the leading warriors. The sights were lowered and a further six rounds ran out before the dramatic and chilling sound of the Gardner jamming to a stop was heard. Major Parry, who served in Suakin under General Graham, wrote, 'The Gardner guns often appeared to jam, but of course, in a complicated weapon of this kind, the conditions under which it was tried in the Sudan were a severe test. The expansion of the metal from the heat, and the dust which was always flying about, were sufficient in a great measure to account for its failure...'[19] Of course we cannot know for sure why Beresford's Gardner jammed at this critical moment but we do know that as a result many British lives were lost.

All seven men of the Naval Brigade under Beresford's command were butchered in a matter of seconds. Miraculously their commander, although badly wounded in the hand, survived and was swept by a tidal wave of warriors into the Heavies. The force was such that these men were hurled into the Sussex Regiment which in turn was forced back into the baggage camels in the middle of the square. Amongst this crush and confusion British and Arab alike struggled to free themselves to fight in deadly hand-to-hand combat. The razor sharp blades of the warriors claimed many British lives, whilst the soldiers fought back with bayonets, swords, revolvers and the occasional Martini–Henry cartridges, which were hastily forced into breeches. Wounded men upon the baggage camels received no mercy and were speared where they lay. Lieutenant Percy Marling of the Mounted Infantry was engaged on the top left of the square. He quickly realised that the men of the Heavies and the Sussex were fighting for their lives and that the British formation was in imminent danger of collapse. Marling ordered the second row of his command to turn around and fire volleys into the warriors who had broken through, whilst the front row of Mounted Infantry continued to engage the enemy facing them. The crossfire brought down enemy and soldiers alike but relieved the immediate threat and as more warriors fell those British troops caught in the crush were able to direct their fire at the Mahdists. Soon there were no Sudanese alive in the remains of the square and the British were again able to direct their attention to those of the enemy that were still facing the position.

Yet, the remaining warriors had had enough and begin to withdraw downhill, their slow retreat followed by Martini–Henry bullets and fire from Beresford's now-working Gardner. Colonel Talbot, commanding the heavy Camel Regiment at the Battle of Abu Klea, recorded:

> At last the Gatling guns [Gardners] were got into action and that practically ended the battle. The Soudanese were simply mowed down. Their bodies flew up into the air like grass from a lawn-mower. But their pluck was astonishing. I saw some of the natives dash up to the Gatling guns [Gardners], and thrust their arms down the muzzles, trying to extract the bullets which were destroying their comrades! Of course, they were simply blown to atoms.[20]

Similarly Beresford was later to write of the destructive power of the Gardner, 'As I fired [the Gardner], I saw the enemy mown down in rows, dropping like ninepins. . .' . After the battle Beresford was able to examine the effect of the Gardner's firepower upon the bodies of the enemy and he wrote, 'I observed that the rows of bullets from the Gardner gun, which was rifle calibre .45 inch, with five barrels, had cut off heads and tops of heads as though sliced horizontally with a knife.'[21]

British technological superiority, immense bravery, disciplined training, and an element of fortune had won the day and the wells of Abu Klea were secured and the parched and exhausted British were able to drink their fill of the milky brown water. Yet, the butchers' bill was high. The British lost eighty-six men in a matter of a few minutes, and many wounded, whose suffering in the awful desert conditions must have been dreadful. A large number of these men would later succumb. There is no accurate figure for the number of Mahdist warriors who died but it is likely to have been over a thousand.

Stewart's command had survived a harsh encounter, the immediate need for water was met and the men had the luxury of a day's rest. Yet, still the problem remained of how to travel on to Metemma, now encumbered with 106 wounded, many of them severely so. Stewart resolved to leave these men, with a garrison of the Sussex Regiment, at Abu Klea and the following day, 18 January 1885, Stewart and his remaining force marched on to Metemma. On the morning of 19 January the Nile and the fortified town of Metemma were sighted. The British halted at 7am for breakfast and by 8am they came under sniper fire, the intensity and accuracy of which increased as the morning progressed. Sometime at around 11am, Stewart himself was hit by a bullet to his groin, which proved to be a mortal wound. He was to die several weeks later in excruciating pain. Stewart was forced to hand over command immediately to his second in command, Charles Wilson (1836–1905), who ordered the construction of a zariba for the stores and the ever increasing number of wounded. Wilson would then march with a force to secure a position on the riverbank and from there return for the wounded.

Unfortunately the enemy sniper fire continued to intensify and both the number of wounded and fatalities rose. Count Gleichen, in his work *With the Camel Corps Up the Nile*, described a number of occasions when his men were hit by enemy fire,

> Another man was knocked down by a bullet lodging in his bandolier. M— got one through his helmet, D— one on his scabbard, and N— a stone, which nearly broke his ankle. I happened to be walking alongside C—, when suddenly he gave a terrific jump, and clapped his hand to his face: a bullet had skimmed through his beard, and passed over his shoulder.[22]

Gleichen himself had a narrow escape when a sniper bullet ricocheted off one of the brass buttons on his uniform and although he was knocked to the ground, he suffered no more than a bruise. Amongst the fatal casualties were two newspaper war correspondents, St Leger Herbert, a freelance, and John Cameron, of the *Standard*.

Despite the high rate of fire and corresponding casualties, the British were so exhausted by their latest night march that many, including Percy Marling, slept, despite the whizzing bullets. Finally, at around 3pm, having endured nearly 7 hours of constant sniping, Wilson declared that the zariba was complete. Leaving the exhausted 19th Hussars, half the Heavies, most of the Naval Brigade and the artillery to guard the wounded and stores, a force of a mere 900, accompanied by a Gardner, set out for the river.

Again, Count Gleichen was able to write a very descriptive passage:

> At length, about 3.30, Sir Charles made up his mind that it was no use waiting for reinforcements, and that the whole force could not fight its way successfully to the river, encumbered as it would be with wounded and stores; the only alternative was the risky one of half of us fighting our way on foot, whilst the baggage remained behind with the other half. It was neck or nothing, for the fighting force could only muster some 900 bayonets, and the enemy were swarming round in thousands. Still we moved on, slowly, very slowly, avoiding

all dips and hollows which might contain the enemy, and every now and then halting to send a few volleys wherever the smoke appeared thickest.[23]

Wilson and his 900 men walked over the desert ground, strewn with rocks and boulders, trying to maintain the cohesion of the square. The enemy snipers still claimed victims and the British began to fear that they would be simply 'picked off' without ever really being able to engage the Mahdists. Both Marling and Beresford would later write that they believed that they were marching to their deaths. The square managed little more than 2 miles an hour and the mass of men was an easy target. More and more fell; Marling was splattered with the blood and brains from a Royal Marine who was standing by him when a bullet thumped into his head. In one brief moment seven men were shot dead. Nerves must have been at breaking point but Wilson realised that a retreat was out of the question and the men set themselves to move slowly on. Finally, and much to the relief of Wilson and his men, the enemy could not resist the temptation to charge. Gleichen described the moment:

> At length the Arabs began to collect in large bodies in front, and the long wished for moment arrived. 'Thank God! They're going to charge!' was the sigh of relief on all sides; and on they came. Several thousand had massed on the slopes on the left front, and they came straight at us. The square was at once halted, and volley after volley poured into the black mass.[24]

As Wilson ordered the square to halt, the discipline and training of his men came to the fore and the British acted automatically. The troops in the front rank sank to their knees, and both they and the men of the rear rank held their Martini–Henry rifles to their shoulders. With a low growl the enemy rushed downhill in a three-pronged attack. What became known as the Battle of Abu Kru was about to begin.

Wilson screamed the order for volley fire and the first rounds seemed to have little effect for the speed and determination of the enemy attack did not appear to lessen. Wilson ordered the bugler to sound 'Cease Fire' and amazingly, despite the terrifying approach of the warriors, the troops obeyed. This allowed for rifles to be reloaded and the smoke to clear. At around 400yd from the square Wilson gave the order for 'Continuous fire' and round after round slammed into the charging dervishes. This time the British fire had the desired effect. Count Gleichen described this moment, 'As they got within

400 yards, the volley-firing became a continuous roar of musketry, and hundreds fell beneath the well-directed fire of the Mounted Infantry and ourselves. Aiming low, and firing steadily as on parade, our men mowed the Arabs down like grass; not one got within eighty yards of the square.'[25]

One officer noted that there seemed to be a 'death zone' between 100 and 200yd from the square, beyond which the Martini–Henry fire would not let the enemy pass. Not more than a dozen dervishes who entered this zone escaped and these few men left around 300 of their comrades dead on the field.[26] The British artillery, left behind in the zariba, was able to support the square and several well-directed shells fell upon the enemy. Corporal F.H. Middleton wrote that at Abu Kru the British had 'a beautiful little square this time; all infantry. Received charge without a wave in any flank. Enemy fell like rotten sheep.'[27]

The surviving dervishes quickly withdrew towards Metemma and Wilson and his men knew that they had won the Nile. Like many of the battles in the Sudan, Abu Kru had been brief and bloody, yet it was here that British firearms clearly demonstrated their superiority and claimed a complete victory. On reaching the Nile the British were finally able to drink their fill and many collapsed with exhaustion.

It took Wilson two days to bring all his troops and stores to a new position at Metemma. Here his force, on 21 January, did indeed rendezvous with four steamers which had left from Khartoum. Wilson was criticised subsequently for the delay in sailing to Khartoum with at least some of his command. However, he had to try and establish whether a supposed threat by the enemy to attack his men at Metemma was real, as well as supply and reinforce the steamers before their hazardous return. So it was not until 8am on the morning of 24 January that the steamers *Talahwiya* and *Bordein* left with Wilson, Beresford and men of the Royal Sussex onboard. Their dangerous journey was full of mishaps, the *Bordein* struck rocks and ran onto a sandbank, which added to the delay and all the time the vessels neared Khartoum so the level of resistance from dervishes on the river bank increased, as did the rumours that the city had fallen. It was not until the morning of 28 January that Khartoum was sighted. Wilson looked through his binoculars for the Egyptian flag flying over the Governor-General's Palace which would have told him that Gordon was still alive, but he searched in vain. Reluctantly, Wilson gave the order to return to Metemma, knowing that to have tried to disembark his small force in the face of stiff enemy opposition would have been suicidal. By doing so, he was to return to face strong criticism. A clamour soon began for Gordon to be revenged and this was to culminate on 2 September 1898 with the British victory at the Battle of Omdurman.

Much has been written about the British errors at Tamai and Abu Klea which allowed the 'square' if not to be 'broken', then at least threatened. Yet, Abu Kru showed what the British could achieve with discipline, tactical awareness and stunning firepower, and these facts are sometimes overlooked by historians. During the Sudanese campaigns of the 1880s, despite setbacks and occasionally high battlefield casualties, the British were masters of the tactical defensive formation, which was ably supported by their technological weapons superiority.

Chapter 6

Technological Slaughter – Omdurman, 2 September 1898

> It was nothing but pure butchery, the way we killed them
>
> 'A Private's View of the Battle',
> *The Times*, 29 September 1898

By the early 1880s technological advancements had produced another European arms race. At the forefront of this competition was the introduction of both a reliable machine gun and a bolt-action magazine rifle. Although slow to enter the race, for once British forces quickly embraced these new weapons and they were soon to be turned upon colonial foes in such diverse places as Sudan, Nigeria and on the North West Frontier.

Potential European adversaries were the first to adopt repeating rifles. The French, in 1879–80, began converting their Gras rifles into the Gras–Kropatschek, by adding a tubular magazine. Germany joined the race in 1884 with a repeating Mauser rifle. The Martini–Henry, after some initial reticence from detractors, was considered one of the best rifles of the late 1870s and early 1880s, and early British designs for magazine-fed rifles focused on adapting this single-shot, breech-block loading rifle. In 1881 a Committee on Small Arms was established with the aim of obtaining an arm for the British Army that was superior to Martini–Henry, whilst examining the possibility of magazine-fed rifles. Interestingly, the Committee first focused on the choice of cartridge and this was led by developments in the field of smokeless propellant. The crucial breakthrough came when a French chemist named Paul Vieille (1854–1934) perfected a formula for pyrocellulose (modern name nitrocellulose).

This new propellant burned faster and at greater temperatures than the black powder propellants then in use. The result was both increased velocity and higher pressure which allowed for bullet diameters to be reduced. In addition, Vieille's discovery did not expose the shooter's position as the pall of white smoke created by the existing propellants was not produced. Pyrocellulose also had the extra advantage in that it did not create the corrosive fouling of gunpowder.

Such developments enabled the Committee on Small Arms to fix the proposed new calibre bullet at .4in or .402in. During nearly five years of experimentation a number of magazine-fed variants of modified Martini–Henry rifles were tried and tested. One of the earliest attempts to modify the Martini–Henry was by an American gun designer, Owen Jones, most famous for his design of the Enfield .476in revolver. The main external alteration feature of this slide-action rifle was the provision of a gravity fed hopper magazine fixed to the right body. Although the Royal Navy was extremely keen to order this converted rifle, and indeed a further Pattern was trialled alongside other designs, the high cost of converting the Owen Jones design eventually led to the demise of this variant.

However, much to the later embarrassment of the Committee, it did approve, on 17 April 1886, the Enfield Martini, .4in, First Pattern. Most of the design of this Pattern, including a radically altered Martini action, chambered for a .4in cartridge, was introduced by Colonel H.T. Arbuthnot, then Superintendent at the Royal Small Arms Factory (RSAF), Enfield, and a member of the Committee on Small Arms. It was intended to produce just 1,000 arms of this new Pattern, but with the urgent need for a new magazine-fed rifle and the incorrect assumption, based on Colonel Arbuthnot's assurances, that this new Pattern would be a success, production pressed ahead whilst trials were ongoing. Unfortunately, the results of the trials were highly unfavourable, due mainly to jamming issues, and production was halted after nearly 22,000 arms had been made. A Second Pattern, approved on 13 May 1887, overcame many of the design faults of the First Pattern, but this too was soon abandoned mainly due to the move towards the smallbore .303.

True British success in the development of a bolt-action, magazine-fed rifle was led by two inventors; William Metford (1824–99) and James Paris Lee (1831–1904). Both men were, from their childhood years, obsessed with firearms and this obsession carried on into their adult lives. Metford was a firm believer that smaller calibre bullets were more efficient than traditional calibres and he created a barrel of seven, shallow grooves, with left-hand twist rifling that proved exceptionally stable for black-powdered ammunition.

James Paris Lee's genius lay in recognising that the future of small arms was in a rifle in which multiple cartridges could be stored in a magazine and fired as quickly as they could be loaded into the breech by the bolt action. Born in Scotland, Lee emigrated to Canada when he was 18, and then went to Wisconsin in the late 1850s. He had some success in adapting existing rifles into magazine-fed variants with his most successful being a conversion of the Springfield rifle. Lee then turned his attention to the Martini–Henry and added a side-mounted magazine, which was capable of firing twenty-eight rounds per minute. However, difficulties with chambering and ejecting cartridges led Lee to look at alternatives. True success came with the realisation that these issues could be overcome by fitting a magazine underneath the receiver body. Five cartridges were stacked vertically in the magazine, on top of a feed plate that rested upon a Z-shaped spring. Although this design meant that the magazine could only be reloaded when the magazine was detached, Lee foresaw that the infantryman of the future could carry additional, loaded magazines on his person, meaning that reloading could be carried out rapidly.

As with the history of the introduction of the Martini–Henry rifle in the 1870s, the final adoption of the Lee–Metford rifle in the 1880s saw a similarly drawn out process of submissions by various manufacturers to the Small Arms Committee of the War Office for testing and evaluation. In March 1880 nine models were presented to the Committee. These included the Gardner rifle, the Hotchkiss Model 1880, the Winchester Model 1876, the Kropatschek system rifle and the Lee Model 1879 rifle. The tube magazines were considered potentially dangerous by the Committee, and this was reinforced during testing when a near fatal accident occurred when a cartridge detonated in the magazine of the Winchester. Consequently, three models, the Winchester, the Hotchkiss and the Kropatschek, all of which used the tube magazine, were eliminated from the selection process. Only the Lee Model 1879 rifle and two other manufacturers' submissions were thought worthy of further consideration.

By 1882 Remington was now contracted to manufacture Lee's rifles and the Model 1882 Remington–Lee was submitted to the Small Arms Committee and this variant overcame some initial concerns the Committee had with the Lee extractor. This 1882 Model was much liked by the Committee, particularly the robust nature of the rifle, the limited number of components in the breech action and the detachable nature of the magazine. The weapon was also found to be quick and easy to load and fire – 5.6 seconds for six rounds and 22.3 seconds for ten rounds. The accuracy of the .45in bullet was considered to be favourable. It was found capable of a grouping of just over 2in at 100yd and an 8in grouping at 500yd.[1]

The decision process ground on to the end of 1886 with just two models, the Owen Jones and the .402in Lee, under serious consideration. Tests, undertaken now by both the army and the Royal Navy at HMS *Excellent*, the weapons testing and training establishment in Portsmouth, both concluded that the Lee offered a much more robust and simple option which was much more likely to be reliable. The Owen Jones was eliminated as a result of its poor performance at HMS *Excellent*.[2] Yet, just when a decision from the Committee seemed imminent, two more models entered the marketplace, the Rubini and Schulhof rifles, and it was felt that these should also be tested and evaluated.

Although this further delay must have been frustrating for Lee, it perversely worked in the inventor's favour for Remington–Lee were able to submit an improved Model 1886 in January 1887 with a simplified bolt design to allow for easier disassembly and the introduction of a new design for a five-round box magazine, mounted underneath the receiver. Finally, the Small Arms Committee recommended the adoption of the Lee action and magazine system to the War Office, but with three crucial considerations. The first was to decide upon the best form of rifling, the second that the bolt be improved and the third was to ensure that a suitable cartridge by found to complement the new bolt-action rifle.

It is interesting to consider how Lee's magazine action performed. The magazine itself consisted of a sheet-steel box, inserted from under the body of the rifle in an opening in front of the trigger guard. It was held in position by a spring in the body engaging in a notch in the magazine. Initial approved marks contained eight cartridges, although this was later to increase. The magazine could be filled when in position in the rifle, or when detached, by inserting the cartridges one by one. A spring at the bottom of the magazine pressed upwards a moveable platform, forcing the column of cartridges also upwards into the breech. A 'cut-off' was fitted to the right side of the body, which, when pressed inwards, stopped the supply of cartridges from the magazine, so that the arm could be used as a single loader, and this action pacified those on the Small Arms Committee who were obsessed with the potential waste of ammunition if troops were allowed to fire rapidly in training. When the 'cut-off' was pulled out, the lower edge of the bolt, on its being driven forward, engaged the top edge of the uppermost cartridge in the magazine and forced it into the chamber, and so on, until the magazine was emptied. The magazine was removed by pressing a small lever inside the trigger guard. One magazine was attached to each rifle, being secured from loss by a chain link.

The War Office became increasingly interested in smaller calibre ammunition to be used in its service rifle when reports were received in June 1885 of successful trials of the Swiss Rubini cartridge. Combined with news from France of Vieille's introduction of smokeless propellant, as well as the adoption by the French Army of the Modele 1886 Lebel 8mm rifle, the War Office realised the proposed use of the new .402in cartridge with the Lee Model would quickly make the rifle obsolete. Trials of the Model 1889 Swiss Rubini, chambered for a 7.5 x 53mm rimless cartridge, proved excellent. With a 130-grain bullet it achieved 3,000ft per second with a range in excess of 1,500yd and with a flatter trajectory than that produced by any black-powder load.[3] The Small Arms Committee, although impressed with the Rubini cartridge, considered the round difficult to massproduce and disliked the bottlenecked design which the Committee felt would be prone to jamming and difficult to chamber in machine guns and ordered the cartridge to be altered to a rimmed, tapered, body of .303in calibre. Manufacture began at the Royal Laboratories in Woolwich. The new cartridge was officially adopted as the 'Cartridge, S.A. Ball .303 inch Powder, Mk 1' on 2 February 1889 and although initially loaded with black powder as a stopgap measure, a cordite load was used from early 1892.

With the matter of the cartridge resolved and improvements made to the bolt action, the last recommendation from the Committee, that of the rifling, was resolved with the adoption of a barrel devised by William Ellis Metford. The barrel had seven shallow segmental grooves, a left-hand twist, with a pitch of one turn in 10in. Over 350 Model 1888 Lee Trials Rifles were manufactured at Enfield and sent for trials to both army and navy units. Reports were very favourable and this resulted in the adoption for service on 22 December 1888 of the Rifle, Magazine, Mark I. In August 1891, the two inventors were given official public recognition when the weapon as renamed the 'Rifle Magazine, Lee Metford'.[4]

Over subsequent years a number of alterations were made to the Lee–Metford rifle. In early 1892 a Mark I (Second Pattern) was approved which incorporated a number of 'hidden' improvements, such as special hardening treatments of parts under high stress, as well as the significant alteration to the Lewes Pattern sight that was required with the use of cordite in the .303in cartridge and with it the subsequent increase in velocity and range of the bullet. This saw the introduction of a long-range dial sight graduated for ranges from 1,600 to 2,900yd. A Mark II variant was approved on 12 April 1892 with the notable adoption of a ten-round double column magazine with a corresponding change to the body. Three years later, on 22 April 1895, an improved Mark II was approved with the most obvious alteration being the addition of a safety catch on the right side of the cocking piece, operated by a thumb piece which rotated a bar housed within the cocking piece.

On 29 September 1894, the Cavalry Service was issued with the 'Carbine, Magazine, Lee Metford, .303in, Mk I'. Compared with the Mark II rifle's dimensions of length, 49.4in, barrel length 30.2in and weight of 9lb 6oz, the carbine had a length of 40in, barrel length of 20.75in and a weight of 7lb 8oz. Apart from the dimensions, the most obvious difference in the carbine and the rifle variants was that the carbine was not fitted with the long-range sight and the backsight was limited to 2,000yd.

Throughout the 1890s the Lee–Metford was issued to all arms of the British forces, and it saw service in the Sudan, Nigeria, South Africa and India, including the North West Frontier. Yet, the introduction of cordite had an unforeseen consequence in that as this propellant burns at a much higher temperature than black powder, the shallow groove rifling of the Metford barrel soon became worn and pitted. A cordite Mark I cartridge was initially approved on 3 November 1891, and underwent some minor changes within a short space of time, until the Mark II cordite round was approved on 17 July 1893. Cordite was so named because it resembled cords of interwoven material, and it was composed of 58 per cent nitro-glycerine, 37 per cent gun cotton and 5 per cent mineral jelly. It was much more stable than black powder and it produced little or no fouling. However, as discussed, the greater heat generated by cordite resulted in a reduced barrel life.

Metford's rifling was designed to overcome problems associated with black powder fouling and was not intended for use with cordite. It was found that after around 6,000 rounds of the new ammunition were fired through the Metford rifled barrel it became pitted and consequently dangerously unreliable. Thus, a new design of rifling had to be found and this was developed at the Royal Small Arms Factory (RSAF), Enfield. The new barrel had five grooves with a left-hand twist, cut to a depth of .005in. Unlike the segmental rifling of the Metford barrel, the Enfield barrel employed a square cut to the grooves. Although the overall length and barrel length were the same as the Lee–Metford, the Enfield was 5oz lighter. 'The Rifle Magazine, Lee Enfield, .303 inch, Mark I' was introduced from 1895 and saw service alongside the Lee–Metford, which was gradually withdrawn from service. However, in the major battles along the North-West Frontier and in the Sudan in the late 1890s it was the Lee–Metford that was most commonly used by British troops in action.

A young officer, Winston Churchill, wrote, in his work *The Story of the Malakand Field Force*, of his experiences of the Lee–Metford/Enfield when fighting on the North West Frontier. The range accuracy of the new rifle enabled the British soldier to counter the accuracy of the breech-loading jezails used by Afghan sharpshooters, as well as enabling them to fire up to ten rounds in rapid succession. The weapon's effectiveness was greatly augmented by the introduction of the exploding dum-dum bullet, which Churchill regarded as being 'of the greatest value', as 'its stopping power is all that could be desired'. As Churchill noted, the bullet:

> [I]s not explosive, but expansive . . . the result is a wonderful and from the technical point of view a beautiful machine. On striking a bone this causes the bullet to 'set up' or spread out, and it then tears and splinters everything before causing wounds which in the body must be generally mortal and in the limb necessitate amputation.

Churchill reserved particular praise for the troops of the Buffs for the accuracy of fire which covered the withdrawal of British forces from one of the native villages that the British had destroyed. 'At the bottom of the hill the Buffs took up the duty of rear-guard, and the deliberate care with which the fire of that terrible weapon the Lee-Metford, with its more terrible dum-dum bullet, was directed effectually checked any pursuit.'[5] Not long afterwards use of the dum-dum bullet in armed conflicts was banned by international law on account of the appalling injuries it inflicted on victims; a prohibition that exists to this day.

It was the basic design of the Mark I Enfield which would later evolve into many different variants of the Lee–Enfield rifle. This rifle, with a few further modifications, outlasted soldiers, politicians and monarchs. As the Short Magazine Lee–Enfield, or SMLE, it remained in service throughout the two world wars and on to 1968 when it finally gave way to a modern automatic weapon, the SLR (L1A1 Self-Loading Rifle).[6]

Contemporary with the introduction of the bolt-action rifle into British service were huge strides taken in the development and improvement of the machine gun, which saw the adoption of the Maxim machine gun in the late 1890s. Although the machine gun, in the form of the Gatling, the Gardner and Nordenfelt guns, had been in British service for nearly twenty years, all these early weapons had similar faults or design problems. These largely centred on jamming and the relatively slow rate of fire as a result of the various mechanisms employed to reload cartridges into the breech.

Hiram Maxim (1840–1916) was originally from rural America, the son of a miller. From an early age Maxim demonstrated a naturally enquiring mind that gave him the rare ability to quickly understand mechanical concepts and apply his own thinking to solving issues or improving designs. His greatest innovation came to him after firing a Springfield rifle, soon after the end of the American Civil War (1861–5). Surprised by the degree of recoil, Maxim had the thought that if a belt of cartridges were fed through a machine gun the firing of one cartridge, with the resulting recoil and energy created, could be utilised to load the next cartridge into the breech, thus rapidly increasing the rate of fire. However, after approaching his father with his idea, both men felt that the technology available at that time was not sufficient to be able to produce such a machine gun in an economic way.

For the next eighteen years Maxim turned his fertile mind to the new science of electricity which put him in direct competition with Thomas Edison (1847–1931). Although Edison is perhaps better remembered for his contribution to developments in electricity use and supply, it was Maxim who produced two important innovations in the field. He beat Edison to produce a practical incandescent light bulb and it was also Maxim who first devised an efficient current regulator. Edison's financial backers had the sense to make Maxim a generous offer to work for them in Europe as a technical advisor on the basis that he ceased all work in the field of electricity innovation for a period of ten years. This offer, which Maxim readily accepted, allowed him to be financially independent and placed him in the heart of Europe at a time when the technological arms race was at its height.

Maxim decided London, the centre of the world's manufacturing at that time, was to be his new home and with shortage of investment money no longer an issue he decided to revisit his idea for a machine gun. His first patent, dated 26 June 1883, was actually for a recoil-operated Winchester rifle which utilised the recoil of the weapon when fired to operate the lever action to load the next cartridge. In the following year Maxim patented his locked-breech recoil system, specifically for machine guns, although both patents offered concepts for other weapon designers and laid down the principles for weapon development in the late nineteenth century. Indeed, the Austrian Ferdinand Ritter von Mannlicher (1848–1904), when working for the weapons manufacturer Steyr, adopted Maxim's recoil innovations as the bases for the Steyr Mannlicher rifle, which saw service in both the Greek and Austrian armies.[7]

Maxim's next great innovation was to focus on designing a magazine-fed mechanism which used the 'blowback', the force produced by firing the cartridge, to repel the breech block backwards after discharging a cartridge. Maxim's ideal was that the breech block was then returned forward by use of a hydraulic spring and as it did so another cartridge was collected and chambered. The main difficulty was not designing the loading mechanism but of developing a means by which cartridges could be reliably fed into the breech. This issue came to dominate Maxim's thinking and would result in several design headaches over the next few years.

By 1884 Maxim had established a small workshop in Hatton Garden, London and it was here that he began to focus on his initial feed mechanism of a weave fabric belt drawn into the breech by metal star wheels. With each new development that solved one issue it seemed another problem would manifest itself, whether this was the requirement to cool the gun as the rate of fire increased or the need to use better quality ammunition. However, Maxim was clearly heading in the right direction and this was reflected in the increased interest from the War Office and investors. He was able to form 'The Maxim Gun Company' on 5 November 1884 with the release of £50,000 worth of £20 shares. Amongst the many investors was Albert Vickers, a major backer and joint owner of the Vickers, Son & Company Ltd. He was elected Chairman of the new company, with Maxim as its Managing Director.[8]

With financial support now in place, Maxim focused on trying to make the gun much lighter and more economical to produce and in this he received help and advice from many quarters, including Britain's most famous general at the time, Sir Garnet Wolseley, who, with his vast experience of colonial warfare, recognised that Maxim's invention would change the face of battle.[9] In addition, General Sir Andrew Clark, Inspector of Fortifications, advised Maxim that to really attract interest from the War Office his machine gun would have to be stripped, cleaned and assembled with no tools, but just the hands of the operators.[10] With such advice ringing in his ears, Maxim again returned to his design.

Knowing that his original concept design of using 'blowback' to facilitate the recoil of the breech block was correct, Maxim refined his thoughts. A new internal mechanism was created and he abandoned the fragile fabric belt-feed mechanism so that a belt of loaded cartridges was now drawn into the breech by a stronger sliding pawl system. By March 1887 three prototypes of .45in calibre had been produced, firing the old .450in Martini–Henry cartridge, two water cooled and one air cooled. All met the War Office requirement of weighing no more than 100lb and were able to fire 400 shots in a minute. Indeed, the prototypes achieved a rate of fire of 670 rounds per minute and all also met the War Office requirement of passing strenuous wear and tear tests and of being able to be stripped in the field with no tools. The War Office purchased all three models and Maxim's career as the world's most successful machine-gun maker had begun.

Maxim received an order for a further six guns from the War Office and later in 1887 he and Albert Vickers were invited to demonstrate their weapon in Thun, Switzerland, where it would be pitted against the latest versions from the Gatling, Gardner and Nordenfelt companies. The results from the demonstration astonished the observing military from across Europe. At a further presentation in Vienna, Field Marshal the Archduke William Franz-Karl of Teschen (1827–94) observed to Maxim that 'it [the Maxim machine gun] is the most dreadful instrument that I have ever seen or imagined'.[11]

These demonstrations were a huge success, and the orders began to pour in; 26 guns for the Italian Army, the Austrians ordered 131 and contracts from the War Office and the Crown Agents, in such places as South Africa, became regular. The premises in Hatton Garden were now rendered inadequate and in July 1888 the 'Maxim Gun Company' was wound up and Maxim and Vickers established an unlikely and short-lived agreement with Thorsten Nordenfelt to produce the weapon in their factory in Erith in Kent. In addition, the new Maxim-Nordenfelt Company opened a small factory site close by in Crayford. The new company was able to secure a twenty-year sales agreement with the vast German arms manufacturer Krupp which saw the machine gun being produced under licence in Germany. History would show how devastating these weapons would be when used against British troops in the First World War. The year 1891 saw the first Enfield-produced Maxim, and in total 2,568 were made at the government arsenal.

There is no doubt that Maxim was a perfectionist and although his design was now a huge commercial success, he was always looking to improve. One area on which he now focused was to realise that the new propellant invented by Paul Vielle, smokeless powder, although allowing for higher bullet velocity and smaller calibre cartridges, did not produce enough recoil for the Maxim breech mechanism. With all the major European powers switching to smaller cartridge calibres Maxim was astute enough to act quickly, and by the start of 1890 he had recalculated the operating parameters for his weapons so as to accommodate the lesser recoil forces generated by the smaller, smokeless calibres. All weapons now produced were chambered for modern high-velocity rifle calibres and were capable of an average rate of fire of 450 rounds per minute.

The business seemed to be going from strength to strength, but behind the scenes the relationship with Nordenfelt was close to breaking point for not only had the Maxim virtually obliterated sales of the Nordenfelt machine gun, but the works at Erith had over expanded and the company's finances were in dire straits. Albert Vickers quickly stepped in and bought out the old Maxim-Nordenfelt Guns and Ammunition Company and from 1 October 1897 the new company was called Vickers, Sons and Maxim Ltd. Maxim's design became the Vickers-Maxim Machine Gun. Maxim himself ceased to be the company's managing director after 1899 but the company, and his invention, went from strength to strength.

The Maxim gun was first used by British troops in campaigns on the North-West Frontier of India. Prior to this, British Colonial Forces had used them with remarkable effect in the Matabele War of 1893. The troops engaged were the armed police of the Rhodesian Chartered Company. They were heavily outnumbered by the enemy, who invariably attacked with reckless courage. The Rhodesians acted on the defensive, provoking the Matabele to charge. A handful of white troops fortified themselves behind a wagon laager with Maxim guns at the angles. A large Matabele army commanded by Chief Lobengula was decimated and routed by a stream of bullets from the Maxim gun, tearing lanes of death through the warriors.

The Maxim was also used in 1897 by a Royal Niger Company Force composed of 32 Europeans and 507 African soldiers, armed with artillery and Maxim guns, which defeated the 31,000-man army of the Nupe Emirate of Sokoto. Here the issue was one of logistics for the terrain did not allow for vast amounts of ammunition to be carried in the field. With five porters required for each Maxim machine gun and its ammunition, fire had to be used sparingly. In two battles in Northern Nigeria, each lasting two days, Maxim machine guns were fired for no more than 3 minutes to conserve ammunition, but the devastating results in stopping the charges of the enemy were very clear to see.[12]

During the Chitral expedition of 1895, Maxim guns were in action against the rushes of the Ghazis in the Malakand Pass and were also useful in driving the enemy from their sangars (stone breastworks) on the hillside. A single Maxim stopped a rush of hill-men near Gumbat in April, having been brought into action against their flanks as they advanced. By a stroke of luck, six .303 Maxims reached India just six weeks before the operation began. Three of these were issued to the troops, with an unlimited supply of ammunition of the same kind as that used in the Lee–Metford and Lee–Enfield rifles. The guns were sent out from England on wheeled carriages, but each was soon fitted on a tripod for mule transport – each gun weighed only 40lb compared with the 100lb of the Gardner. The British also found that Maxims were invaluable for the defence of frontier posts where the ranges could be pre-marked and ammunition stored in large quantities. The experiences of the value of even this small number of Maxims in mountain warfare quickly settled the question of their general adoption in the British Army.[13]

Both the Lee–Metford rifle and the Maxim machine gun became synonymous with the Sudanese campaign of 1898 which culminated in the British and Egyptian armies defeat of the Mahdist forces at the Battle of Omdurman on 2 September 1898. Ever since the death of Gordon and the capture of Khartoum in 1885, the British public, and the country's generals, had sought revenge over the followers of the Mahdi, now led by the Khalifa, Abdallahi. Yet, for over ten years British governments did not press for another expeditionary force to be despatched and when forces were directed more again against the Mahdists, revenge was not the initial motivation for the reconquest of the Sudan.

The defeat of Italian forces by the Abyssinians at the Battle of Adowa (1 March 1896) created a power vacuum in the region and to counter an alliance of Abyssinia and the Khalifa, as well as deterring French imperial meddling in the area, the Conservative Prime Minister, Lord Salisbury (1830–1903), and the British Consul-General in Egypt, Lord

Cromer (1841–1917), authorised a military diversion by Egyptian forces south along the Nile towards Dongola. Egyptian and Sudanese forces, frequently led by British officers, provided the vast majority of troops in the initial advance. The commander, or Sirdar, of the Egyptian Army was Major General Herbert Kitchener (1850–1916) and his initial command was named the River Column as it largely followed the banks of the Nile and utilised the river where possible to transport men and supplies. Although Kitchener's men were not supplied with the latest Lee–Metford or Lee–Enfield rifles, a number of Maxim guns accompanied the advance and saw service.

The Maxim gun sections of two British battalions, then serving in Lower Egypt, were detached from their units and sent forward with Kitchener's advance. Each battalion had two Maxims in its machine-gun section, organised as a battery of four guns mounted on wheeled carriages, but also having mule pack-transport.

A special precaution had to be taken to prevent the mechanism of the gun from being jammed by the desert sand, which forms almost a fog on windy days in the Sudan. Each gun had a silk cover, in which it was kept wrapped until it was brought into action.[14]

A most successful and secret night march over 6–7 June 1896 placed Kitchener's command within striking distance of the strong Mahdist defensive position at Firket. It was strategically vital that the River Column nullified the threat from the enemy at Firket for the planned railway, which would be so important to Kitchener's ultimate success, could then be safely extended. The resulting action began at 5am on 7 June 1896 when five enemy riflemen fired at the advancing Egyptian troops. A short burst of Maxim fire promptly put an end to this fire, but alerted the defenders to the presence of Kitchener's force. The Egyptian and Sudanese troops advanced rapidly towards the town of Firket, added by supporting fire from the Maxim guns and horse-artillery batteries. The battle became a close-quarters affair in which the discipline and training of the men of the River Column prevailed. The action was over in little more than 2 hours and the result was a crushing victory for Kitchener and his men.

The River Column's further advance was delayed by both unheard of torrential rain storms in Sudan which swept away a length of the railway and seriously slowed the laying of track, as well as some further enemy resistance. The Mahdists in the region, led by one of the Khalifa's trusted commanders, Muhammad Wad el-Bishara, opposed Kitchener's advance at Kerma, on the banks of the Nile. Using both

Nile steamers and the recently repaired railway, Kitchener was able to move 13,000 troops, including for the first time a British battalion, the North Staffords, within striking distance of Kerma. At daybreak on 19 September 1896, Kitchener discovered that the enemy had withdrawn to the village of Hafir, about half a mile upstream. Here they had formed a defensive position, with trenches and gun pits, which ran for over 900yd on the opposite bank to where Kitchener's force now found itself. Through his field glasses Kitchener could survey the enemy and the strength of the position. At 6.30am he ordered his artillery, five Krupp breech-loaders, to commence firing, and his steamers to sail towards the enemy. In a scene reminiscent of a Napoleonic naval battle the steamers sailed alongside and up to the dervish emplacements but instead of delivering a broadside, the Royal Marines gunners traversed the enemy parapets with Maxim fire. Although the enemy suffered many casualties, the steamers, and their crews, were in a very exposed position and the steamer *Metemma* was hit three times by shell fire. In addition, dervish riflemen concealed in the heads of palm trees, which lined the riverbank, were able to fire down and over the protective plated shields onto the men and crew onboard the steamers. On the *Metemma* Sergeant Richardson of the Royal Marines Artillery was shot dead whilst manning his Maxim gun and a further thirteen men were wounded.[15]

Under such an onslaught, and taking serious casualties, the steamers withdrew and Kitchener realised that the steamers themselves could not knock out the dervish defences. He ordered Major Parsons of the Royal Artillery to advance across the shallows to a midstream island and from here two field batteries, one horse battery and a Maxim battery were able to unleash a more directed fire upon the dervish defences. Kitchener also deployed infantry and a Maxim battery directly opposite the dervish positions. Once again the steamers returned in a combined assault, and with eighteen field pieces and the Maxims pouring fire down, three of the five enemy guns were knocked out and the steamers finally passed the dervish defences. Lieutenant Pritchard of the Royal Engineers described how the Maxim battery nullified the dervish sniper fire, 'Several Dervishes could also be seen firing from the tops of the palm trees, from which they were soon dislodged by the Maxims, and if they were not killed by the bullets, they certainly must have been by their fall to the ground.'[16]

With the steamers through his defences, Muhammad Wad el-Bishara, already wounded by shrapnel himself, realised that his remaining forces risked being outflanked and cut off so he withdrew under cover of darkness leaving behind 200 dead. Kitchener was able to claim yet another victory and the path to Dongola now lay undefended. Making full use of the abandoned dervish nuggars, or small boats, his force crossed over to the east bank. By 21 September 1896 the entire force of 3,200 horses and camels and 13,000 troops were ready for the last march on Dongola. At 3am on the morning of 23 September Kitchener's command began to descend upon this small, but strategically significant, town. Major Farley, of the North Staffords, recalled that, 'The men of the Maxim Battery wore red. It was a sight never to be forgotten, 15,000 men of every shade of colour, from white to sooty black, moving slowly and relentlessly towards a common goal; if it did not inspire a feeling of dismay in the hearts of Wad-el-Bishara's army they were made of very stout material.'[17]

But the large force under Kitchener's command convinced Muhammad Wad el-Bishara not to make a stand. A group of Baggara horsemen made an impressive display as they charged at Kitchener's men, but they then wheeled away before the Maxims could be fired at them. These were the only enemy to demonstrate, for the main dervish force escaped south into the Bayuda Desert. Although a number of stragglers were captured, Kitchener's men met with no resistance as they occupied the town and thus liberated Sudan's northern province from the Khalifa's rule.

The Khalifa, Abdallahi, realised that with the fall of Dongola the way was open for the reconquest of Omdurman and thus summoned his emirs in the regions of Darfur and Kordofan to bring their armies to Omdurman to face the predicted onslaught. However, Lord Salisbury had not envisaged a further advance at this stage and even Lord Cromer thought that a period of consolidation would be required before an advance on Omdurman could be considered. Kitchener, aware of the British public's mood for avenging Gordon's death and knowing that his personal prestige was high after his recent victories, decided to return to London to seek political support for British troops and funds with which to continue the advance.

On reaching London in November 1896, Kitchener found himself a celebrity, worshipped by the public, knighted and invited to Windsor Castle. Here he took the opportunity to convince Her Majesty of the desirability of advancing on to Omdurman. For the Queen the death of Gordon and the fall of Khartoum had been a very personal loss and she was very sympathetic to Kitchener's ambitions.

162 Bayonet to Barrage

Although opinion was in Kitchener's favour, the issue was one of money. Whilst Lord Cromer was persuaded by the argument that to continue the advance now would be cheaper than beginning again in a few years, Kitchener had to convince the Chancellor of the Exchequer, Sir Michael Hicks-Beach (1837–1916), to find the £500,000 needed. Again circumstances were in Kitchener's favour for news was released that a French officer, Captain Marchand (1863–1934), had been authorised by his government to strike a claim to the Upper Nile. Marchand's intervention became a symbol of the European 'Scramble for Africa' which came to dominate the end of the nineteenth century. The British government could not sit back and allow such a blatant act and so Kitchener was given the funds and British troops, if required, to retake Khartoum and restore the British imperial presence in the region. He returned to the Sudan almost immediately, ecstatic that he had been trusted with the task of avenging Gordon.

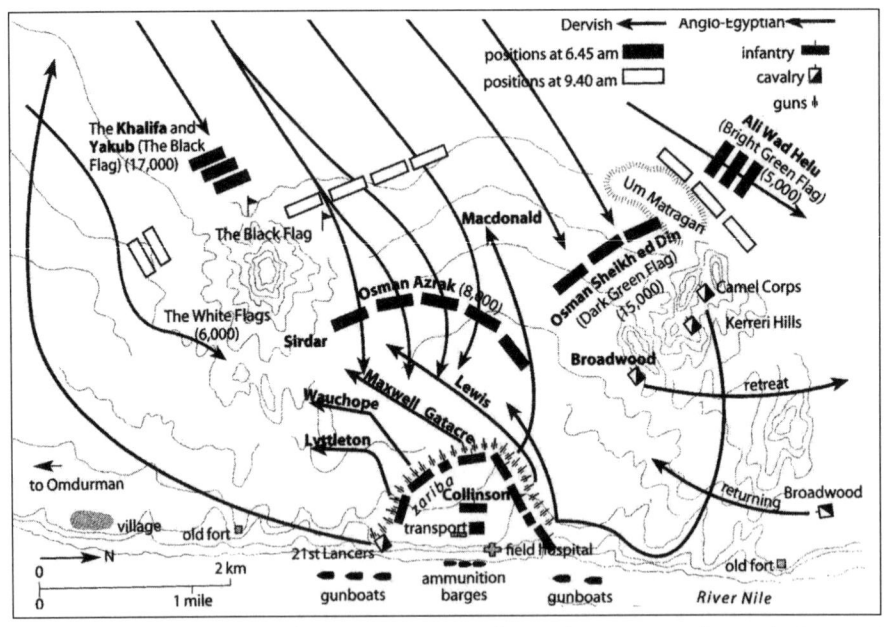

The Battle of Omdurman. The development of the battle in its two phases, before and after the two main allied forces left the zariba. Both, though, were contests between dervish numbers and Anglo-Egyptian firepower. (ML Design after Churchill, W.S., *The River War: An Account of the Reconquest of the Sudan* (London, 1899). From *The Seventy Great Battles of all Time*, edited by Jeremy Black, published by Thames & Hudson Ltd, London)

Kitchener was always an engineer first and a soldier second and he viewed the success of his latest campaign in terms of what we call today logistics or transport and supply. He never considered Wolseley's line of advance of 1884–5, across the Bayuda Desert as feasible but rather focused on the 250-mile stretch of desert between Korosko and Abu Hamed, which had for centuries been a caravan route. Kitchener's plan was to span the desert with a railway. In all the Sudan Military Railway ran for 383 miles and ensured the flow of supplies, water, troops and the prefabricated sections of the armed river steamers which as the Nile rose with its seasonal floods made the passage through the various cataracts possible. Construction of the railway, in the inhospitable environment of Sudan, was at best difficult and at times Kitchener was close to physical and mental breakdown as setback followed setback. Throughout 1897 and into 1898 work continued and ultimately the railway was completed. Men and supplies were transported and the armed steamers constructed and launched into the Nile so that the advance continued and Kitchener's command could be safely and reliably re-supplied. Such was the importance of the railway link that Winston Churchill declared, 'The Khalifa was conquered on the railway'.[18]

It seems clear that the Khalifa had no understanding of the strategic importance of the railway for the ultimate success of Kitchener's advance as no significant attempt was made to attack or disrupt the railway as it inched closer and closer to its ultimate target. The Khalifa decided to risk all on a pitch battle at the gates of Omdurman where he thought his numerical advantage would result in a decisive victory. There was only one significant engagement during the advance and this was at Atbura where the Mahdist warriors had created a defensive zariba, or square, out of thorn bush which was considered a formidable obstacle.

At Atbura, the Mahdists, led by Mahmud Ahmed, one of the Khalifa's youngest and most headstrong commanders, presented a difficult obstacle. Kitchener could not simply bypass the position and Mahmud Ahmed would not be enticed out from his strong defensive zariba. Therefore, on the morning of 8 April 1898, Kitchener led what has to be considered a rather unimaginative assault. On this occasion Kitchener had in support of his Egyptian and Sudanese troops a number of British regiments.

Men of the Cameron Highlanders, Seaforth Highlanders, the Royal Warwickshire Regiment and the Lincolnshire Regiment, all armed with the Lee–Metford, advanced upon the zariba. Whilst the 1st and 2nd Egyptian brigades were deployed in lines and advanced in rushes, the British brigade was ordered to walk towards the enemy with the Camerons leading. The battle began at 6.15am with a combined artillery barrage supported by Maxim fire which lasted for 90 minutes. At its cessation the advance was sounded and the various brigades moved towards the zariba.

The Camerons, walking in close formation, stopped to fire 'beautiful volleys' from their Lee–Metford rifles.[19] Only when the advance was within 300yd of the zariba did the defenders return fire and it was then that the Camerons begin firing independently on the move. Although the Sudanese troops entered the zariba first, the Camerons soon followed and they were joined by other regiments as the battle developed into a fierce hand-to-hand struggle in which the bayonet was much used. The British troops benefited from the magazine fire of the Lee–Metford which allowed them to fire repeatedly at the defenders. Corporal Farquharson recalled, 'Everyone . . . had either to be bayoneted or shot, and some got both'.[20]

By 8.30am the surviving dervishes had fled across the river leaving over 3,000 dead. Although the Sudanese suffered the most casualties, the British brigade had proportionally higher casualties losing twenty-six officers and men and ninety-nine wounded. Of the British it was the Camerons, leading from the front, that sustained the heaviest losses of fifteen killed and forty-five wounded. Kitchener was fortunate that the enemy's rifle fire was not more accurate, for his plan of attacking across open ground, with no cover, in close formation, showed little vision. Perhaps the most significant benefit of the battle was that British troops had now faced the fearsome dervishes and had proven themselves equal to the task and all now knew that they had in the Lee–Metford and Maxim machine gun a technological superiority over the enemy.

Within the army there was muted criticism of Kitchener and particularly of Major General William Gatacre (1843–1906), who led the British brigade from the front with flags flying. Yet, at home and, critically amongst British politicians, Kitchener had achieved another notable victory and his popularity continued to increase. There was now no sizeable enemy force with which to oppose the advance. Kitchener concentrated on constructing the final miles of the railway, re-supplying and reinforcing his troops. A second British brigade composed of the Grenadier Guards, the Lancashire Fusiliers, the Northumberland Fusiliers and the 2nd Battalion of the Rifle Brigade arrived as well as two additional Maxim batteries and a vast array of field artillery, including two massive 40pdr guns designed to destroy fortifications. In addition, the railway brought forward, in prefabricated sections, the gunboats *Shiekh*, *Sultan* and *Melik*. These three vessels, armed with between five and six artillery pieces and four Maxims, were part of a naval flotilla of ten gunboats that were to provide transport, reconnaissance and additional firepower.

As this naval force could not cross the sixth cataract until the waters of the Nile had risen, the final advance could not commence until August 1898. For four months the British waited at Wad Hamid. This time was both monotonous and exhausting and trying to escape the worst of the desert heat became the daily battle. In this harsh environment exercise and training continued and every week the men were marched at dawn into the desert in square formation for field firing. It was already clear that Kitchener perceived that the forthcoming battle would be one in which his command would be on the defensive and reliant on the overwhelming firepower it possessed and thus the men trained accordingly.

Although advanced Egyptian and Sudanese troops began a tentative march in early August, it was not until the third week of the month that Kitchener had the whole of his command ready to advance. This comprised 17,600 Egyptian and Sudanese soldiers, 8,200 British troops with 44 artillery pieces and 20 Maxims on land and a further 36 guns and 24 Maxims on the various steamers. The latter was used to protect Kitchener's left flank. The right flank was guarded by the Camel Corps and the cavalry whilst the bulk of the infantry marched in regimental order. The whole force stretched over 2 miles as it advanced along the banks of the Nile.

As the infantry and cavalry moved towards Omdurman the steamers went ahead. Although, at this stage, they were used primarily for reconnaissance, the guns on board were used to silence any opposition from the small villages and defensive positions that the steamers passed along the river bank. The infantry and cavalry, much to the men's astonishment, were frequently soaked by sudden downpours which slowed the march. Although the enemy cavalry was frequently observed, there were no skirmishes as they simply withdrew each time an encounter looked likely. By the morning of 1 September 1898 Kitchener's force had reached the village of Egeiga, a mere 6 miles from Omdurman. His cavalry located the Khalifa's main army, between 40,000 to 50,000 strong, at around midday. The enemy, advancing slowly on a 3-mile front with flags flying, seemed to be intent on battle.

Kitchener, on receiving the news, issued an order for his men to fall in and form up ready to receive an attack. However, further reconnaissance reports informed him that the Khalifa's force had halted and was making camp. For the rest of the day the two opposing armies sat just 5 miles apart.

The steamer force under the leadership of Commander Keppel (1862–1947) of the Royal Navy had advanced to within 3,000yd of Omdurman. Keppel landed the guns of the 37th Field Battery on the east bank of the Nile and from here lyddite shells slammed into Omdurman itself and seriously damaged the Mahdi's tomb.

Keppel, and his guns, would play an important part in the forthcoming battle as they assisted Kitchener to halt the Khalifa's attacks. News from deserters informed Kitchener that the enemy was planning a night attack, and indeed this was urged upon the Khalifa by many of his commanders. This was one thing Kitchener feared for he knew such an attack would neutralise his advantage in weaponry and would allow the enemy to close on his forces so that their swords and spears could inflict injury and death. If this were to happen, then the butcher's bill would be high and indeed might even threaten Kitchener's whole force. Fortunately, the Khalifa, despite being implored to launch a night attack by the likes of Osman Digna and Ibrahim al-Khalil, considered that his men would be difficult, if not impossible to control, and some might even resort to desertion so he decided upon a massed attack at dawn the next day.

Kitchener and his men could not know of the Khalifa's decision so naturally defensive positions were prepared. The British managed to construct a thorn brush zariba, although this proved somewhat difficult as materials were in short supply. Elsewhere the Egyptian and Sudanese troops dug slip trenches. All men spent a nervous night with little or no sleep, fearful of a night attack and anxious of what the following day might bring.

Major Watson, who was present at Omdurman, and clearly close to Kitchener throughout, wrote two letters home to his father which have survived. Watson's words have left a vivid image of the scenes, and anticipation, within the zariba as the battle neared:

> 4 a.m. we stood to arms and the gunboats on either flank threw their search-lights over the ground to our right and left. From either flank our Cavalry patrols crept out. Dawn came, and our Cavalry screen was completed and out in a line with signal hill . . . We waited for news from our Cavalry,

Sirdar [Kitchener] got impatient, sent me out to Cavalry, and a mile from our Zereba, I met an Egyptian officer with message 'Whole Dervish force rapidly advancing in E. direction on Zareba'. So they were really coming. Unload the ammunition mules, open the boxes and put ready behind the troops, better have a couple of maxims here, and get that battery up to that corner. In comes Broadwood, at the rate they are coming, Dervishes will be over the sky-line (1200 yards off) in ten minutes. Sirdar up and down the line to see if anything more can be done to improve position. The blacks [Sudanese troops] tapping down their earth parapets, forming rough sorts of head cover, stretchers ready Doctors ready. There was a lot done in those few minutes. Very gradually back fell our Cavalry, working away to flanks to clear fronts. Then came the tips of banners, and then the host. Like a rising sea, swirling around signal hill, stretching far up into Kerrari range, right across our front, in an almost unbroken line, thousands and thousands of them, a sight never to be forgotten. Nearer and you can hear the roar of sound as they shout. There seemed to be too many to stop.[21]

Similarly, Lieutenant David Henry Graeme, of the 1st Battalion Seaforth Highlanders, wrote of the moment that the enemy first advanced,

When news came that the Dervishes were coming towards us and would soon be in sight, and so they were, the first thing seen being their white flags appearing over the ridge over a mile away. Then one could make out a long line of white figures and one could soon see how great their numbers were, and how steadily they were coming.[22]

Lieutenant The Honourable E.D. Loch wrote in his diary of the first opening shots of the battle:

The first Dervish Army advanced yelling and shouting to the front ridge which they crossed, they were allowed to advance about a couple of hundred yards and then the 32nd Battery [from the Nile steamers and the east bank] opened on them with common shell. The first shot pitched short the second over this gave the range, they then opened with shrapnel the first three or four shots pitched beautifully and knocked over dozens, two standards going down at the same time . . . the enemy halted and yelling their best loosed off their guns into the air. But they did not halt for long but came on gallantly. The infantry opened with long range fire at 2,400 yards.[23]

Lieutenant Graeme also recorded the impact of the British artillery:

At least one of our guns opened fire and it was very soon afterwards taken up by the infantry, British and Egyptian, and the Maxims, and continued steadily, and they were not long in replying to it; it was a wonderful sight to watch our shells bursting in the air one after another from different points in the line, but you could not see that much damage was being done, though occasional gaps seemed to be refilled; their standards, white and good many coloured ones, gave good marks to aim at . . .[24]

Kitchener had decided upon a large, semi-circular encampment backing onto the Nile, with the thorn wall, or zariba, erected on the desert side facing a flat plain which gave a clear field of fire for both his Maxim guns and rifles. On the right of the battlefield were the rising Kerreri Hills which were patrolled by the Camel Corps and on the left were the Jabel Surkab Hills. Both these hills at first hid the movements of the Khalifa's army which had been divided into four forces; those led by Osman Azraq, which comprised the first full frontal attack at around 6.45am, and those of the Green Standard led by Osman Sheikah ad-Din, the White Standard or Kara Army and the Black Standard led by the Khalifa himself. The combined force has been described as, 'one of the last medieval armies ever mustered . . . armed mostly with double-edged "crusader" swords, straight daggers in arm-sheaths, elephant and rhino-hide shields, javelins and broad-bladed fighting spear . . . they chanted . . . "La ilaha illa-llah – There is no god but Allah". . .' .[25]

In addition, around 10,000 men were armed with ancient Remington rifles, captured over many years from Egyptian troops. These rifles had been poorly cared for and their effectiveness was further reduced as they fired 'home made' cartridges made with poor quality gunpowder, which lessened the bullets' velocity and penetrating power. The total force, which extended for no less than 5 miles, was in excess of 40,000 men and could have been close to 50,000.

Most historians agree that there were two distinctive phases in the Battle of Omdurman. The first, which began with the first British shells slamming into the advancing forces led by Osman Azraq, was largely defensive, in which the firepower of the Maxim and Lee–Metford claimed thousands of victims. The second saw Kitchener move out of the zariba in an attempt to stop the enemy retreating into Omdurman, for he feared that if this was allowed to happen then his men would be forced into costly street fighting.

A certain Winston Spencer Churchill was attached to the 21st Lancers, whose role in the early stage of the battle was one of reconnaissance. Churchill led a patrol up into the Jabel Surkab Hills and from here they were forced to retire as the Khalifa's army first advanced and Remington bullets whistled around them. As the force led by Osman Azraq passed these hills they wheeled towards Kitchener's zariba. Churchill led his men down the ridge and into the path of this vast advancing army. Churchill ordered four of his troopers to fire a few rounds from their carbines into the enemy mass and thus he was able to claim the first British shots of the battle. He then led his men back up to a sheltered position on the Jabel Surkab Hills as the enemy passed by.

Churchill knew that as soon as the Mahdists topped the ridge in front of them they would be seen by the men in the zariba and those on board the steamers. Churchill waited, 'fascinated by the impending horror. I could see it coming. In a few seconds swift destruction would rush on these brave men.'[26]

As predicted by Churchill, the full force of British weapons technology was now unleashed upon the Khalfia's men.

Churchill and others were initially surprised by the fact that it was the Khalifa's artillery that opened fire first. Two shells fell harmlessly 50yd short of the zariba. This fire drew an immediate response from the British artillery and within moments shells and shrapnel slammed into the advancing enemy. The British unleashed volley fire by company from their Lee–Metford rifles when the enemy was within 2,000yd of the zariba. Lieutenant Meiklejohn of the Royal Warwicks observed:

> A volume of fire burst out from the whole length of the zariba . . . Continued repetition on my part of the words of command 'Ready' – 'Present' – 'Fire' – 'Ready' in this rhythm, only varied by a shortening of the range . . . I could see little trace of 'sand spirits' from bullets in front of them,

so concluded our elevation was correct, yet it seemed almost as if nothing could stop them.[27]

Although the Lee–Metford was, of course, a magazine-fed rifle, many of the British troops were ordered to fire the weapon as a breech-loader, thrusting one cartridge in at a time so as to allow for fire by company. Even so, each man was able to unleash twelve rounds a minute into the advancing mass of enemy. Rifles became too hot to handle and had to be swapped for weapons held in reserve, whilst the water in the Maxim barrels boiled. As the enemy got within 1,000yd the Martini–Henry rifles of the Sudanese and Egyptian troops also began to take a toll upon the enemy. Major Watson wrote:

> Now they are getting closer and the Martinis of Blacks [Sudanese] and Egyptians speak. Guns, Maxims, Rifles, a terrible concert. Our mens' black powder [from the Martini–Henry rifles] stopped the view but you could hear the shouts, and occasionally through a rift in the smoke catch sight of a banner and black face. This part of the fight was at its height. Modern weapons versus numbers, the din was terrific and stretchers were plying. Then their fire slackened, and great cheers began to go up. They were stopped. Cease fire sounded. We got the first clear view of what we had done, and it was sufficiently appalling . . .[28]

Lieutenant Loch wrote of the effects of the Maxim upon the enemy:

> They kept on advancing till about 1,000 yards off then the fire was too much for them and they were obliged to halt. The Maxims simply wiped out thousands. Meanwhile the lot halted in the middle of the plain in desperation sent a charge of about 500 hundred Bajara horse against our centre. This charge was useless but magnificent.
> The instant they started they were subject to a perfectly hellish fire from rifles and Maxims. They rode on and were wiped out to a man. One gallant old fellow rode on to within about four hundred yards of the zereba before he fell. He was the only man who got anywhere near all day. A few sharp shooters managed to creep up to within about 750 yards and did a bit of damage. All our casualties were I think caused by these fellows.[29]

Captain D.W. Churcher, of the 1st Battalion of the Royal Irish Fusiliers, was in command of a Maxim battery and wrote in his diary:

> About 7.00 am we saw the whole Dervish Army, a perfect horde of them about 40,000, I believe they were estimated, coming out from behind the little ridge of hills in front of us, and they immediately advanced in column to the attack, and we opened fire and I never heard such a fiendish row in all my life; I got the maxims on a body of men to the left at about 1700 yards and as far as I could tell they didn't come any further then I turned them on the right, and kept on firing away at any body of men I could see . . . the maxims came in very handy at times . . . Everyone seems to be delighted with our maxims as we did not have a hitch with them all day long, which is a good deal to say, as we fired nearly 8000 rounds.[30]

The value of the Maxims was also recorded by the German military attaché, Major von Tiedemann, who told how he rode to watch the effect of the Maxim gun battery on the right flank:

> The gunners did not get their range at once, but as soon as they found it the enemy went down in heaps, and it was evident that the six Maxims guns were doing a large share of the work of repelling the Dervish rush. They were firing .303 cartridges, with smokeless powder, and besides the rapidity of the fire, they had the advantage of longer range with a flatter trajectory then that of the Martini rifles, with which the Egyptian troops to right and left of them were armed.[31]

The historian Donald Featherstone wrote of the Maxim at Omdurman, 'the Maxims opened fire with tremendous effect, the attack began to thin and waver; a rigid line would gather itself up and rush on evenly, then suddenly quiver and stop; then other lines would gather themselves up again, again and yet again but, they went down'.[32] Colour Sergeant Fraley of the Rifle Brigade stated that under Maxim fire the Mahdists, 'simply fell down in a line, just the same as if they had been told to lie down, some of the bodies they saw afterwards had been hit with bullets five and six times across their bodies before they fell'.[33]

The slaughter was appalling. Whole tribes of warriors were wiped out. No man could advance against such firepower and at about 800yd from Kitchener's zariba the attack lost momentum and faltered. One final gesture, as recorded by Lieutenant Loch, was made by the commander, Osman Azraq, who led 500 Baggara cavalry in a futile charge directly at the Maxim battery in the centre of the defensive line. Not one man got within 300yd of the British position; all were simply wiped out in a few seconds. Within the space of little over 50 minutes more than 2,000 of the Khalifa's best warriors had been slain and over 4,000 wounded. Churchill thought the slaughter 'a mere matter of machinery'.[34] The war correspondent G.W. Steevens wrote, 'It was not a battle, but an execution.'[35]

Yet, Kitchener's force did not have a bloodless victory. The cavalry force, led by Lieutenant Colonel Robert Broadwood (1862–1917), was forced to retreat from its position on the Kerreri Hills and was ably assisted by supporting artillery fire from the gunboats as it fell back. Several British soldiers were hit by Remington bullets from the few sharpshooters that used what available cover there was to get within 750yd of the zariba. However, the majority of British losses came from an unnecessary cavalry charge by the 21st Lancers at Osman Digna dervishes, many of whom were concealed in a depression in the ground.

After the annihilation of the enemy's first charge, Kitchener advanced out of the zariba towards Omdurman. This move was premature for he failed to realise how many of the Khalifa's reserves were still in place behind the cover of the hills. The rush for the city resulted in the abandonment of the standard echelon formation and left the Egyptian infantry, commanded by Lieutenant Colonel Hector Macdonald (1853–1903), exposed on the north-west flank. Here it was attacked by the Khalifa's forces from the west and also the north. Macdonald steadied his men who first defeated the enemy from the west and then calmly realigned his force to face north and beat off the attack from that direction. Although supported by artillery fire from the gunboats, Macdonald's success owed much to his own calmness and the steadfastness of his troops.

One interesting feature of this last engagement was that the Egyptian and Sudanese troops were armed with the Martini–Henry rifle, the effective range of which was significantly less than that of the Lee–Metford. Whilst the British opened fire at the enemy at 2,000yd out and stopped them with their Lee–Metfords at 800yd, the Egyptian and Sudanese troops began firing at 1,000yd and stopped the Khalifa's men within 500yd with their Martini–Henry fire.[36] This illustrates how rifle effectiveness had advanced in a short period of time and was commented on by contemporary newspaper reports such as those in the *Daily Telegraph* of 6 September 1898.

Major Watson described the attack on Macdonald's men and his comment tells of how the Martini–Henry had stopped the dervishes 'in banks', just like the Zulus had been halted at Khambula and Gingindlovu:

> The brunt of it fell on MacDonald's brigade, and the way he handled his men, and his men played up, was splendid. It was a very serious ten minutes, and the charge the Dervishes made there, literally thousands, was enough to try the best troops in the world. Wauchope's brigade was sent off to the right to assist, but the danger was over before they arrived. The Dervish dead in front of Mac's brigade were literally in banks.[37]

One other notable feature of the battle was the artillery support, both defensive and aggressive, that the infantry received from the gunboats. They were used to guard the left flank of the enemy, sending shell after shell into the massed ranks of the enemy as it attacked. When the Camel Corps were hard-pressed, some of the gunboats were able, by dropping down stream, to turn back a large mass of dervishes coming around the Kerreri Hills. The 12pdr shrapnel shell burst with the greatest accuracy, and the crossfire of gunboats from the river, and artillery from the land, had, in addition, a great effect on morale. As Kitchener's army advanced on Omdurman, the gunboats pushed on, and about 5pm went alongside the walls of Omdurman, helping to silence the fire that was still going on from the houses near the river.

Kitchener's Omdurman despatch of 5 September was emphatic in praise of the gunboats:

> The excellent service performed by the gunboats . . . is deserving of special mention. These gunboats have been for a long time almost constantly under fire; they have made bold reconnaissance past the enemy's forts and rifle pits; and on the 1st and 2nd September, in conjunction with the irregular levies . . . and the howitzer battery, they materially aided in the capture of all the forts on both banks of the Nile, and in making the fortifications of Omdurman untenable. In bringing to notice the readiness of resource, daring and ability of

Commander Keppel and his officers, I wish also to add my appreciation of the services . . . of the detachments of the Royal Marine Artillery and the gun crews, who have gained the hearty praise of their commanders.[38]

Such cooperation between British gunners and infantry was to become a notable feature of another conflict in little more than a year's time on the same continent.

Kitchener was victorious. Despite 48 men killed, the majority of whom were lost in the senseless charge of the 21st Lancers, and 434 wounded, Kitchener's men had avenged Gordon and retaken Khartoum. The Khalifa's army had suffered greatly at the hands of the technologically superior British, Egyptian and Sudanese forces and best estimates are that nearly 10,000 warriors were killed, a further 10,000–16,000 wounded and 5,000 captured. It was indeed a slaughter.

The Khalifa fled from the battlefield, escaped and reformed his army on the White Nile. Colonel Wingate (1861–1953) was despatched by Kitchener to finally capture or kill him. Wingate tracked the Khalifa's forces to Umm Diwaykarat, where they had encamped, and attacked them on 25 November 1899. The Maxims opened fire at a range of 800yd from a position on a hill overlooking the encampment. The dervishes charged towards this position but the Maxims beat off the assault, with the foremost of the enemy falling within ninety-four paces of the guns. Then they fell back on their main position. Here the Khalifa, with some twenty of his Emirs, made a last stand. The Maxims opened fire with deadly effect. The Khalifa and most of his Emirs perished in a stream of .303 bullets. Wingate stated, 'To the Maxim Gun primarily belongs the victory which stamped out Dervish rule in the Sudan.'[39] British power and control in Sudan was now total. Yet, at the same time as the Khalifa was dying British troops were falling to a foe armed with similar battlefield technology to their own. Once again the nineteenth-century battlefield was to be changed by technology and thus it was to be the British who would have to learn some deadly lessons.

Chapter 7

Barrage – Pieter's Hill, 27 February 1900

> More than seventy guns concentrated their fire on the entrenchments, scattering the stones and earth high in the air. Then, suddenly, shortly after four o'clock, all further attempts at advancing under cover were abandoned, and the Lancashire Brigade marched proudly into the open ground and on the enemy's works.
>
> Winston Spencer Churchill,
> *London to Ladysmith via Pretoria*

With Kitchener's victory at Omdurman Britain was at the height of its imperial prestige and British arms and technology had swept away its foes. Yet, within fourteen months, upon the same continent, Britain was in conflict with the Boers of South Africa who were armed with battlefield weapons which were at least as good as, if not superior, to anything the British Army possessed. Although the first battle, that of Talana Hill on 20 October 1899, was a British victory, it came at a high price in terms of dead and wounded troops and was a foretaste of the bloody battles that were to follow.

As with most wars in history there was no one specific act that triggered war between Britain and the Boers. The road to war was a long one that had fermented for twenty years or more. However, and again like most wars, the real and ultimate cause was that each opposing side held an uncompromising stance and never understood each other's position.

After Britain's humiliating defeat at the Battle of Majuba Hill (27 February 1881) during the First Boer War (1880–1), the British government had been forced to recognise the independence of the Transvaal State. In 1886 the discovery of huge gold deposits in the Transvaal enhanced the State's financial security and independence.

British political dreams of a Federation of South Africa, which began in the 1870s, seemed very far away.

Yet, although in a stronger financial position, the Transvaal was very dependent on British capital and technological expertise to successfully develop the gold fields. British citizens flocked to Johannesburg and its surrounds and within a few years these immigrants, or Uitlanders, outnumbered the Transvaalers. There was no doubt a cultural difference, and lack of understanding between the local Boers and the British immigrants. Crucially the shrewd and pious President of Transvaal, Paul Kruger (1825–1904), refused to allow the Uitlanders full civil rights and the vast majority were not allowed to vote. Kruger feared that if the Uitlanders were fully franchised then an English-speaking government might be the logical result and this would have gone against sixty years of Afrikaner determination to avoid British rule. Kruger expressed his view in his usual plain way when he said of the Uitlanders, 'Their rights! Yes, they'll get them over my dead body.'[1]

Although not in itself a cause for war, Kruger's refusal to grant rights to the Uitlanders did provide the British government with some moral justification for its tough negotiating position. Of course the government did have a responsibility to its citizens overseas but the new Colonial Secretary, Joseph Chamberlain (1836–1914), saw in the financial strength of the Transvaal both a threat and an opportunity which needed to be controlled. Although not proven, there was a belief that Chamberlain had been involved in the botched attempt to overthrow Kruger's republic in December 1895, in the Jameson Raid. This act had been financed and orchestrated by Cecil Rhodes (1853–1902), the ultimate British imperialist, millionaire and business man and then Prime Minister of the Cape Colony. The failure of the raid to ignite an uprising of popular support from the Uiltander community in the Transvaal ultimately forced Rhodes to resign. The longer term result was that the Afrikaner position was strengthened with Boers residing in the Orange Free State and in the Cape expressing their solidarity with the Transvaal. There was now complete distrust between Britain and the Afrikaners.

Chamberlain was not to be thwarted in his attempts to secure British suzerainty over the region and now turned to diplomatic manoeuvring. Over the next three years Chamberlain worked to isolate the Transvaal both politically and diplomatically. His biggest coup was to secure the Anglo-German Agreement of 1898 which agreed to apportion the Portuguese colonies of Angola and Mozambique should the near bankrupt Portuguese government be forced to mortgage these territories. In the event this was not to happen but the price of the Agreement was that Germany, a one-time strong supporter of the Kruger republic, distanced itself from the Transvaal.

In 1897 the British government appointed a new High Commissioner and Governor of the Cape, Sir Alfred Milner (1854–1925). Although initially not averse to following the path of mediation and reconciliation between Britain and the Transvaal, within a year Milner had concluded that war was likely. Both he and Chamberlain enhanced the campaign for Uitlander rights and each portrayed the Uitlanders as a persecuted group. In May 1899, Milner and Kruger met in Bloemfontein to try and hammer out a settlement of the Uitlander issue. Perhaps neither party truly understood the other's position and although Kruger did offer some concessions, these were deemed insufficient. In Britain the government portrayed Kruger as intransient. The British public was being prepared for a war to free the Uitlanders. The conclusion of British military operations in the Sudan allowed for troops to move to South Africa and in June 1899 Milner and Chamberlain had agreed upon further reinforcements.

By October 1899 the British had 70,000 troops either in South Africa or en route. On 9 October 1899 Chamberlain and Milner negotiated their last diplomatic and political coup by teasing the Transvaal government into issuing an ultimatum demanding the withdrawal of all British troops on the Transvaal border and that those at sea should be sent back. The British government was never going to back down in the face of such a challenge and when war broke out on 12 October 1899 it was not a shock to either the Afrikaners or the British public.

What was a surprise to the world was the poor performance of British forces in South Africa in the remaining weeks of 1899. A string of reversals, or outright defeats, were as a result of tactical ineptitude and arrogance from the British High Command. The military skill of the Boer commanders, the fighting quality of the enemy and the deadly effect of modern rifle and artillery fire were seriously under estimated by the British, who seemed slow to learn and adapt.

Many of the weapons that the British had utilised at Omdurman, such as the Lee–Metford magazine rifle and the Maxim machine gun, would again see service in South Africa. At the start of the war the Royal Artillery was organised into three parts: siege, horse and field. Each branch was under strength, frequently by as much as 50 per cent, and the ordnance in use was rapidly approaching obsolescence due to lack of modern quick-firing field guns and long-range heavy artillery. Indeed, field commanders, such as Buller, would soon come to depend on the work of the guns of the Naval Brigade for long-range support of the infantry. As the war progressed, and after several battlefield reversals, the British learnt the importance, and how to effectively use, the artillery they possessed. In 1885 the British introduced the 12pdr RBL (Rifled Breech Loading) gun to both field and horse artillery batteries. A lighter version was issued to Royal Horse Artillery units in 1892, and the 12pdr was converted to accept a 15pdr shell for the Royal Artillery. Firing case shot and shrapnel canisters with cordite as the propellant, the 12 and 15pdrs were the two most commonly used British artillery pieces of the Second Boer War. In addition, the British would have the service of 4.7in guns from detachments of the Naval Brigade, which, after mounting on carriages, were able to fire a lyddite projectile, at extreme elevation, a distance of 12,000m. These guns were to play a prominent role during the siege of Ladysmith and in the subsequent attempts to relieve the town.

Lyddite, a high-explosive containing picric acid, was first used in British shells from 1898 and performed well against the walls and tombs of Omdurman. Lyddite shells also saw service in South Africa where it was hoped they would drive an entrenched force from defensive positions. Indeed, it was later evident that if the lyddite shells could be placed on or near a Boer trench then the explosive power was tremendously effective, but that their detonation was very uneven. Indeed, due to problems with the shell casing up to 75 per cent of shells failed to detonate fully. However, the main issue remained that throughout the conflict the Boers' ability to camouflage their positions made the task of the British artillery extremely difficult.

The Boers' opening strategy was founded firmly on speed of movement based on the thinking that time was not on their side for the British would only get numerically stronger as the weeks and months passed. Initial battlefield success would, the Boers hoped, dishearten both the British military and public enough for a favourable settlement to be negotiated. The Boers concentrated their first advance upon British forces in north Natal, primarily the 4,000 troops stationed at Dundee, under the command of General Sir William Penn Symons (1843–99), and the 8,000 men at Ladysmith who were led by Sir George White, VC (1835–1912). White was in overall command of British forces in Natal and despite advice to the contrary, he decided to advance across the Tugela River thus isolating his troops from immediate support and offering the Boers tempting targets in the first weeks of the war.

Crossing the Drakensberg Mountains and advancing from the west, the Boers pressed towards Ladysmith. Newcastle was occupied without a shot being fired and the Boers managed to secure positions on both Talana Hill and Lennox Hill above the British position in Dundee. Dawn on 20 October 1899 revealed to Penn Symons and his men the strength of the Boer position. The warning signs of British ineptitude and Boer tactical awareness were seen in this first major battle of the conflict at Talana Hill. Although the British artillery successfully and rapidly nullified the Boer artillery, Symons' plan of a full-scale infantry assault, backed by artillery, showed contempt for the enemy. Lacking cover and struggling uphill, the British were easy targets for Boers' Mausers, the fire from which claimed many lives. The Boers concentrated upon the British officers and many were killed or injured, including Penn Symons himself who would die of his wounds three days later. Although the British were ultimately successful, driving the Boers from their positions, the victory was a pyrrhic one, with nearly 500 men killed or wounded against Boer losses of around 150 men. Furthermore, the remaining British troops now withdrew to Ladysmith and the Boers occupied Dundee.

The following day a British assault, led by General John French (1852–1925) and Colonel Ian Hamilton (1853–1947), upon the Boers at Elandslaagte was a clear British victory. The Boers were driven from their defensive positions by a combined artillery, infantry and cavalry assault, although the infantry casualties at the hands of accurate Mauser fire were again high. This tactical success was reduced however as all British forces withdrew to Ladysmith as the Boers gradually encircled the town. Numerous British attempts to now break what was rapidly becoming a siege, the most significant being on 29 October 1899, failed and within the space of little more than a week the Boers had very much gained the strategic upper hand. For the next four months the British were forced to direct their energies largely towards the relief of Ladysmith and more setbacks were soon to follow.

Overall command was now in the hands of General Sir Redvers Buller, VC (1839–1908), who, after a sixteen day sailing, arrived in South Africa on 30 October 1899 onboard the *Dunottar Castle*. He journeyed with his staff officers and several newspaper journalists, including Winston Churchill (1874–1965), then working for the *Morning Post*. En route, first at Madeira and then as the party neared Cape Town, Buller and his entourage learnt of the initial Boer attacks in Natal and the Cape Colony, the latter which had cut off British forces in Kimberley as well as Cecil Rhodes himself. If these reports were accurate, then Buller would have to radically alter his plans for an advance on Pretoria via Bloemfontein.

As the gangplank crashed down onto the dockside, the journalists, Churchill amongst them, rushed to find Cape newspapers to see if the reports were correct. At the same moment, Buller and his staff read the secret war telegrams which confirmed the worst fears of British defeats and the sieges of Kimberley and Ladysmith. Buller then met a very despondent Milner who expressed his fears of a potential uprising in the Cape Colony.

Buller clearly had to amend his plans in light of the Boer advances and battlefield successes. Focus, for both military and political reasons, had now to be centred on the relief of the besieged British troops. By 4 November 1899, Buller had decided to break up his army. He would personally lead in excess of 20,000 men to Natal to rescue White in Ladysmith whilst Lord Methuen (1845–1932), and the 13,000 men of his command, would be tasked with the relief of Kimberley.

Like many senior British officers in the late nineteenth-century army, Methuen was unimaginative in his thinking. His lessons from the British victories at Talana and Elandslaagte were that direct attacks against the Boers would prove fruitful, whilst at the same time he disregarded the high number of casualties the British had suffered in these and other engagements. To relieve Kimberley Methuen's force would have to overcome a number of physical obstacles en route including the hills of Belmont and Graspan, the Modder River and the triangular hills of Magersfontein, all of which were ideal locations from which the Boers could ably defend against a British advance. To one officer who suggested to Methuen that a detour round Belmont might be prudent, Methuen is recorded as responding, 'My good fellow, I intend to put the fear of God into these people [the Boers] and the only way is to fight them.'[2]

Methuen's advance was along the railway line from Orange River Station towards Kimberley. His engineers repaired sections of rail that the Boers had sabotaged and this allowed the force to be readily supplied. Resistance was first met at Belmont Station where a number of hills were occupied by the Boers. A night march was planned to get the British troops in place at dawn for an attack on 23 November 1899. Unfortunately, a number of unseen obstacles held up the night march and the element of surprise was lost. Belmont was to be a foretaste of future battles for the Boers, superbly camouflaged and hidden in defensive trenches, maintained their discipline and the first the British knew of their presence was when thousands of Mausers erupted. Troops dropped all around but the British showed great tenacity as they continued their advance and this seemed to unnerve some of the

Boers whose fire became erratic. The Boers were eventually driven from their defensive positions but again the price paid in terms of casualties, 53 officers and men killed and 245 wounded, was high.

The success at Belmont, although costly, was something of a morale-booster for the British after a series of reversals. Indeed, it seemed to Methuen that his tactic of frontal assault was the correct one. The next encounter, the Battle of Graspan, was a slightly different affair. The battle began on the morning of 25 November with an artillery duel, which the British won. This was followed by an infantry attack in open order with rushes which demonstrated that at least the infantry officers were learning and the lesser casualties of twenty killed illustrates this. Unfortunately, the Naval Brigade, attacking for the first time across open ground, continued to advance in close order and consequently suffered over a hundred casualties, although they did have the honour of storming the Boer hill position.

Methuen's advance was now somewhat slowed as the Boers had seriously damaged the railway line. This delay gave the Boers some time for soul searching for although they had inflicted serious casualties upon the British, it had been them that had been forced to flee the field from the last two battles. Some of the Free State Boers were dispirited and returned to their homes, but Koos De la Rey (1847–1914), a formidable leader of a commando unit, argued for a change of tactics at the Modder River. Instead of taking positions on top of hills which attracted both British artillery and rifle fire the Boers, in his opinion, should adopt defensive positions lower down where the British would not be expecting them to be and from where their fire would benefit from a flat trajectory which would correspondingly improve accuracy. The smokeless Mauser ammunition would not reveal their new positions to the British and it was envisaged that they could be halted at such a distance that the final feared bayonet charge would be nullified. De la Rey successfully convinced his fellow commanders, including Piet Cronje (1836–1911), and the Boers prepared their defensive positions at the Modder River. These included white range markers so as to further improve the accuracy of their rifle fire.

When Methuen advanced upon the Modder River crossing on the morning of 28 November all seemed quiet. Indeed, the British commander was later to write to his wife, 'I thought the enemy had cleared off, as did everyone else, whereas Kronje [Cronje], De la Ray [Rey] and 9,000 men were waiting for me in an awful position. I never saw a Boer, but even at 2,000 yards when I rode a horse I had a hail of bullets round me.'[3]

Methuen was not short of bravery and he himself even led a charge towards the river. This came to nothing, like the British advance across most of the battlefield. For 10 hours the British were pinned down by Mauser fire from a foe they never saw.

Hunger and above all thirst drove men to try and retreat towards water carts and many were killed in the attempt. Errors were made on both sides. Cronje's men fired too early and failed to completely trap the advancing Scots Guards. In addition, Cronje positioned most of the Boer artillery to support De la Rey's trenches and had not provided enough men or artillery to defend Rosmead Drift on the west of the battlefield. Eventually after 3 hours of stalemate, men of the 9th Division, led by Major General Pole-Carew (1849–1924) crept forward in rushes and utilising a small fold in the ground were able to reach the drift. Men of the North Lancashires were the first over and by the early afternoon British troops had dug themselves into the north bank and driven the Boers back. Pole-Carew now directed his men to a position behind the centre of the Boer position but a counterattack by De la Rey stalled the advance, although the British still held their position on the north bank. As darkness fell the British reinforced Pole-Carew's position and the artillery readied itself to re-launch the bombardment in the morning. However, morning revealed that the Boers had withdrawn and now only one final natural obstacle, the Magersfontein Hills, remained between the Modder and Kimberley.

The British, apart from their success at Rosmead Drift, had been pinned down by the Boer fire for hours. Private Snape of C Company of the North Lancashires described in a letter home the intensity of the fire, 'for bullets came flying at us like hail stones, and I had three men shot dead within ten yards of me . . .'.[4] Similarly Colonel B. Lang of the Argyll and Sutherland Highlanders wrote of his experiences:

> We had not gone very far when we came under fire, so we got into extended order and continued to advance. There was no cover of any sort and we soon began to suffer casualties. Finally the firing line was brought to a standstill by the Boer fire from the deep banks of the River which gave them excellent cover, and completely concealed them from us. Our firing line thus was almost stationary the whole day, and all ranks suffered from the blazing sun on the backs of our exposed legs.[5]

Clearly this was a new type of war, never experienced by British troops in action, where intense modern rifle fire could completely stall an advance at distances of a mile or more. The British casualties of 24 officers and 460 men were high but also did not really reflect the static nature, for much of the days' fighting, of the battle. Only the British artillery and the Boer errors at Rosmead Drift allowed Methuen to claim his third victory in a row.

Before advancing upon the last strong Boer position at the Magersfontein Hills, Methuen allowed his troops a two-week recovery period to rest and re-equip. Although this delay was probably essential, it did allow the Boers to receive reinforcements from Mafeking and, with African labour, to dig a 12-mile-long defence line under the shadow of the Magersfontein ridge. Most of the defences consisted of broken lines of breastworks, built securely of stone or earth, 5ft deep and camouflaged so as to be invisible to the British eye. Indeed, British scouts never got within a mile of these Boer positions as they were driven back by Mauser fire. Methuen had no idea of the complexity or quality of the defences he would have to overcome, nor of the fact that the defenders had increased in number to over 8,000 committed Boers.

During Methuen's rest period, the first British disaster in what was to become known as 'Black Week' occurred at the Battle of Stormberg on 10 December 1899. A force of 2,500 British troops, under the command of Lieutenant General William Gatacre (1843–1906) attempted a disastrous night march to try to surprise the Boer force of 800 men holding the important junction at Stormberg. Many of the British troops became hopelessly lost in the dark, local guides proved incompetent and the chain of command broke down. The result was that the British arrived exhausted and already demoralised. The Boer picquets opened fire, alerting their comrades, and within seconds the British were caught in a deadly crossfire. After 30 minutes Gatacre ordered the retreat but unfortunately 600 men of the Northumberland Fusiliers failed to receive the order and were subsequently taken prisoner. On top of the loss of the Northumberlands, there were ninety British casualties. Black Week had begun.

Despite Gatacre's disastrous night march, Methuen, now facing the Magersfontein Hills, decided upon the same risky tactic. Major General Andrew Wauchope (1846–99), the commander of the Highland Brigade, was tasked by Methuen to march his command to the foot of the Magersfonein kopje before launching a surprise dawn attack.

Methuen also placed his trust in the vastly superior British artillery, including a newly arrived 4.7in naval gun, to deliver a devastating bombardment upon the Boer position. Yet, with at best stretchy intelligence where was the British fire to be targeted?

On the moonless night of 10 December 1899 Wauchope lined up his command of four battalions in a compact formation: 3,500 troops all compressed into a column just 45yd wide and 160yd long. Despite this close formation, the darkness of the night made it difficult to maintain cohesion. Furthermore, the plain in front of the kopje was strewn with rocks, anthills and thorn bushes which ripped at the Highlanders' kilts. To add to the misery a storm deluged the men. Against such odds Wauchope and his men stoically arrived at dawn a thousand yards from the ridge and more or less in the right position. Now Wauchope, against the advice of some of his battalion commanders, displayed a complete ignorance of the power of the modern rifle upon a closed formation for he continued to advance at the head of this massed column of men. A single shot rang out from the Boer defences, followed by a great roar as thousands of Mausers fired at Wauchope and his men.

Still the battle could have been saved for the British had indeed achieved surprise and the initial Boer fire sailed over the heads of the Highlanders. Yet, vital seconds were lost as the Highlanders attempted to deploy and some of the troops panicked. By the time order was restored the Boers had begun to find their range and the British started to take casualties. Just like at Modder River, they were pinned down, seeking any cover that was available. The British artillery was able to give some support to the infantry and the Boer artillerymen decided not to return fire.

During the battle the Naval Brigade, firing both common shell and lyddite, restricted the Boer movement behind the kopje. The effects of the lyddite shells were spectacular; clouds of rocks and dust were thrown 200 or 300m into the air and these could be seen for 10 miles or more. However, the large number of Boer infantry reinforcements, secure in their trenches, was able to surprise Methuen and his men with a deadly wall of fire. The British commander was little more than a spectator to events as, with the failure of the Highlanders to achieve their objective, he now had to focus on supporting these troops and had little opportunity to probe for any weaknesses in the Boer position.

After hours under fire, there was no sign of an end to the ordeal for the Highlanders. Around 200 men of the Black Watch and Seaforths had advanced to the east face of the kopje but here they were either killed or captured. At around 1pm the Colonel of the Seaforths noticed some Boers attempting to outflank them and ordered two companies to move back a few hundred metres to counter the enemy's movement. At the same time the Colonel of the Gordons gave a similar order and these two movements seemed to have triggered a panic amongst the men who had been pinned down under a withering fire for nearly 8 hours. The retreat which began as a trickle rapidly became a flood and despite the Highlander officers attempting to restore order, often with threats from their revolvers, all cohesion was lost. One officer wrote: 'I saw a sight I hope I may never see again: men of the Highland Brigade running for all they were worth.'[6]

The following morning when ambulances searched the battlefield for the dead and wounded 902 were found on the British side and 236 on the Boer. Wauchope was amongst the dead, his body within 200m of the Boer trenches, his face to the enemy. However, the majority of his Brigade's dead had died from wounds to their backs. As Methuen watched the disaster unfolding around the Highlanders he must have known that the battle was lost. However, there was the hope that as at Belmont, Graspan and Modder the Boers might abandon their defences overnight and leave the route open to Kimberley. Yet, the day after the battle, the British observation balloon's crew reported that the Boers were still secure in their trenches and the way to Kimberley was still blocked.

The British were experiencing a new type of warfare in which the enemy was rarely seen but their threat was ever present. The men of the Highlander Brigade, who were renowned for their stoicism and had a long tradition of bravery, fortitude and battlefield success, had clearly been affected by what could be classed as psychological warfare. Fuller has written:

> In the small battles fought during the opening months of the war, it became apparent that, due to smokeless powder, the old terror of a visible foe had given way to the paralysing sensation of advancing on an invisible one. A universal terror, rather than a localized danger, now enveloped the attacker, while the defender, always ready to protect himself by some rough earth-or stone-work, was enabled,

because of the rapidity of fire, to use extensions unheard of in former battles, and in consequence overlap every frontal infantry attack.[7]

Thus, although outnumbered and frequently out-gunned in terms of artillery, the Boers were able to hold defensive positions with much fewer men than had been the case in previous wars. According to Fuller, at the Battle of the Modder River, the Boers extended 3,000 men on a frontage of 7,700m; at Magersfontein, 5,000 on 11,000; and at Colenso, 4,500 on 13,000. Yet, in spite of the human thinness of the defences, these fronts could not be penetrated due to the effectiveness of modern rifle fire combined with smokeless ammunition and secure, well-concealed trenches.

The solution for the attackers to succeed in this new style of warfare rested on new open order infantry formations and the effective use of artillery to not only nullify the effects of fire from the defenders but also to allow the attackers to advance under the cover of an artillery umbrella. However, of all the European powers the British had been the slowest to adopt and improve their artillery capabilities. The introduction of quick-firing artillery arose out of proposals made in 1891 by General Wille in Germany and Colonel Langlois in France. They concluded that increased rate of fire was impossible unless recoil on firing was absorbed. This led to much experimental work on shock absorption, and to the eventual introduction of a non-recoiling carriage, which permitted a bullet-proof shield being attached to it to protect the gun crew. Until this improvement in artillery was introduced, the magazine rifle would dominate the battlefield, but, by the end of the nineteenth century, it was challenged by the quick-firing gun, which not only out-ranged it and could be fired with almost equal rapidity, but could be rendered invisible by indirect laying by a physical feature, such as a slope of hill. The British, as demonstrated by the early battles of the Boer War, had not fully realised the potential of their artillery to support the infantry attack and instead frequently focused on trying to destroy or nullify the enemy's artillery. Unfortunately, it would take several more significant British battlefield reversals before these lessons were learnt.

The next battle and the last of Black Week took place at Colenso on 15 December 1899. Although historians have been critical of General Buller for the British reversal at Colenso, it could be argued that almost from the start of the battle Buller was let down by his subordinate officers, who showed a complete lack of understanding of the dangers of rapid and accurate rifle fire and how to most effectively utilise their artillery. With the relief of Ladysmith the number one priority for the British, it was Buller's task to find a way through or around the Boer positions. The Tugela River was a natural defensive line and the Boers used the cover and strength of the hills and mountains behind to their usual great effect.

Buller halted at the town of Frere and it was here that the British consolidated and brought up men, arms and ammunition. Buller was undecided as to how best to cross the Tugela River but was limited in his options. Buller summed up his predicament in a letter to the War Office:

> I am in great doubt how to attack Ladysmith. The main road through Colenso goes through a ghastly country exactly the sort made for the Boer tactics and they have strongly fortified it. I can turn it by going across the Tuglea at Potgieters Drift some 15 miles up the River, and should better ground to advance over but I should not be in so good a tactical position to help White [in Ladysmith], as I should be if I came up the main road from Colenso . . . I don't know that I ever had a problem which has bothered me more.[8]

On arriving in Frere Buller seemed to have decided upon the Potgieters Drift route as being the easier of two difficult options. Yet, his mind was to change for several reasons. Logistically Buller was hampered by a lack of animal transport to move his force towards Potgieters Drift and certainly, with the Boers' telescopes trained upon his force, there would be no element of surprise. Crucially Buller would be forced to leave at least one full brigade behind near Frere and would thus have the risk of splitting his force and threatening his line of communication. Thus, with some reluctance, an attack to force a crossing at Colenso was decided upon.

The railway bridge had been dynamited but there still remained a wagon bridge and two drifts which Buller hoped his men could use to cross the Tugela. Although it seems clear that the British underestimated the quality of the Boer trenches, Buller's force, with a strength of 14,000 infantry, nearly 3,000 mounted troops and 44 guns, would, it was hoped, be sufficient to cross the river and form a bridgehead. At just after 5am on Friday, 15 December 1899 the two British 4.7in naval guns began a bombardment and at around 6am the Boers detected the first movement of British troops heading towards the Tugela.

General Louis Botha (1862–1919) watched as the British divided into three columns, with the central column, Hildyard's Brigade, heading for the wagon bridge. Yet, to Botha's amazement it was not infantry that led this advance but twelve 15pdr field guns and six naval 12pdrs, under the command of Colonel Charles Long. The Colonel positioned his guns within 1,000m from the Tugela and ordered them to prepare to fire. The artillerymen, within range of the Boer Mauser fire, were too tempting a target and Botha gave the order to fire.

Elsewhere on the battlefield another of Buller's subordinate officers was making a similarly fatal error. Major General Fitzroy Hart was personally leading his Irish Brigade towards the Bridle Drift, but crucially his African guides led the men incorrectly into a loop of the river, a small confirmed space which was open to sweeping Boer crossfire from three sides. Botha ordered the hidden Krupp howitzer to fire at the advancing Irish men. The fourth shell landed in the centre of the Brigade and with this Mauser fire poured into the British. Not only had Hart ordered his men to move in close formation but the loop into which the British had advanced was only a thousand metres wide and within this confined space 4,000 troops now tried to survive the onslaught of lead. Buller gave the order for Hart and his men to withdraw from the loop and over several hours those Irish men who were physically able gradually returned. Many were in a terrible state, suffering from sunburn, dehydration and utter fatigue.

Buller had watched the unfolding disaster of Long's guns with horror and now did his best to rectify the situation. By 8am Buller had decided that with the failure of Hart's advance and Long's fatal positioning of the guns the British attack should be suspended with only one of his brigades even committed. The next hours were spent trying to extract Long's guns from their advanced position whilst the artillerymen, who had not already been killed or wounded, tried to find cover. Whilst the men who manned Long's field guns had blundered into a zone of fire, and men and horses fell together, the naval guns were positioned slightly behind and suffered much less, for the Mauser fire was at its extreme range. Buller asked for volunteers to try and save the twelve field guns and men stepped forward including the son of Lord Roberts, Freddy, who was to earn a posthumous Victoria Cross in the attempt. Two guns were saved at a high cost whilst the remaining ten were lost to the Boers.

The British reversal had demonstrated that many of the British senior officers had entered the battle with little or no recognition or respect of modern concealed artillery and rifle fire. In addition, the basic tactics of the artillery, discounting Long's blundering, were shown to be inferior to those displayed by the Boers. Whilst the British, and to be fair most European powers, assumed that the role of artillery was to first nullify the enemy's artillery, the Boers realised that the key to the success of their artillery was concealment and the use of smokeless powder. The British were simply unable to locate the Boer artillery and much time and energy was wasted, which could have been spent supporting the infantry. In addition, although the British lyddite shells had shown their worth against fortifications, they were proving almost useless against dispersed infantry for the blasts they created were very concentrated.

In addition, the smokeless cartridges of the Mauser rifles firing from invisible trenches meant that the British had no clue where to direct their own fire. The effective killing range of the Mauser, at around 1,000m, had proved deadly against Hart's Irish Brigade as well as the artillery men of Long's command. Hart's men in close order columns were easy targets and the Boer's stopped the advance before it had even begun. In contrast, Buller had ordered men of Hildyard's Brigade to take Colenso village and by advancing in rushes of half-companies, with 6–8m between each man and 50–80m between each half-company, this very open order allowed the men of the Queen's Regiment and the Devons to successfully advance despite the storm of Mauser fire. Clearly the lessons were there for all to see. The casualties for the day were high. The British lost 143 killed and over 1,000 wounded; the Boers a mere 7 killed and 22 wounded.

The reversal at Colenso, and the earlier defeats, sent a shockwave all the way to London which culminated in Buller being replaced as Commander-in-Chief in South Africa by Lord Roberts, although Buller would retain command of British forces in Natal. It is clear that Buller was let down by some of his subordinates, but he can, however, be considered to be at fault for not keeping a tighter rein on their actions and movements. This was very apparent during the next major clash of arms at the Battle of Spion Kop (23–4 January 1900).

Whilst civilians and troops alike were forced to spend the Christmas of 1899 besieged in Ladysmith, Buller was preparing for his next attempt to break the Boer lines on the Tugela River. By the beginning of January, with the addition of a new division under the command of General Sir Charles Warren (1840–1927), Buller had around 30,000 troops available for his new advance. His plan was to cross the Tugela at Trichardt's Drift with the troops of Warren's Division who would then move on a sweeping left flanking movement round the Rangeworthy Hills onto the town of Dewdrop where they would combine with General Lyttelton's brigade which would have forced a crossing at Potgieter's Drift. These two movements would effectively turn the Boer entrenchments, and force the enemy to fall back thus allowing a free path to Ladysmith. Whilst the plan was innovative, its success would require a great deal of coordination between Warren and Lyttelton and ultimately between them and Buller.

Initially the advance went well. Both divisions successfully crossed the Tugela in good order but once across Warren found the terrain too difficult for his wagons. He halted for days at the foot of the Rangeworthy Hills, racked by indecision and inertia. Buller failed to intervene directly and left Warren to finally decide upon the next course of action which proposed to dislodge the Boers by a direct attack upon the hills and he chose the highest peak in the range, Spion Kop, as the first target. If this was gained, Warren considered that he could then enfilade the enemy's trenches and dominate the route towards Ladysmith. Buller was somewhat grudging in his support for the plan but approved it. On the night of 24 January 1,900 British troops, stumbling in the dark, succeeded in surprising the small Boer picquet and by 4am Spion Kop was in British hands.

For the next few hours a false sense of security pervaded the British. Attempts were made to dig entrenchments but the ground was rocky and the troops had only twenty shovels between them. When, at around 7am, the morning mist was burnt off it revealed to the British the precariousness of their position. In the dark they had settled on a false summit which was exposed to the Boers now above them and from the enemy positions in the surrounding hills. Soon the British were taking heavy causalities from Mauser rifle fire, from pom-poms and field artillery. The inadequate trenches soon became filled with British bodies. For the rest of the day the British, by constantly sending reinforcements up the slopes were just about able to cling on to their position. Private T. Neligan of the Lancashire Fusiliers wrote of the intensity of the fire that the British had to endure:

> Shells and bullets of every description rained unmercifully into the trenches, and the enemy seemed to be able to place their fearful Hotchkiss or pom-pom shells anywhere they liked. Some of the sights on that hill were terrible to behold, and one man, who was hit behind the neck with a pom-pom shell that set his clothes on fire, actually simmered where he fell. One might be speaking to the man on his right and left

one moment and, after firing a round from his rifle, might turn round the next and find them both dead. Some had their limbs torn clean away, and if a man was only slightly wounded he considered himself extremely lucky.[9]

Elsewhere Lyttelton's division was achieving their objectives and the twin peaks east of Spion Kop were taken. Whilst this success should have been considered an opportunity to relieve the pressure on the beleaguered troops on Spion Kop it was not supported and instead Buller's confused efforts focused on feeding troops into the maelstrom of Spion Kop. By the time darkness fell the British could no longer take any more punishment and withdrew back down leaving Spion Kop to the Boers to reoccupy the following morning. Buller ordered Lyttelton to also give up his hard-won position and once again the British crossed the Tugela, with the relief of Ladysmith apparently no nearer. The slaughter of Spion Kop had claimed 1,750 men killed, wounded or captured whilst the defending Boers suffered 300 casualties. The British government and public were shocked by yet another debacle. Buller had lost the confidence of some of his subordinate officers. Lyttelton, for example, was very critical of his commander.

Perhaps surprisingly, many of Buller's troops remained loyal to him, with many veterans recognising the difficulties encountered by the British fighting in harsh terrain and facing a new type of warfare against a frequently invisible enemy. Father Matthews wrote that, 'My Soudan experiences were mere child's play in comparison [with the Boer War]'. Private H. Worth of the 2nd Battalion of the Devonshire Regiment stated that his experience in the Tirah campaign was eclipsed by the Battle of Colenso. Private Louis Wilshaw of the 2nd Battalion of the Lancashire Fusiliers claimed that 'Omdurman was a picnic' by comparison with Spion Kop.[10] Many, including the maligned Buller, were beginning to realise that modern warfare was moving away from the one-day pitch battle towards a series of movements (some of which might be a reversal), often over many days, to achieve the objective of final battlefield success. This new thinking was to be displayed in Buller's last two attempts to relieve Ladysmith.

After the reversal at Colenso, Buller had become somewhat melancholy, a feeling that remained with him for weeks. Yet, after the even more crushing defeat of Spion Kop he remained surprisingly positive and soon began to focus on a new attempt to break the Boer defences. Buller's plan was to move the bulk of his force to the east to assault a group of hills, Vaal Krantz and Doorn Kop, which the Boers had entrenched to defend the eastern approach to Ladysmith. Buller proposed a divisionary attack to the west of Vaal Krantz to draw Boer forces, before committing the main attack further east. On 5 February Buller's force again crossed the Tugela.

The Royal Engineers worked magnificently to construct two pontoon bridges, one for the main eastern attack and the other for the divisionary assault. The eastern one was built in 50 grueling minutes with the engineers under constant Boer fire. Unfortunately, 3 vital hours were lost when field batteries assigned to the main assault crossed over the western bridge and had to relocate and move into the correct position. Troops of the Durham Light Infantry and the Rifle Brigade made the initial assault upon Vaal Krantz but Boer fire from Doorn Kop was heavier than expected and Buller, therefore, decided not to support the attack with further troops, although he did later concede to Lyttelton's request for the 60th and the Scottish Rifles to be committed. Lyttelton's men eventually took the southern-most hill of the Vaal Krantz ridge and avoided heavy casualties by hiding behind rocks and boulders despite enfilading fire from Doorn Kop. The troops tasked with securing Doorn Kop were not sent forward by Buller and with the terrain restricting the effectiveness of the British artillery, the Commander ordered a British withdrawal under cover of the night.

Yet, again the British troops crossed the Tugela and a joke began to circulate that Buller was 'the Ferryman of the Tugela'.[11] Criticism from politicians and many of his officers was once again directed at Buller. Yet, amongst his troops support remained high. Many applauded him for breaking off an attack which seemed destined to incur a high number of casualties. Sergeant A. Kean, of the 2nd Battalion of the Somerset Light Infantry, affirmed that:

> There is no doubt General Buller deserves the greatest praise for the way in which he has manoeuvred the troops ... I think it is General Buller's great motto to manoeuvre and take the positions with as few casualties as possible and not to rush a position which means sure death, especially against such positions and fortifications as our enemy possessed.[12]

Yet, from another reversal there were lessons to be understood. Private Neligan stated that the initial advance had clearly learnt from Hart's formation at Colenso and that, 'The movement was admirably carried out. Each regiment acted independently, but in line, moved out in skirmishing order, and marched to within a mile or thereabouts of the enemy's position ...'[13]

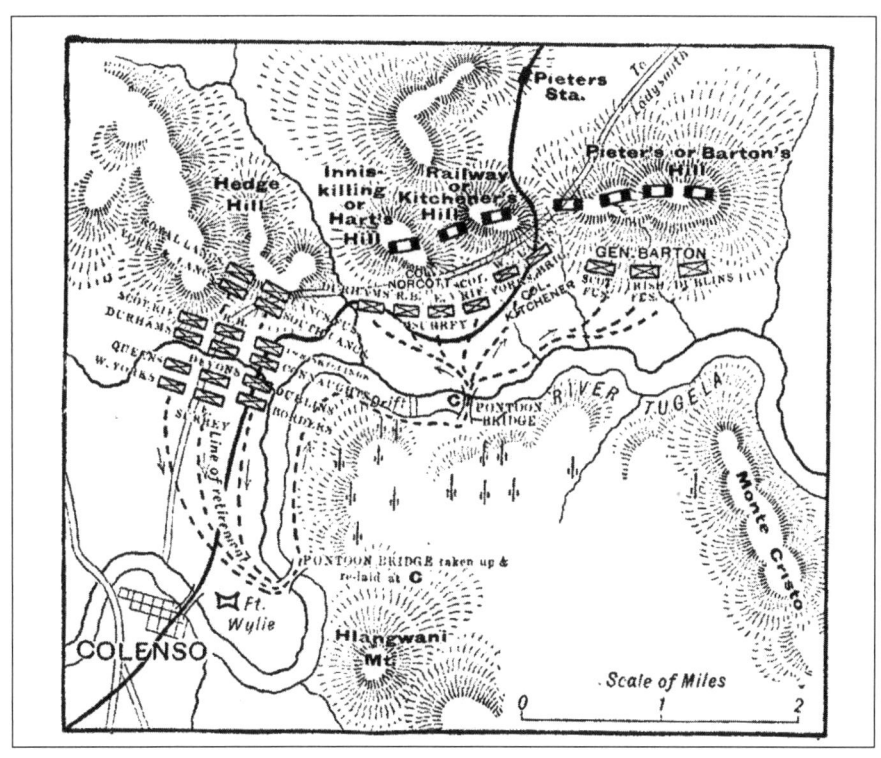

The Battle of Pieter's Hill. Plan of the final attack on the Boer positions north of the Tugela.

Buller, and most of his subordinates, were realising that in this new type of warfare there were no easy wins or solutions and certainly no short cuts to success. To counteract the superb defensive tactics, particularly those displayed by General Botha, a new system of offensive warfare was required. The effective use of artillery to support an infantry advance was being understood by artillery commanders such as Colonel Parsons, and Generals such as Hildyard. Whilst the inability to position the artillery at Vaal Krantz cost the British the initiative, it was becoming increasingly understood that the effective use of artillery would be critical. The use of a creeping barrage of artillery fire ahead of the advancing infantry would, it was felt, reduce the effectiveness of the defenders' fire. Battles would need to be considered as a series of interlocking events, spread over perhaps many days or even weeks. Infantry would have to display greater individual initiative and a better use of cover. Close order formation would have to be consigned to the history books. Somewhat miraculously, the understanding of this new type of offensive warfare came to fruition in Buller's next assault across the Tugela.

The key to Buller's next advance was to place the field artillery in a favourable position from which it could clearly and easily support an infantry advance. With this at the forefront of his thinking Buller turned his attention back towards Colenso and the hills occupied by the Boers on the south eastern side of the Tugela, on the British side of the river and within a great loop of it. The hills were specifically Hlangwane, Hussar Hill and Monte Cristo, the last of which rose over 350m above the surrounding plain. The Boer trenches spread across the two western hills, or kopjes, Hlangwane and Green Hill.

The first hill to be captured by the British was Hussar Hill, which was the forward ridge joining north to Green Hill. In the early hours of 14 February 1900 a small British raiding party seized Hussar Hill from a handful of Boer defenders. Over the following two days Buller placed thirty-four heavy guns on the summit, including a battery of 12pdrs. Despite accurate Boer artillery fire, which forced the British to construct redoubts around each of the guns, the British artillerymen, many of them from the Naval Brigade, were able to support the advancing British infantry. Men of Barton's and Hildyard's brigades moved forward under a blistering creeping barrage, or protective veil of exploding shells, to their respective targets. One by one the hills fell to the infantry, first Cingolo and then Green Hill until only Monte Cristo remained in Boer hands.

Throughout these sets of action the British upon Hussar Hill were subjected to accurate Boer fire. One piece in particular, located near Bloy's Farm, was particularly troublesome. Men of the Naval Brigade directed shells from their 6in guns and the third one scored a direct hit upon the Boer gun at a range of 16,500m![14] By Sunday, 18 February 1900 the struggle for Monte Cristo began. The hill was assaulted by Hildyard's 2nd Brigade, whilst simultaneously Barton's 6th Fusilier Brigade attacked the opposite ridge of Green Hill. Although the sound of the Boer's pom-poms filled the air, the British infantry advanced under the cover of a creeping barrage from Hussar Hill and suddenly a thin cheer rang out as the British claimed the summit.

Arriving at dawn the following morning, the men of the Naval Brigade, with help from men of the Devonshires, hauled the 12pdr battery up the challenging slopes of Monte Cristo and from there they were able to direct fire upon the Boer artillery pieces shelling Ladysmith. Later in the day, with a supreme effort, the 4.7in guns were manhandled up and within moments were also firing. British troops now strolled into Colenso without a shot being fired and the railhead was brought swiftly into action. Within a few hours trains were steaming into Colenso station bringing men and supplies and critically fresh shells for the artillery pieces now massing for one final push.

On 20 February Buller climbed to the top of Monte Cristo to survey his recently acquired gains. Ladysmith was tantalisingly close. With the capture of the hills the British were now masters of the south bank of the Tugela. With Monte Cristo in British hands the trench lines at Hlangwane had effectively been turned and had led to its capture. Overnight the Boers had fled across the river leaving many supplies behind and the British were able to install further artillery on this summit. The British were impressed by the Boer defences they found on Hlangwane. There were trenches, 5ft 6in deep, sometimes cut through solid rock, quite invisible from the front, and three rows of barbed wire running from tree to tree around the hill. Boulders added to the strength of the defence and, to make a noise if anyone tried to cross the wire, the wire was hung with jam-pots.[15] Indeed, if the British had not forced the Boer withdrawal by the capture of Monte Cristo, then the cost of having stormed Hlangwane would have been undoubtedly high.

Yet, despite this tactical victory the issue still remained that beyond the Tugela the terrain was dominated by high hills where the Boers were still entrenched in strong defensive positions. How to crack these last obstacles would see the British coordinating an infantry advance supported by a creeping barrage and would culminate in the relief of Ladysmith. Yet, this final victory was not to be a dramatic flourish but a series of movements over several days which again demonstrated that the Victorian battlefield had very much entered a new phase of twentieth-century warfare.

However, before the final victory Buller's troops would be further checked. On 22 February Major General Wynne's 11th Brigade and Major General Hart's Irish Brigade crossed over a pontoon bridge east of Colenso and began to advance north-eastwards. By the end of the day, troops of Wynne's Brigade had gained a foothold on the first of a pair of hills, which became known as Wynne's Hill. The following day Hart led his men across difficult terrain towards Hart's Hill. Unfortunately, the Boers here were very well entrenched which nullified the effects of the British artillery which was trying to support the advance. Even more unfortunate, Hart demonstrated that he had learnt nothing from the debacle of his advance at Colenso and he ordered his men to advance in columns of four, fully exposed to the rifle and artillery fire of the enemy's firing line in the hills above. Lieutenant Colonel Jourdain recorded, 'Hart ordered his men to march on with eyes front, leaving seven men smashed and dying at either side of the track as a single shell crashed down on sixteen men of E Company, Connaught Rangers.'[16] Lyttelton described Hart as 'a dangerous lunatic'.[17]

Men of the Connaughts and Inniskillings became stalled by accurate Boer rifle and artillery fire. Rather than wait for support from the Dubliners, Hart became impatient and sent company after company up the hill in what became a weak narrow attack which predictably not only failed but resulted in huge casualties. The Colonels of both the Dublins and the Inniskillings were killed, whilst the latter regiment lost 72 per cent of its officers and 27 per cent of its men. These were the highest losses of any regiment in the war.[18] Next morning the Irish Brigade, shattered and demoralised, drifted back towards the valley. For the wounded, left on the slopes of both Wynne's and Hart's Hills, two further days were spent without food, water or medical care. Finally a 6-hour armistice was agreed on Sunday, 25 February for stretcher bearers to provide help. Unfortunately, for many of the men, help came too late.

Buller and his Chief Intelligence Officer, Colonel A. Sandbach (1859–1928), now examined the topography of the gorge of the Tugela, and Sandbach was able to report that a second crossing point of the river, a mile or so downstream from the first pontoon, had been considered and thought possible. This position would offer the additional advantage in that once across the infantry could be ably supported by the artillery whilst at the same time they would have some shelter from the gorge which would hide them from the worst of the Boer fire as they assembled for an assault.

Buller now confirmed his plan for the final assault, set for 27 February, which was, by coincidence, the anniversary of the Battle of Majuba, the notorious British defeat of 1881 during the First Boer War. Buller decided upon an all-out offensive with three infantry brigades, supported by massed artillery. The three hills – Hart's Hill, Railway Hill and Pieter's Hill – which dominated the intended route to Ladysmith were the primary targets. Barton's 6th Brigade would take Pieter's Hill whilst the 11th Lancashire Brigade commanded by Walter Kitchener (1858–1912) was tasked with assaulting Railway Hill. On the left Major General Charles Norcott (1849–1931) with his 4th Brigade was to renew an attack upon Hart's and Wynne's Hills which, it was thought, would tie down the bulk of Botha's defenders.

In the early morning of 27 February 1900 Buller himself addressed the men of the Lancashire Regiment who had been tasked with the final assault upon Pieter's Hill. The moment was recorded in the diary of Lance Corporal Matthew Kelly of the 1st Battalion of the South Lancashire Regiment, as was the initial advance:

> Leave Hlangwane Hill and move down to River. General Buller addresses our Regt. And says he has decided to assault Pieters Hill. He says he knows our Regt. well and has decided to let them attack the central position. He points the hill out to us.
>
> Looking from where we are it appears to be a long flat hill on the far side of the Railway. On the right is a valley and a hill further on. On the left is Railway Hill. The Innerskillings lost 400 men trying to take it on the 23rd. Before we move off great joy is caused by our hearing the Cronje has surrendered at Paardeberg [Lord Roberts' forces had successfully surrounded the main Boer forced commanded by Cronje].
>
> Buller tells us to do our best and remember Majuba of which this day is the anniversary. We move off and cross the Tugela below the waterfall. Halt for half an hour. Move along the banks of the river and on the way pass a signpost on which is written 'The Road to Hell'. It is supposed to have been written by one of the wounded Inniskillings. We climb the high banks, sight the Railway alongside which we halt. Then the order is received to advance in two lines A.B.C.D. first line, E.F.G.H. second line. First line moves off. We reach the railway, scramble through the barbed wire and cross the rails to have to cross another lot of barbed wire. All this time the Boers are pouring it in us hot as they can and as we have 95 guns in action the uproar is deafening. But somehow we get through the wire and make for the valley between the hill.[19]

Similarly, Private Neligan recorded that at the start of the assault:

> Everyman carried 200 rounds of ammunition. About 7.30am, the battle was opened by an Artillery duel, our Naval Guns doing grand work in the enemy's trenches. News of Cronje's surrender reached the troops – 'Such shouting and cheering I never heard before. Strong men wept of joy, chums shook

hands with each other, the bluejackets ceased firing for the moment and commenced to dance the sailor's hornpipe around their guns. The infantry stood up and cheered again and again; some threw, whilst others kicked their helmets in the air, and everywhere could be seen manifestations of joy at the good news, which seemed to make all ranks, from the General downwards, only too eager to get at the foe.[20]

By 9am the bulk of forces had crossed the Tugela over the second pontoon, ably supported by a constant rolling of thunder from the British artillery placed on Monte Cristo and Naval Hill. Botha had apparently thought the crossing by the second pontoon and the terrain would be too difficult for the British infantry so the Boer left flank at Pieter's Hill was lightly defended. For the first time Colonel Parsons and his artillerymen could, from their advanced and heightened positions, cover the infantry attack across the river with converging fire. Skimming over the heads of the advancing infantry and landing just 100yd ahead of them, a creeping curtain of fire made the ground in front of the attackers shake and rocks and earth and shrapnel rise into the sky. Into this maelstrom the infantry moved only to see the curtain lift and advance in front of them. Barton's Hill was swept with artillery from both Monte Cristo and the Hlangwane spur and this made the Boer position there untenable. In addition to this 'curtain of fire', the naval gunners, manning their 4.7in pieces, were particularly adept at neutralising Boer firing positions. On one occasion a naval gun, firing from Gun Hill, placed three shells in quick succession into a Boer gun pit at a range of 9,000m, destroying both the enemy gun and its crew.[21]

Earlier in the day Buller had watched the three brigades cross the pontoon but then vanish down a gorge to the right. At around midday, having taken Barton's Hill, the infantry reappeared as small dots some 2 miles away on the first kopje of the Pieter's plateau. However, as the British advanced further, the British gunners struggled with the distance now between the two forces, and the artillery support slackened. Botha had now realised that Pieter's Hill was the main target and he threw as many reinforcements as could be found to stop the British turning his flank. By 2.30pm the increased Boer fire from the northern kopje of Pieter's, combined with a raking fire from the Boers still entrenched on Railway Hill, had stalled the advance. However, within a few minutes men of Kitchener's Brigade could be seen moving from rock to rock on Railway Hill. Men of the West Yorkshires and South Lancashires moving swiftly and in open skirmish order succeeded where Hart's Irishmen, constrained by their rigid formations, had failed. With fixed bayonets they won the spur of ground between Railway Hill and Hart's Hill to the left. On reaching the Boer trenches Lance Corporal Matthew Kelly recorded that many of the Boer dead were a yellow colour, killed by the shock of lyddite.

Now only remained the eastern positions of the Boer line centred on Pieter's Hill itself, and here the men of Norcott's 4th Brigade fanned out ready for the final assault. The naval guns now concentrated their efforts on the summit. Captain Limpus, of HMS *Terrible* wrote:

> The shells burst seemed almost continuous, lyddite and shrapnel throwing up earth and stones at each trench. The bombardment was now terrible, especially at a little mischievous entrenched kopje near the top of the nek; several times the Boers had to be brought back by a determined man who seemed to be in charge, until he himself disappeared in a great Lyddite shell-burst – and that trench was silenced.[22]

E Company of the Lancashire Regiment was then called to the front with orders to cover the advance of the rest of the Battalion by firing, with maxim guns and rifles, at the Boers in the trenches on the slopes. E Company having taken up their position, the rest of the Regiment began their attack on Pieter's Hill. At a given signal, they rose up, crossed the embankment in widely dispersed lines and charged up the hill with fixed bayonets. Their advance was aided by the fire from the guns on Monte Cristo and Hlangwane.

Private Neligan wrote of the attack:

> About 4 pm, the grass within three hundred yards of the enemy's position had caught fire from the blazing of the Lyddite shells, and the khaki clad figures showed up most prominently against the dark and sombre back-ground. When about two hundred and fifty yards from the main position the firing was terrible, and the bullets came so thick that my regiment attempted to take cover behind a small rise in the ground, but this proved to be quite inadequate for the purpose. Seeing this the commanding officer gave the order to 'fix bayonets and charge' saying at this time, 'Remember, men, the eyes of Lancashire are watching you to-day!'
>
> At his words the whole regiment rose like one man, and the black slope fairly twinkled with the glitter of the

bayonets as they flashed in the sun. Like a wall of rock the gallant 40th closed upon their foe, and the best disciplined troops in the wide world could not have withstood that irresistible rush.[23]

Deneys Reitz, a 17-year-old Boer Commando, arrived to reinforce Pieter's Hill just as the British attacked and survived to record his experiences:

> As we went along a bombardment more violent than that of yesterday broke out ahead of us, and when we came to the rear of the Heights we saw the ridge on which lay the Bethal men (and our own) going up in smoke and flame. It was an alarming sight. The British batteries were so concentrating on the crest that it was invisible under the clouds of flying earth and fumes, while the volume of sound was beyond anything that I have ever heard. At intervals the curtain lifted, letting us catch a glimpse of the trenches above, but we could see no sign of movement, nor could we hear whether the men up there were still firing, for the din of the guns drowned all lesser sounds. We reined in about four hundred yards from the foot of the hill at a loss what to do; to approach our men through the inferno was to court destruction, while not to try seemed like desertion. For a minute or two we debated, and then, suddenly, the gun fire ceased, and for a space we caught the fierce rattle of Mauser rifles, followed by the British infantry swarming over the skyline, their bayonets flashing in the sun. Shouts and cries reached us, and we could see men desperately thrusting and clubbing. The rout of burghers broke back from the hill streaming towards us in disorderly flight. The soldiers fired into them, bringing many down as they ran blindly past us, not looking to right or left. We went too, for the troops, cheering loudly, came shouting and running down the slope.[24]

The literary giant Sir Arthur Conan Doyle wrote in his work, *The Great Boer War*, of the moment of victory, 'The Boer fire lulls, it ceases – they are running! Wild hat-waving men upon the Hlangwane uplands see the silhouette of the active figures of the stormers along the skyline and know that the position is theirs. Exultant soldiers dance and cheer . . .'[25]

The Boer centre and left had been turned and the way to Ladysmith had been opened. Those watching across the Tugela at the battle in front of them were jubilant, Buller amongst them. Although history has been rather unkind to Buller's reputation, and indeed there are definite areas over which he can be criticised, he does deserve credit for constantly thinking about how he was to overcome the problem that he faced; that being how to breach the Boer defensive line and so relieve Ladysmith. His ultimate success can perhaps be considered to have been as a result of his concern for his men. At Colenso, Spion Kop and Vaal Krantz Buller decided against funnelling more men into a lost cause, despite the urging of many of his subordinates. His final successful advance at Pieter's Hill can be viewed as one in which he had learnt from his errors, had finally appreciated and understood the role of artillery and above all wished to use tactics that reduced the number of casualties amongst his fighting men.

One observer amongst Buller's staff wrote:

> Surely nothing as beautiful was ever seen as the advance . . . The bursting lyddite clothed the summit with a yellow veil; through this flashed the exploding shrapnel, and up and in through the smoke advanced a stately line of infantry, without a pause, until they had command of the kopje, and drove the enemy forever from the banks of the Tugela.[26]

Ladysmith was finally relieved after 112 days when mounted troops rode into town. The war itself would now move away from pitch battles to one of guerrilla warfare by the Boers and counter-insurgency tactics from the British which would be revolutionary in their approach, although not always of the highest moral code. The use of concentration camps to imprison Boer families in unsanitary conditions resulted in the deaths of over 25,000 Boer women and children and received worldwide condemnation. Peace would not be secured until 31 May 1902 with the signing of the Treaty of Vereeniging.

Despite the revolutionary and successful tactics introduced by Buller at Pieter's Hill, the man himself was to receive little credit. Indeed, a move soon started to denounce Buller and blame him for many of the failings of late 1899. The likes of Spenser Wilkinson of the *Morning Post* and Leo Amery, *The Times*'s chief correspondent, who would write an influential history of the Boer War, led the way amongst the newspaper men, whilst Ian Hamilton was perhaps Buller's most ardent critic within the serving military. However, few men realised the difficulties faced by Buller; the terrain over which he fought, the lack of quality subordinates and the need to learn fast and to adopt new tactics, to name just three. The last words regarding what the British had achieved at Pieter's Hill can be left to General Henry Rawlinson (1864–1925), who during the First World War was to be the chief proponent of the rolling barrage on the Western Front. At first as critical of Buller as Hamilton had been, Rawlinson later travelled over the ground which the British had fought to relieve Ladysmith and wrote in his diary, 'Most interesting – it was marvellous they got through at all . . .'.[27]

Conclusion – Lessons Forgotten

> The proper use of cover, of infantry advancing in rushes, co-ordinated in turn with creeping barrages of artillery: these were the tactics of truly modern war, first evolved by Buller in Natal.
>
> T. Pakenham, *The Boer War*

The argument of some historians, such as Thomas Pakenham, is that modern warfare, arguably first seen in the British Army at the Battle of Pieter's Hill, is a product of the Boer War. This is a view that was also expressed by contemporary witnesses. Soon after experiencing this new type of warfare Winston Churchill wrote:

> Personally, I am convinced that future warfare will be to the few, by which I mean that to escape annihilation soldiers will have to fight in widely dispersed formations, when they will have to think for themselves, and when each must be to a great extent his own general; and with regard to artillery, it appears that the advantages of defensive action, range, concealment, and individual initiative may easily counterbalance numbers and discipline.[1]

Churchill's opinion was shared by the military thinker Colonel G.F.R. Henderson who, writing soon after the conclusion of the Boer war, stated that:

> The success for this fourth attempt [Buller's attack at Pieter's Hill to break the siege of Ladysmith] was mainly due to a change in military tactics to a more modern concept that is seen thereafter; the Artillery located behind the infantry, shelling the areas in front to clear the way ahead. In addition, the infantry were permitted to fight as individuals, taking

cover where they could and selecting their targets rather than being forced ahead as 'cannon fodder' as they had been in the past.[2]

Even in the early weeks of the Boer War there was a realisation amongst some commentators that the war would alter warfare completely. For example, on 13 December 1899 Maurice Brett, the future Lord Esher, received a letter from Sir Francis Mowatt, a senior civil servant, indicating that 'this war will do two things – change our whole military system in England, and alter military tactics throughout the world'.[3] Yet, despite some very obvious lessons from the war it was not the British that led the debate as to the future of warfare. There were several reasons for this but perhaps at the heart of the issue was that there had never been a culture of intellectual thought and debate within British military circles. For example, in 1900 Germany produced 50 per cent of the world's military literature, France 25 per cent and Britain just 1 per cent.[4] After the war much critical literature was published which focused on the failings of the British in South Africa, however not much of it was constructive criticism. Undoubtedly the most widely read was *The Times History of the Boer War*, written by the paper's war correspondent, Leo Amery, who was particularly damming of Buller's record.

Lord Esher was charged to chair a Commission to look at some of the lessons that could be learnt from the war and statements were taken from those that had been at the heart of the conflict. The Commission took evidence in private and focused on the army organisation and administration as well as the inefficiencies that had been found during the war. The Esher Report was published in 1904 and as Britain's main official response to the performance of its army it undoubtedly missed an opportunity to consider a doctrine for how the British Army would fight future conflicts. Instead, the Report focused on organisational changes. The position of Commander-in-Chief was abolished and a General Staff created with three distinct Directors with responsibility for military operations, staff duties and military training. The War Office was also to be radically reformed with a division of duties shared between the Chief of the General Staff, the Adjutant General, the Quartermaster General and the Master General of Ordnance. The Report's recommendations were implemented throughout the army and emphasis was given to the commanders of field units to train for war.

Critically, although the Esher Report did address many of the administrative inefficiencies of the army, which would ensure that the

British Expedition Force of 1914 was despatched efficiently to France, it did not provide a doctrine for future warfare. There were no suggestions as to attacking, or defensive, formations or dispositions and no considered thought as to how to address the issue of cooperation between the infantry and artillery in future wars. Whilst the lack of formal guidelines can be criticised, there are a number of reasons why the British Army, after the painful lessons of the Boer War, did not lead the debate on the future of warfare.

As has already been considered, there was a genuine lack of intellectual debate amongst the British military and this can perhaps be explained by the very nature of the army itself. The Royal Navy was still very much considered to be the pride of British military might, and it took the majority of the defence budget. Army finances were always under pressure during the period from 1902–14 and just when the army needed to have the funds for increased expenditure on practice ammunition, whether bullet or shell, or funds for regular full-scale training manoeuvres, monies were denied in the amounts required. In addition, the army had the issue of having to regularly supply troops to India which placed a huge drain on the Home Army and the battalion system. Linked to this was the perceived observation that the army was still viewed as something of a colonial policing force which saw men and resources diverted all over the world. Finally, compared with the armies of France, Russia and Germany, the British Army was small and, with conflicting demands on its limited manpower, thinly stretched.

Those training manuals that were issued to the British Army after the Boer War can be viewed as advisory and certainly not as a doctrine. Infantry Training Manual 1905 stated:

> It is impossible to lay down a fixed and unvarying system of attack or defence. Although such system might appear capable of modification to meet different conditions, yet constant practice in a stereotypical formation inevitably leads to want of elasticity, accustoms all ranks to work by rule rather than by the exercise of their wits and cramps both initiative and intelligence...[5]

In the Combined Training Manual, also issued in 1905, the lessons of the Boer War were embodied and summed up in the following paragraph:

> Mounted troops and infantry compel the enemy to disclose his position and thereby afford a target to the artillery, whilst

the latter by their fire enable infantry to approach the hostile position. Infantry, unaccompanied by mounted troops, is hampered by ignorance of the enemy's movements, cannot move in security, and is unable to reap the fruits of victory; unaccompanied by artillery, it is unable to fire beyond rifle range, and is generally powerless against entrenchments . . .[6]

Combined Training urged officers to gain knowledge of the principles of the other arms and this view was reinforced in the Field Service Regulations of 1909 with the phrase, 'The full power of an army can be exerted only when all its parts act in close combination.'[7] Although urging closer cooperation, these regulation manuals were far from producing a firm doctrine, nor did they suggest a systematic way in which closer cooperation could be achieved. This was highlighted in 1912 by the inspector general of forces who noted that the 2nd, 3rd and 4th Divisions each had a preferred method of attack which differed markedly. The inspector general commented that the army had failed to achieve 'anything approaching uniformity of practice, which is so divergent in different divisions that it would be difficult for them to combine into an army that acts with full effect'.[8]

It is, therefore, perhaps not surprising that the debate on the future of warfare was driven by other armies than the British and by the experiences from other conflicts in the immediate post-Boer War period. Although the experiences of the Boer War provoked a discussion across the armies of the world on how to attack successfully at a time when machine guns, magazine rifles, artillery and entrenchments were becoming common place, the conclusions drawn were perhaps rather surprising.

Whilst the evidence from numerous Boer battles was that advancing into the 'fire zone' produced by modern weapons would be costly, if not suicidal, there still remained an emphasis on the offensive as the way to achieve an ultimate victory. This view gradually began to dominate military thinking as the respect for modern firepower eroded as time passed. Historians, such as Spencer Jones and Tim Travers, have used the phrase 'the primacy of the offensive' or the 'unofficial cult of the offensive' to describe this thinking which was to dominate the outlook of both the French and German armies.[9]

The central thinking behind the 'cult of the offensive' was fundamentally flawed. Whilst the fact that new weaponry had transformed the battlefield to a huge degree was largely accepted, many also felt that the lessons from the Boer war were abnormal, due to the unique conditions there. These included wide open spaces and the unusual atmospheric conditions that allowed bullets and shells to travel longer distances. So it was thought by some that to place too much emphasis on the lessons from the war would be to undermine the future thinking of offensive strategy. It was considered that future wars would see high losses but that eventually sheer weight of numbers would always succeed against a defensive strategy. Both the soldier and the civilian would have to be prepared for high battlefield casualties and thus both would have to display a high level of discipline, as well as a lofty sense of self within a nation which was prepared for sacrifice.

Much of this flawed offensive strategy was taken from the example of the Russo-Japanese War of 1904–5, fought between the two empires of Russia and Japan over their imperial ambitions in Manchuria and Korea. Although there were numerous naval conflicts, the major theatres of land operations were the Liadong Peninsula and Mukden in Southern Manchuria. Both armies had modern magazine rifles, artillery and machine guns and the nature of the brutal warfare was a foretaste of the battles of the Western Front. During the conflict the Russians largely adopted a defensive posture, with their troops fighting behind earthworks against waves of Japanese attacks. The Japanese were frequently forced to move under cover of darkness to approach the Russian positions and the 'fire zone' was even more deadly than that experienced in South Africa for both sides had large quantities of artillery and machine guns. Despite often horrendous casualty figures amongst the attackers, the Japanese were largely successful in their assaults. This fact seems to have resulted in misplaced lessons. Whilst at the tactical level the Japanese had demonstrated that although a night advance could reduce casualties, crossing the 'fire zone' would inevitably be costly. Yet, at the strategic level the ultimate Japanese success indicated that a powerful offensive would, eventually, overcome a passive defensive, even if the defenders possessed a numerical advantage and strong field works.

The fact that the Japanese had won the war with an offensive strategy led some observers to believe that this was a vindication of the power of the attack. Although many tactical observers, such as Ian Hamilton, had placed emphasis on the Japanese use of close artillery support and entrenchment this was sometimes lost to the belief that morale and willpower had ultimately been the deciding factors in the Japanese success. The Japanese warrior spirit of Bushido had, it was believed by some, been the difference between the protagonists, and even the Russian Commander, General Kuropatkin (1848–1925), wrote after the war that 'our moral strength was less than that of the Japanese . . . This lack of martial spirit, of moral exaltation, and of heroic impulse, affected particularly our stubbornness in battle. In many cases we did not have sufficient resolution to conquer such antagonists as the Japanese'.[10]

This belief that moral strength in the offensive, as seen in the Japanese, could overcome the 'fire zone' again led to lessons from the Boer War being lost to some in the British Army. In Europe the British tactics of flanking movements, as employed by Lord Roberts against Cronje, in the Boer War had largely been viewed in a negative light. Major William Balck of the German Army claimed that the Japanese had succeeded because they had spurned the British tactics and had 'pushed doggedly forward like angry bull dogs, never halting, until, bleeding and exhausted, they had fastened themselves on the enemy and won the victory'.[11] Such views became more widely held throughout Europe, particularly in France, and began a resurgence in the belief that morale, training and martial spirit could overcome defensive positions.

Within the British Army the Japanese victory was not viewed in the same way or degree as it was elsewhere, but the apparent success of the offensive spirit did serve to dilute some of the lessons from the Boer War, particularly that associated with the ability of determined troops to cross the 'fire zone'. There was a slight change in wording between *Combined Training*, 1905, and the *Field Service Regulations*, 1909, which saw a new emphasis placed upon the final assault and similarly the stress placed upon flank attacks in the previous manuals was altered to underline the need to find weak spots in the enemy's defences and delivering a decisive assault there. If nothing else these subtle shifts increased the level of confusion as to the best way to ensure a successful offensive and did nothing to help the establishment of a doctrine within the British Army. Indeed, there was still a great emphasis on overwhelming firepower, fire by volley and concentration of fire at ranges of 450m, as compared, for example, with 600–1,000m for the German Army.[12]

At its most extreme the dilution of the lessons from the Boer War saw some senior British Generals and commentators even returning to the view that the use of the bayonet was the key to a successful offensive. This was seen at the 1910 General Staff Conference when Brigadier General Lancelot Kiggell offered the opinion that:

> After the Boer War the general opinion was that the result of the battle would for the future depend on fire-arms alone, and

that the sword and the bayonet were played out. But this idea is erroneous and was proved so in the late war in Manchuria [Russo-Japanese War] . . . Victory is won actually by the bayonet, or by the fear of it, which amounts to the same thing so far as the conduct of the attack is concerned. This fact was proved beyond doubt in the late war [Russo-Japanese War]. I think the whole question rather hangs on that; and if we accept the view that victory is actually won by the bayonet, it settles the point.[13]

This quote can be viewed as an example of some of the archaic thinking amongst senior British officers, yet it was part of a wider debate on the use of firepower to facilitate movement in an offensive and should thus be viewed in that context. Kiggell was widely criticised by other attendees at the conference. His comments do at least illustrate some of the confused thinking present at senior levels of the army at this time.

The lack of a firm doctrine within the British Army as to the offensive, and the confusion and uncertainty this created, was perhaps most felt in the area of cooperation and coordination between the infantry and the artillery. The relationship, even after the Boer War, was never strong, even despite the encouragement of senior officers such as Ian Hamilton who, at the Southern Command, pioneered the secondment of infantry and artillery officers to each other's units. By 1913 cooperation at manoeuvres had improved, although the inspector general reported that more needed to be done. The British emphasis on flexibility in the offensive did, unfortunately, mean that the artillery had no systematic approach to providing infantry support. The result was that the success of the artillery/infantry coordination depended to a large extent on the enlightenment of individual artillery officers which, although providing some localised successes in the early years of the First World War, produced flaws across the large battlefields of the Western Front.

However, the Royal Artillery should not be criticised too severely for its performance during 1914–16. The tactics of concealment, accurate long-range fire and cooperation with the infantry were widely understood. These lessons had been learnt in the Boer War and reinforced by the experiences of the Russo-Japanese War. It was the lack of artillery pieces, insufficient resources for regular large-scale manoeuvres so as to reinforce these beliefs, and the absence of a formal doctrine which hampered performance in the early stages of the First World War.

Despite the lack of a formal doctrine and the blurring of the lessons from the Boer War, there is no doubt that against overwhelming numbers, in the first months of the First World War the British Army performed well against their German adversaries. In contrast the British were aided and the Germans hampered by the latter's focus on operations and grand offensive plans that had been laid down in the years proceeding the war. This thinking was at the expense of tactical awareness and was perhaps most vividly demonstrated at the First Battle of Mons (23 August 1914) and the First Battle of Ypres (19 October–22 November 1914), when, to the amazement of the British, the German infantry advanced in close order formation and suffered dreadful casualties at the hands of the British Lee–Enfield rifle. However, the small size of the British Army, combined with a lack of formal doctrine, meant that when, by the end of 1914, this army had been effectively annihilated by high battlefield casualties much of the lessons learnt from previous conflicts was lost. It would take the British two more painful years of bloodshed to again really understand and appreciate these lessons as they struggled to rebuild their army.

Some enlightened thinkers, such as J.F.C. Fuller, wrote, as early as November 1914, that the key to battlefield success in the First World War was the employment of infantry to penetrate the enemy's lines with support from quick-firing artillery and machine guns. In contrast, there existed a belief that artillery was only an auxiliary to the battlefield and that it was the infantry that won the offensive. Regrettably this seems to have been the view held by Field Marshal Douglas Haig (1861–1928), Commander of the British Forces, who struggled to see the infantry and the artillery as an equal arm.

In comparing the experiences of the First World War and Victorian colonial warfare Daniel Headrick has written:

> The soldier going over the top of a Flanders trench was as vulnerable as any Dervish warrior. The surprise of World War One was that the offensive had become suicidal, that vigour, élan vital, courage, espirt de corps, and all the other presumed virtues of the European fighting man were irrelevant against the hail of bullets from these same rifles and machine guns. The effect of modern infantry weapons on the battlefields of Europe was quite the opposite of what it had been in Africa. Instead of bringing about the quick and easy access the European powers had become used to, the new firearms made victory impossible.[14]

Not until the Allied forces rebuilt their armies and remembered the lessons from the Boer War did the offensive once again became possible. Tragically many were to die before this was to happen.

Victoria's reign witnessed a technological advance in battlefield weaponry which was unparalleled in human history, before or since. It is perhaps only in recent years with the developments of drones, robots and cruise missiles that the battlefield has altered to a similar extent. From the start of Victoria's reign in 1837, when the bayonet still decided the success of an offensive, to the end in 1901, when artillery firing from hidden positions could eliminate enemy positions many miles away, technological advances altered completely the size and nature of the battlefield. Commanders were sometimes slow to understand and appreciate these changes and it was the British soldier that paid the price when this happened. Yet, ultimately, the British prevailed and this is surely a reflection not just of British industrial strength but also of the skill, bravery and tenacity of the Victorian soldier.

Notes

Introduction
1. N. Ferguson, *Empire How Britain Made the Modern World* (Allen Lane, 2003), p. xi.
2. H. Strachan, *From Waterloo to Balaclava – Tactics, Technology and the British Army, 1815–54* (Cambridge University Press, 1985).
3. B.M. Add MSS 49107, f20, C. Napier to Robertson, 29 October 1838.
4. D.F. Harding, *Small arms of the East India Company 1600–1856*, 4 vols (Foresight Books, 1999).
5. D. Headrick, *The Tools of Empire – Technology and European Imperialism in the Nineteenth Century* (Oxford University Press, New York, 1981). D. Headrick, *Power Over Peoples – Technology, Environments and Western Imperialism, 1400 to the Present* (Princeton University Press, 2010).
6. Headrick (2010), p. 257.
7. Headrick (1981), p. 101.
8. H. Bailes, 'Technology and Imperialism – A Case Study of the Victorian Army in Africa', *Victorian Studies*, 24 (1980), pp. 83–104, 85.
9. Colonel Sir Charles Callwell, *Small Wars: Their Principles and Practice* (1st edn, HMSO, 1896), p. 21.
10. Lieutenant R. da Costa Porter, 'Warfare against Uncivilised Races', Professional Papers 6 (1881), pp. 305–60 and Colonel J.C. Gawler, 'British Troops and Savage Warfare', *Journal of the Royal United Services Institution*, 17 (1873).
11. H. Bailes, 'Technology and Tactics in the British Army', in R. Haycock and K. Neilson (eds), *Men, Machines and War* (Wilfrid Laurier University Press, Waterloo, Ontario, 1988), p. 35.
12. Hansard Parliamentary Debate, 3rd ser., 338 (1889), col. 989; and 349 (1891), cols 1631–84 (debate on new rifle).
13. O. Figes, *Crimea – The Last Crusade* (Allen Lane, 2010), p. 210.
14. L. Amery (ed.), *The Times History of the War in South Africa*, 7 vols (Sampson and Low, 1900–9), Vol. II, p. 40.
15. Bailes (1980), p. 87.
16. J.F.C. Fuller, *Armament and History – A Study of the Influence of Armament on History* (Eyre & Spottiswoode, 1946), p. 122.
17. Bailes (1988), p. 23.
18. W. Churchill, *The River War: An account of the Reconquest of the Sudan* (Carroll & Graf, New York, re-issue, 2000), p. 300.
19. E. Spiers, *The Late Victorian Army, 1868–1902* (Manchester University Press, 1992), p. 315.

Chapter One
1. D. Chandler, *Waterloo the Hundred Days* (George Philip, 1980), p. 172.
2. Harding, Vol. III, p. 275.
3. Wolseley, Field Marshal Viscount Wolseley, *The Story of a Soldier's Life*, 2 vols (Archibald Constable & Co., 1903), p. 80.
4. B. Farwell, *Eminent Victorian Soldiers – Seekers of Glory* (Viking, 1985), p. 24.
5. D. Featherstone, *Weapons and Equipment of the Victorian Soldier* (Blandford Press, Poole, 1978), p. 35.
6. B.S. Nijjar, *Anglo-Sikh Wars* (K.B. Publications, New Delhi, 1976), p. 2.
7. P. Duckers, *British Military Rifles* (Shire Books, Princes Risborough, 2005), p. 11.
8. Harding, Vol. III, p. 237.

9. Duckers, p. 15.
10. H. Woodend, *Catalogue of the Enfield Pattern Room British Rifles* (HMSO, 1981), p. 2.
11. Harding, Vol. IV, pp. 515–17.
12. Harding, Vol. III, p. 303.
13. Ibid., pp. 510–11.
14. OIOC: P/41/51, IMP No. 175 of 22 Sep 1849, BIMB Report 1847–48, paras 384–6. (NB: BIMB – Bengal Imperial Military Board Report; OIOC – British Library, Oriental and India Office Collections, London).
15. OIOC: P/41/51, IMP No. 175 of 22 Sep 1849, BIMB Report 1847-8, 'Extract from a Memorandum from Lieutenant Colonel J.T. Boileua of Engineers, dated Simla 19th May 1846.
16. Harding, Vol. III, p. 513.
17. OIOC: P/40/37, IMP No.7 of 21 May 1847, Adjutant General's ltr No. 315 dated 9 April 1847. (NB: IMP – India Military Proceedings).
18. D. Featherstone, *At them with the Bayonet – The First Anglo-Sikh War 1845–6* (Leonaur, repr. 2007), p. 143.
19. H. Bolitho, *The Galloping Third – The story of the 3rd King's Own Hussars* (John Murray, 1963), p. 158.
20. Featherstone (2007), p. 167.
21. A.S. Sidhu, *The First Anglo-Sikh War* (Amberley Publishing, Stroud, 2010), p. 36.
22. Ibid., p. 63.
23. Ibid., p. 69.
24. Ibid., p. 70.
25. Featherstone (2007), p. 178.
26. Letter 2/Lieutenant Thomas Haydon to his mother, dated 21 February 1846, NAM 1987-11-49.
27. G. Bruce, *Six Battles for India: The Anglo-Sikh Wars 1845–6, 1848–9* (Arthur Baker, 1969), p. 183.
28. Sidhu, p. 155.
29. Featherstone (2007), p. 181.
30. Sidhu, p. 157.
31. Bruce, p. 185.
32. C. Allan, *Soldier Sahibs – The Men Who Made the North-West Frontier* (John Murray, 2000), p. 62.
33. Sir H. Smith, *Autobiography* (John Murray, 1901), p. 192.
34. J.W. Baldwin, *A Norfolk Soldier in the 1st Sikh War* (Leonaur repr., 2005), pp. 55–6.
35. R. Burford, *The Battle of Sobroan* (George Nichols, 1846), p. 9.
36. Letter Pvt. R. Perkes to family, undated, NAM 7505-57.
37. G. Bruce, p. 190.
38. Smith (1902), p. 194.
39. R.S. Rait, *The Life and Campaigns of Hugh First Viscount Gough Field Marshal*, Vol. II, (Constable, 1903), pp. 76–7.

Chapter Two

1. D. Headrick, 'The Tools of Imperialism: Technology and the Expansion of European Colonial Empire in the Nineteenth Century', *The Journal of Modern History*, Vol. 51, No. 2 (June 1979), p. 250.
2. H. Raugh, Jr. *The Victorians at War, 1815–1914 – An Encyclopaedia of British Military History* (Clio, Oxford, 2004), p. 182.
3. M. Barthorp, *Heroes of the Crimea – The Battles of Balaclava and Inkerman* (Blandford, Poole, 1991), p. 14.
4. B. Wilson, *Heyday: Britain and the Birth of the Modern World* (Weidenfeld & Nicolson, 2016), pp. 14–15.
5. P. Smithurst, *The Pattern 1853 Enfield Rifle* (Osprey Publishing, Oxford, 2011), p. 14.
6. Featherstone (1978), p. 17.
7. H.O. Mansfield, *Charles Ashe Windham – A Norfolk Soldier Soldier (1810–1870)* (Terence Dalton, Lavenham, 1973), p. 79.
8. QLRM 962A, 47th Regimental Letters.
9. S. David, *Victoria's Wars* (Viking, 2006), p. 188.

10. Mansfield, p. 86.
11. F. Myatt, *The British Infantry 1660–1945 – The Evolution of a Fighting Force* (Blandford Press, Poole, 1983), p. 114.
12. J. Spilsbury, *The Thin Red Line* (Weidenfeld & Nicolson, 2005), p. 89.
13. Ibid., p. 88.
14. O. Wheeler, *The War Office Past & Present* (Methuen, 1914), p. 136.
15. C. Woodham-Smith, *The Reason Why* (Constable, 1953), p. 223.
16. Figes, p. 244.
17. T. Royle, *Crimea – The Great Crimean War 1854–56* (Little Brown, 1999), p. 268.
18. Spilsbury, p. 147.
19. Smithurst, p. 33.
20. LIM Archive Box 14a.
21. R. Chapman (ed.), *Echoes from the Crimea* (The Green Howard's Museum, Richmond, 2004), p. 155.
22. Ibid., p. 156.
23. Spilbury, p. 198.
24. LIM Archive Box 14A Farren Letters No. 5, 7 November 1854.
25. NAM 6706-30.
26. Figes, p. 269.
27. Royle, p. 290.
28. A. Lambert, *The Crimean War. British Grand Strategy Against Russia, 1853–56* (Manchester University Press, 1991), p. 344.
29. Figes, p. 215.
30. Wilson (2016), p. 172.
31. Smithurst, p. 32.
32. Ibid., p. 33.
33. Myatt (1983), p. 116.
34. Ibid., p. 115.
35. Spilsbury, p. 266.
36. Smithurst, p. 32.
37. Ibid., p. 37.
38. Ibid., p. 46.
39. Ibid., p. 48.
40. A. Massie, *The National Army Museum Book of the Crimea War* (Sidgwick & Jackson, 2004), p. 254.
41. Wilson (2016), p. 283.

Chapter Three

1. R. Haycock and K. Neilson (eds), *Men, Machines and War* (Wilfrid Laurier University Press, Waterloo, Ontario, 1988), p. 23.
2. Headrick (June 1979), pp. 231–63, 249.
3. J. Black, *Tools of War – The Weapons that Changed the World* (Quercus, 2007), p. 111.
4. Ibid., p. 112.
5. Ibid., p. 123.
6. Raugh (2004), p. 183.
7. Black (2007), p. 98.
8. I. Skennerton, *A Treatise on the Snider – The British Soldier's Firearm 1866–c.1880* (Hollingsworth & Moss, Leeds, 1977), pp. 85–6.
9. E. Wallis Budge, *A History of Ethiopia: Volume II* (Routledge, 2014), p. 510.
10. P. Smith, *Victoria's Victories* (Spellmount, Tunbridge Wells, 1987), p. 110.
11. F. Myatt, *The March to Magdala* (Leo Cooper, 1970), p. 140.
12. B. Bond (ed.), *Victorian Military Campaigns* (Hutchinson, 1967), p. 140.
13. I. Knight, *Go to Your God Like a Soldier* (Greenhill Books, 1996), p. 97.
14. Smith (1987), p. 118.
15. E. Wood, *From Midshipman to Field Marshal: Vol. I* (Methuen, 1906), p. 265.
16. S. Manning, *Evelyn Wood V.C., Pillar of Empire* (Pen & Sword, Barnsley, 2007) p. 78.
17. Bond, p. 189.
18. Colonel E. Wood, 'The Ashanti Expedition of 1873–4', *Journal of the Royal United Services Institution*, Vol. XVII (June 1874), p. 351.

19. Wolseley (1903), p. 338.
20. H. Brackenbury, *The Ashanti War of 1873–4*, Vol. 2 (Frank Cass, repr. 1968), pp. 157–8.
21. J. Lehmann, *All Sir Garnet: A Life of Field-Marshal Lord Wolseley* (Jonathan Cape, 1964), p. 185.
22. A. Lloyd, *The Drums of Kumasi – The Story of the Ashanti Wars* (Longman, 1964), p. 128.
23. Bond, p. 191.
24. Lloyd, p. 130.
25. E. Spiers, *The Scottish Soldier and Empire 1854–1902* (Edinburgh University Press, 2006), p. 31.
26. Lloyd, p. 131.
27. Hove Wolseley MSS, W/P4/7, 1 February 1874.
28. NAM 2007-07-32.
29. J. Strawson, *Beggars in Red: The British Army 1789–1889* (Pen & Sword, Barnsley, 2003), p. 194.
30. R. Brooks, *The Long Arm of Empire – Naval Brigades from the Crimea to the Boxer Rebellion* (Constable, 1999), p. 125.
31. H.M. Stanley, *Coomassie and Magdala* (Sampson Low, Marston & Co., 1891), p. 161.
32. Ibid., p. 163.
33. Brackenbury, p. 183.
34. Wood (June 1874), p. 353.
35. Lloyd, p. 131.
36. Wolseley (1903), p. 343.
37. Ibid., p. 354.
38. Woodend, p. 14.
39. B. Robson, *The Road to Kabul – The Second Afghan War* (Spellmount, Staplehurst, 2003), p. 195.
40. E. Spiers, *The Victorian Soldier in Africa* (Manchester University Press, 2004), p. 124.

Chapter Four

1. D. Westwood, *Weapons and Warfare – An Illustrated History of their Impact – Rifles* (ABC-Clio, Oxford, 2005), p. 48.
2. Headrick (1981), p. 98.
3. S. Bull, *The Encyclopaedia of Military Technology and Innovation* (Greenwood Press, Westport, 2004), p. 165.
4. Quoted from the 'Report on Breech Loading Arms', published by the War Office in April 1868.
5. Report of the Small arms Committee, issued 14 March 1865, under the authority of Brigadier General J.H. Lefory, RA, President; War Office Publication.
6. Westwood, p. 57.
7. Ibid., p. 58.
8. Ibid., p. 59.
9. I. Knight and R. Scollins, *British Forces in Zululand 1879* (Osprey Publishing, Oxford, 1991), p. 23.
10. Featherstone (1978), p. 25.
11. H.P. Miller, *A Guide to the Queen's Sixty OR Martini-Henry and Snider Rifles and How to Use Them* (1881), p. 22.
12. W.P.P. Marshall, 'The Comparative Merits of the Martini Rifle and the Westley Richards Rifle', *Engineering*, 27 April 1871.
13. Miller (1881), p. 23.
14. Featherstone (1978), p. 24.
15. D. Morris, *The Washing of the Spears* (Simon & Schuster, New York, 1965), p. 297.
16. Knight and Scollins, p. 22.
17. P. Scarlata, 'The British Martini-Henry Rifle', *Shotgun News* (6 December 2004), pp. 36–40.
18. Headrick (1981), p. 98.
19. R. Kipling, *The Complete Verse* (Kyle Cathie Ltd, 1990), p. 337.
20. I. Knight and I. Castle, *Zulu War* (Osprey Publishing, Oxford, 2004), p. 26.
21. P. Gon, *The Road to Isandlwana* (A.D. Donker, Johannesburg, 1979), p. 136.
22. Ibid., p. 140.

23. S. David, *Zulu* (Viking, 2004), p. 34.
24. Manning (2007), p. 95.
25. J. Laband, *Rope of Sand* (Jonathan Bull, Johannesburg, 1995), p. 208.
26. Alison Papers, p. 27: Letter Clery to Alison, 13 April 1879.
27. M. Prior, *Campaigns of a War Correspondent* (1912), p. 137.
28. Laband (1995), pp. 99–101.
29. R. Lock and P. Qunatrill, *Zulu Victory* (Greenhill Books, 2002), p. 45.
30. D. Moodie (ed.), *John Dunn, Cetywayo and the Three Generals* (Pietermaritzburg, 1886), p. 29.
31. NAM, Lord Chelmsford Papers: Letter to Colonel Wood, 23 November 1878.
32. Knight and Castle (2004), pp. 160–1.
33. A. Greaves and B. Best (eds), *The Curling Letters of the Zulu War* (Pen & Sword, Barnsley, 2001), pp. 89–90.
34. F. Emery, *The Red Soldier – The Zulu War of 1879* (Jonathan Ball, Johannesburg, 1983), p. 80.
35. I. Knight, '"Old Steady Shots", The Martini-Henry Rifle, Rates of Fire and Effectiveness in the Anglo Zulu War', *The Journal of the Anglo Zulu War Historical Society*, XI (June, 2002), p. 1.
36. Wood (1906), p. 64.
37. I. Knight, *Zulu Rising* (Macmillan, 2010), p. 378.
38. Ibid., p. 374.
39. Interview with Zimema, a Zulu veteran, which appeared in the *Natal Mercury*, 22 January 1899.
40. Knight (2010), p. 375.
41. An account in *Ilanga Lase Natal*, 20 June 1936.
42. General Sir H. Smith-Dorrien, *Memories of 48 years Service* (John Murray, 1925), p. 83.
43. Knight (2010), p. 385.
44. An account in the Symons Papers, Killie Campbell Collection, University of KwaZulu-Natal.
45. Morris, p. 387.
46. J. Laband, *Fight us in the Open* (University of Natal Press, Pietermaritzburg, 1985), p. 85.
47. A. Greaves, *Crossing the Buffalo – The Zulu War of 1879* (Weidenfeld & Nicolson, 2005), p. 231.
48. I. Knight, *The National Army Museum Book of the Zulu War* (Sedgwick & Jackson, 2003), p. 60.
49. Knight (2010), p. 497.
50. An account in the *Cambrian* newspaper, 13 June 1879.
51. Emery, p. 130.
52. I. Knight, *Nothing Remains But to Fight* (Greenhill Books, 1993), p. 108.
53. Clery to Alison, 1 February 1879, cited in I. Beckett and S. Corvi (eds), *Victoria's Generals* (Pen & Sword, Barnsley, 2009), p. 118.
54. David (2004), p. 356.
55. The *Daily News*, 12 February 1879.
56. Bailes (1980) pp. 83–104, 85.
57. For a study of the Battle of Khambula see Manning (2007), pp. 120–4.
58. Laband (1995), p. 102.
59. Knight (2003), p. 202.
60. Callwell, p. 76.
61. Laband (1985), p. 280.
62. NAM, Chelmsford Papers, 2 April 1879.
63. Knight (2003), p. 203.
64. B. Blood, *Four Score Years and Ten* (1933), p. 52.
65. Zulu War Journal of Corporal John Hargreaves, Lib. RGJ, D.37.
66. Knight (2003), p. 203.
67. Major Ashe and Captain Wyatt-Edgell, *The Story of the Zulu Campaign* (Sampson Low, Marston, Searle & Rivington, 1880), p. 169.
68. I. Knight and I. Castle, *Fearful Hard Times – The Siege and Relief of Eshowe, 1879* (Greenhill Books, 1994), p. 197.
69. C. Norris Newman, *In Zululand with the British* (Greenhill, 1988), p. 137.
70. Laband (1985), p. 282.
71. Emery, p. 201.
72. Ibid., p. 196.

73. Knight (June, 2002), p. 4.
74. Moodie (ed.), p. 103.
75. Knight (June, 2002), p. 4.
76. Emery, p. 201.
77. Zulu War Journal of Corporal John Hargreaves, Lib. RGJ, D.37.
78. J.J. Guy, 'A Note on Firearms in the Zulu Kingdom with Special Reference to the Anglo-Zulu War of 1879', *The Journal of African History*, Vol. 12, No. 4 (1971), pp. 567–70, 570.
79. Callwell, p. 396.
80. Zulu War Journal of Corporal John Hargreaves, Lib. RGJ, D.37.
81. Knight and Castle (1994), p. 198.
82. Ibid.
83. Ibid., p. 203.
84. Emery, p. 201.
85. 'A Sheffield Soldier in Zululand', *Sheffield Daily Telegraph*, 22 April 1879, cited in Spiers (2004), p. 50.
86. The *Perthshire Advertiser*, 28 April 1879.
87. The *Essex Standard*, 26 April 1879.
88. The *Isle of Man News*, 26 April 1879.
89. *The Times*, 19 May 1879.
90. L. Maxwell, *The Ashanti Ring* (Leo Cooper, 1985), p. 120.
91. KZNA, Wood Mss, II/2/2 Chelmsford to Wood, 11 April 1879.
92. Laband (1985), p. 312.
93. Callwell, p. 387.
94. David (2004), p. 348.
95. *Manchester Guardian*, 6 September 1879, cited in Spiers (2004), p. 52.
96. J. Laband and I. Knight, *The War Correspondents – The Anglo-Zulu War* (Sutton Publishing, Stroud, 1996), p. 139.
97. Diary of R. Wolrige Gordon, REF: ASHM N-C91.GOR.W.
98. Prior, p. 145.
99. Spiers (2004), p. 52.

Chapter Five

1. Major General Sir Garnet Wolseley, *The Soldier's Pocket Book for Field Service* (4th edn, Macmillan, 1882), p. 372.
2. Bailes (1980), pp. 83–104, 85.
3. Pridham, Major C. *Superiority of Fire – A Short History of Rifles and Machine-Guns* (Hutchinson, 1945), p. 31.
4. Ibid., p. 33.
5. Raugh (2004), p. 215.
6. Pridham, p. 30.
7. Ibid.
8. J. Darwin, *Unfinished Empire – The Global Expansion of Britain* (Allan Lane, 2012), p. 134.
9. Segeant William Danby, letter home dated 1 March 1884, NAM 1970-03-2.
10. H. Keown-Boyd, *A Good Dusting – The Sudan Campaigns 1883–1899* (Leo Cooper, 1986), p. 26.
11. Letter dated 1 March 1884 from Sergeant Danby to his cousin Adie, NAM 1970-03-2.
12. Quoted in the *Western Times* of Exeter, Devon, Tuesday, 4 March 1884.
13. Ibid.
14. B. Burleigh, *Desert Warfare – Being the Chronicle of the Eastern Soudan Campaign* (Chapman & Hall, 1884), p. 156.
15. Ibid., pp. 195–6.
16. M. Asher, *Khartoum – The Ultimate Imperial Adventure* (Viking, 2005), p. 156.
17. SPECIAL FIELD FORCE ORDER By Lieutenant-General Sir Gerald Graham,V.C., K.C.B., Commanding Suakin Field Force, Suakin, 16 May 1885, SA 6005/SHYKS/86/0064F.
18. Asher, p. 220.
19. E. Gambier Parry, *Suakin 1885 – A Sketch of the Campaign* (Kegan, Paul, Trench & Co.), p. 197.
20. Strawson, p. 227.

218 *Bayonet to Barrage*

21. C. Beresford, *Memoirs*, 2 vols (Methuen, 1914), pp. 263 and 267.
22. Count Gleichen, *With the Camel Corps Up the Nile* (The Naval and Military Press, repr. Uckfield, 2008), pp. 156–7.
23. Ibid., p. 156.
24. Ibid.
25. Ibid.
26. Asher, p. 243.
27. 'Another Letter from a Melton Man in the Soudon', *Leicestershire Chronicle and Leicestershire Mercury*, 18 April 1885, p. 3.

Chapter Six

1. M. Pegler, *The Lee-Enfield Rifle* (Osprey, Oxford, 2012), p. 10.
2. Woodend, p. 35.
3. Pegler (2012), p. 12.
4. Woodend, p. 41.
5. W. Churchill, *The Story of the Malakand Field Force* (1898), pp. 287–8.
6. J.M. Brereton, *The British Soldier – A Social History* (1986), p. 99.
7. Westwood, p. 116.
8. M. Pegler, *The Vickers-Maxim Machine Gun* (Osprey, Oxford, 2013), p. 17.
9. Headrick (2010), p. 265.
10. Pegler (2013), p. 18.
11. Ibid., p. 19.
12. R. Marjomaa, *War on the Savannah: The Military Collapse of the Sokoto Caliphate under the Invasion of the British Empire, 1987–1903* (Helsinki, 1998), p. 108.
13. Pridham, p. 41.
14. Ibid.
15. Asher, p. 316.
16. M. Simner, *The Sirdar and The Khalifa – Kitchener's Reconquest of Sudan, 1896–8* (Fonthill, 2017), p. 105.
17. Major Farley, 'The Dongola Expedition Recollections', p. 32, Staffordshire Regimental Museum Box AB81, 1226.
18. J. Black (ed.), *The Seventy Great Battles of All Time* (Thames & Hudson, 2005), p. 218.
19. E. Spiers (ed.). *Sudan, The Reconquest Reappraised* (Frank Cass, 1998), p. 59.
20. Ibid., p. 60.
21. Letter to his father from Major J.K. Watson, dated 7 Sept. 1898, NAM 1983-04-112.
22. Letter from Lieutenant David Henry Graeme, 1st Bn Seaforth Highlanders to his father dated 6 September 1898, from Omdurman, NAM 2006-04-33.
23. Diary of Lieutenant The Hon. E.D. Loch, NAM 8608-66.
24. Letter from Lieutenant David Henry Graeme, 1st Bn Seaforth Highlanders to his father dated 6 September 1898, from Omdurman, NAM 2006-04-33.
25. Asher, p. 376.
26. Churchill (1899), p. 115.
27. Asher, pp. 381–2.
28. Letter to his father from Major J.K. Watson, dated 7 September 1898, NAM 1983-04-112.
29. Diary of Lieutenant The Hon. E.D. Loch, NAM 8608-66.
30. Omdurman Diary of Captain D.W. Churcher, 1st Bn The Royal Irish Fusiliers, NAM 7704-53.
31. Pridham, p. 42.
32. Featherstone (1978), p. 65.
33. J. Meredith, *Omdurman Diaries 1898* (Greenhill, 1998), p. 170.
34. Black (ed.), p. 219.
35. G.W. Steevens, *With Kitchener to Khartoum* (William Blackwood & Sons, Edinburgh, 1898), p. 264.
36. S. Manning, *The Martini–Henry Rifle* (Osprey, Oxford, 2013), p. 69.
37. Letter to his father from Major J.K. Watson, dated 7 September 1898, NAM 1983-04-112.
38. E. Fraser and L.G. Carr-Laughton, *The Royal Marine Artillery 1804–1923*, 2 vols (RUSI, 1930), Vol. 2, p. 623.
39. Pridham, p. 42.

Chapter Seven

1. D. Judd, *The Boer War* (Granada, 1977), p. 16.
2. Ibid., p. 57.
3. T. Pakenham, *The Boer War* (Abacus, 1992), p. 195.
4. Private Snape letter dated Modder Rover, 1 December 1899, published in the *Lancashire Daily Post*, 30 December 1899.
5. Diary of Colonel Lang, REF: ASHM N-D1.LAN.
6. Pakenham (1992), p. 206.
7. Fuller (1946), p. 140.
8. Pakenham (1992), p. 211.
9. J. Downham, *Red Roses on the Veldt – Lancashire Regiments in the Boer War, 1899–1902* (Carnegie Publishing, 2000), p. 112.
10. Spiers (2004), p. 165.
11. Pakenham (1992), p. 344.
12. 'The Doings of the Somersets in South Africa', *Somerset County Gazette*, 14 April 1900.
13. Downham, p. 118.
14. T. Bridgland, *Field Gun Jack Versus The Boers. The Royal Navy in South Africa 1899–1900* (Leo Cooper, 1998), p. 127.
15. R. Oakeley, *Oakeley's War 1899–1902* (private publication, 2005), p. 62.
16. Lieutenant Colonel H. Jourdain, *Memories – The Natal Campaign 1899–1900* (private publication, 1948), pp. 99–101.
17. Pakenham (1992), p. 357.
18. Ibid., p. 358.
19. QLRM, Diary of Lance Corporal Matthew Kelly, 27 February 1900.
20. H. Eaves, *From Lancashire to Ladysmith – With the 1st Battalion South Lancashire Regiment – by One of the Regiment* (private publication, Preston, 1900), pp. 41–2.
21. Bridgland, p. 131.
22. Pakenham (1992), p. 363.
23. Eaves, pp. 41–2.
24. Queen's Lancashire Regimental Museum, Preston, Box 97.
25. A. Conan Doyle, *The Great Boer War* (Smith Elder & Co., 1902), p. 295.
26. H.W. Wilson, *With the Flag to Pretoria*, 2 vols (1900–2), Vol. II, p. 475.
27. Pakenham (1992), p. 370.

Conclusion

1. W. Churchill, *The Boer War* (Pimlico, 2002), p. 200.
2. G.F.R. Henderson, *The Science of War – A Collection of Essays and Lectures 1891–1903* (Longmans, 1912), p. 53.
3. J. Stone and E. Schmidl, *The Boer War and Military Reforms* (University Press of America, New York, 1988) p. 3.
4. Ibid., p. 12.
5. War Office, Infantry Training 1905, p. 123
6. War Office, Combined Training 1905, p. 99.
7. S. Jones, *From Boer War to World War – Tactical Reform of the British Army, 1902–1914* (Oklahoma University Press, Norman, 2012), p. 54.
8. WO 163/18IGF, Report for 1912, TNA, pp. 567–8.
9. See T. Travers, *The Killing Ground: The British Army, the Western Front and the Emergence of Modern War, 1900–1918* (Pen & Sword, Barnsley, re-issue, 2003) and Jones.
10. A. Kuropatkin, *Russian Army and the Japanese War,* 2 vols (1909), Vol. 2, p. 80.
11. Jones, p. 64.
12. Stone and Schmidl, p. 13.
13. 'Report on a Conference of General Staff Officers at the Staff College, 17–20 January 1910', p. 28, Joint Service Command and Staff College Library.
14. Headrick (2010), p. 124.

Bibliography

Note – place of publication is London, unless otherwise specified.

Aggett, W. *The Bloody Eleventh – History of the Devonshire Regiment*, Vol. II, *1815–1914* (The Devon and Dorset Regiment, Exeter, 1994).
Alford, H. and Dennistoun Sword, W. *The Egyptian Soudan – Its Loss and Recovery* (Macmillan, 1898).
Alister Williams, W. *Commandant of the Transvaal – The Life of General Sir Hugh Rowlands, VC, KCB* (Bridge Books, Wrexham, 2001).
Allen, C. *Soldier Sahibs – The Men Who Made the North-West Frontier* (J. Murray, 2000).
Amery, L. (ed.). *The Times History of the War in South Africa*, 7 vols (Sampson and Low, 1900–9).
Anon. *A Lieutenant Colonel in the British Army – With an introduction by Major-General F. Maurice, The British Army* (Sampson, Low & Marston, 1899).
Ashe, Major and Wyatt-Edgell, Captain. *The Story of the Zulu Campaign* (Sampson and Low, Marston, Searle & Rivington, 1880).
Asher, M. *Khartoum – The Ultimate Imperial Adventure* (Viking, 2005).
Atwood, R. *The March to Kandahar* (Pen & Sword, Barnsley, 2008).
Baldwin. J. *A Norfolk Soldier in the First Sikh War* (Leonaur, 2005).
Bancroft, N. *Bancroft of the Bengal Horse Artillery – An Account of the First Sikh War 1845–6* (Leonaur, 2008).
Barthorp, M. *The North-West Frontier* (Blandford Press, Poole, 1982).
Barthorp, M. *Heroes of the Crimea – The Battles of Balaclava and Inkerman* (Blandford Press, Poole, 1991).
Baumgart, W. *The Crimea War 1853–1856* (Edward Arnold, 1999).
Beaumont, R. *Sword of the Raj – The British Army in India, 1747–1947* (Bobbs-Merrill, New York, 1977).
Beckett, I. *Victoria's Wars* (Shire, Princes Risborough, 1974).
Beckett, I. *The Victorian's at War* (Hambledon, 2003).
Beckett, I. (ed.). *Wolseley and Ashanti* (The Army Records Society, The History Press, Stroud, 2009).
Beckett, I. and Corvi, S. (eds). *Victoria's Generals* (Pen & Sword, Barnsley, 2009).
Beresford, C. *Memoirs*, 2 vols (Methuen, 1914).
Bidwell, S. and Graham, D. *Fire-Power: British Army Weapons and Theories of War 1904–1945* (Pen & Sword, Barnsley, re-issue, 2004).
Black, J. *Tools of War – The Weapons that Changed the World* (Quercus, 2007).
Black, J. *War in the Nineteenth Century 1800–1914* (Polity, 2009).
Black, J. *The Great War and the Making of the Modern World* (Continuum, 2011).
Black, J. *War and Technology* (Indiana University Press, Bloomington, 2013).
J. Black (ed.). *The Seventy Great Battles of All Time* (Thames & Hudson, 2005).
Blake Knox, E. *Buller's Campaign with the Natal Field Force* (1902).
Blood, B. *Four Score Years and Ten* (1933).

Bibliography

Bolitho, H. *The Galloping Third – The story of the 3rd King's Own Hussars* (John Murray, 1963).
Bond, B. (ed.). *Victorian Military Campaigns* (Hutchinson, 1967).
Boyden, P., Guy, A. and Harding, M. *'Ashes and blood'. The British Army in South Africa 1795–1914* (National Army Museum Publication, 1999).
Boyle, F. *Fanteland to Coomassie* (Chapman & Hall, 1874).
Brackenbury, H. *The Ashanti War of 1873–4*, 2 vols (Frank Cass, repr., 1968).
Brereton, J.M. *The British Soldier – A Social History from 1661 to the Present Day* (The Bodley Head, 1986).
Brice, C. *The Thinking Man's Soldier – The Life and Career of General Sir Henry Brackenbury 1837–1914* (Helion & Company Ltd, Solihull, 2012).
Bridgland, T. *Field Gun Jack Versus The Boers. The Royal Navy in South Africa 1899–1900* (Leo Cooper, 1998).
Brooks, R. *The Long Arm of Empire – Naval Brigades from the Crimea to the Boxer Rebellion* (Constable, 1999).
Bruce, G. *Six Battles for India – The Anglo-Sikh Wars 1845–6, 1848–9* (Arthur Baker, 1969).
Bull, S. *Encyclopaedia of Military Technology and Innovation* (Greenwood Press, Westport, 2004).
Burford, R. *The Battle of Sobraon, with the Defeat of the Sikh Army of the Punjab* (George Nichols, 1846).
Burleigh, B. *Desert Warfare – Being the Chronicle of the Eastern Soudan Campaign* (Chapman & Hall, 1884).
Burton, Lieutenant Colonel R. *The First and Second Sikh Wars* (Government Central Branch Press, Simla, 1911).
Callwell, Colonel C. *Small Wars: Their Principles and Practice* (1st edn, HMSO, 1896).
Carver, Field Marshal Lord. *The National Army Museum Book of the Boer War* (Sidgwick & Jackson, 1999).
Chandler, D. *Waterloo the Hundred Days* (George Philip, 1980).
Chandler, D. and Beckett, I. (eds). *The Oxford History of the British Army* (Oxford University Press, 1994).
Chapman, R. (ed.). *Echoes from the Crimea* (The Green Howard's Museum, Richmond, 2004).
Churchill, W. *The Story of the Malakand Field Force* (1898).
Churchill, W. *The River War: An account of the Reconquest of the Sudan* (Carroll & Graf, New York, re-issue, 2000).
Churchill, W. *London to Ladysmith via Pretoria* (Longman, 1900).
Churchill, W. *The Boer War* (Pimlico, 2002).
Conan Doyle, A. *The Great Boer War* (Smith, Elder & Co., 1902).
Connaughton, R. *Rising Sun and Tumbling Bear – Russia's War with Japan* (Cassell, 2003).
Cook, H.C.B. *The Sikh Wars 1845–6, 1848–9* (Leo Cooper, 1975).
Cope, W. *The History of the Rifle Brigade*, Vol. 2, *1816–1876* (Leonaur, 2010).
Coughlin, C. *Churchill's First War – Young Winston and the Fight Against the Taliban* (Macmillan, 2013).
Darwin, J. *Unfinished Empire – The Global Expansion of Britain* (Allan Lane, 2012).
David, S. *Military Blunders – The how and why of military failure* (Robinson Publishing, 1997).
David, S. *Zulu* (Viking, 2004).
David, S. *Victoria's Wars* (Viking, 2006).
De Cosson, Major. *Days and Nights of Service – with Sir Gerald Graham's Field Force at Suakin* (John Murray, 1886).
De Watteville, Colonel H. *The British Soldier* (J.M. Dent, 1954).
Downham, J. *Red Roses on the Veldt – Lancashire Regiments in the Boer War, 1899–1902* (Carnegie Publishing, 2000).
Duckers, P. *British Military Rifles* (Shire Books, Princes Risborough, 2005).
Duncan, J. and Walton, J. *Heroes for Victoria* (Spellmount, Tunbridge Wells, 1991).

Dundonald, Earl of. *My Army Life* (Edward Arnold, 1926).
Dunn, Captain J.C. *The War the Infantry Knew 1914–1919* (Abacus repr., 2004).
Eaves, H. *From Lancashire to Ladysmith – With the 1st Battalion South Lancashire Regiment – by One of the Regiment* (private publication, Preston, 1900).
Edgerton, R. *Like Lions They Fought* (Southern Books, Bergvlei, 1988).
Emery, F. *The Red Soldier – The Zulu War of 1879* (Jonathan Ball, Johannesburg, 1983).
Farwell, B. *Queen Victoria's Little Wars* (Allan Lane, 1973).
Farwell, B. *Eminent Victorian Soldiers – Seekers of Glory* (Viking, 1985).
Faust, F. (ed.). *The Lineage of the Lee–Enfield Rifle* (Middle Coast Publishing, 2016).
Featherstone, D. *Weapons and Equipment of the Victorian Soldier* (Blandford Press, Poole, 1978).
Featherstone, D. *At them with the Bayonet –The First Anglo-Sikh War 1845–1846* (Leonaur, 2007).
Ferguson, N. *The Pity of War 1914–1918* (Allan Lane, 1998).
Ferguson, N. *Empire – How Britain Made the Modern World* (Allan Lane, 2003).
Figes, O. *Crimea – The Last Crusade* (Allen Lane, 2010).
Fletcher, I. and Ishchenko, N. *The Battle of the Alma* (Pen & Sword, Barnsley, 2008).
Fraser, E. and Carr-Laughton, L.G. *The Royal Marine Artillery 1804–1923*, 2 vols (RUSI, 1930).
Fuller, J.F.C. *Armament and History – a study of the Influence of Armament on History* (Eyre & Spottiswoode, 1946).
Fuller, J.F.C. *The Conduct of War 1789–1961* (Methuen, 1961).
Gleichen, Count. *With the Camel Corps Up the Nile* (The Naval and Military Press, repr., Uckfield, 2008).
Goldfrank, D. *The Origins of the Crimean War* (Longman, 1994).
Gon, P. *The Road to Isandlwana* (A.D. Donker, Johannesburg, 1979).
Gough, C. and Innes, A. *The Sikhs and the Sikh Wars* (Kaveri Books, New Delhi, 2005).
Graham, C.A. Brigadier General. *The History of the Indian Mountain Artillery* (Gale & Polden, Aldershot, 1957).
Greaves, A. *Crossing the Buffalo – The Zulu War of 1879* (Weidenfeld & Nicolson, 2005).
Greaves, A. and Best, B. (eds). *The Curling Letters of the Zulu War* (Pen & Sword, Barnsley, 2001).
Harding, D.F. *Small arms of the East India Company 1600–1856,* 4 vols (Foresight Books, 1999), Vols III and IV.
Harrington, P. and Sharf, A. (eds). *Omdurman 1898: The Eye-Witnesses Speak* (Greenhill Books, 1998).
Haycock, R. and Neilson, K. (eds). *Men, Machines and War* (Wilfrid Laurier University Press, Waterloo, Ontario, 1988).
Haythornthwaite, P. *The Colonial Wars Source Book* (Arms and Armour Press, 1995).
Headrick, D. *Tools of Empire – Technology and European Imperialism in the Nineteenth Century* (Oxford University Press, New York, 1981).
Headrick, D. *Power over Peoples: Technology, Environment and Western Imperialism, 1400 to the Present* (Princeton University Press, 2010).
Henderson, G.F.R. *The Science of War – A Collection of Essays and Lectures 1891–1903* (Longmans, 1912).
Heron, I. *Britain's Forgotten Wars* (Sutton Publishing, Stroud, 2003).
Holden Reid, B. *Studies in British Military Thought – Debates with Fuller & Liddell Hart* (University of Nebraska Press, Lincoln, 1998).
Holmes, R. *Redcoat – The British Soldier in the Age of Horse and Musket* (HarperCollins, 2001).
Hope, R. *A Staffordshire Regiment in the Zulu and Sekukuni Campaigns 1878–9 – 80th Regiment of Foot* (Churnet Valley Books, Leek, 2007).
Hutchinson, Colonel H. *The Campaign in Tirah 1897–98* (Lancer, New Delhi, 2008).
Jones, S. *From Boer War to World War – Tactical Reform of the British Army, 1902–1914* (University of Oklahoma Press, Norman, 2012).

Jourdain, Lieutenant Colonel H. *Memories – The Natal Campaign 1899–1900* (private publication, 1948).
Judd, D. *The Boer War* (Granada, 1977).
Judd, D. *Empire. The British Imperial Experience from 1765 to the Present* (HarperCollins, 1996).
Keown-Boyd, H. *A Good Dusting – The Sudan Campaigns 1883–1899* (Leo Cooper, 1986).
Kingston, W. *Blow the Bugle, Draw the Sword* (Leonaur, 2007).
Kipling, R. *The Complete Verse* (Kyle Cathie Ltd, 1990).
Knight, I. *By the Orders of the Great White Queen* (Greenhill Books, 1992).
Knight, I. *Go to your God Like a Soldier* (Greenhill Books, 1996).
Knight, I. *The National Army Museum Book of the Zulu War* (Sidgwick & Jackson, 2003).
Knight, I. *Zulu Rising* (Macmillan, 2010).
Knight, I. and Castle, I. *Fearful Hard Times – The Siege and Relief of Eshowe, 1879* (Greenhill Books, 1994).
Knight, I. and Castle, I. *The Zulu War* (Osprey, Oxford, 2004).
Knight, I. and Scollins, R. *British Forces in Zululand 1879* (Osprey Publishing, Oxford, 1991).
Kochanski, Halik. *Sir Garnet Wolseley: Victorian Hero* (Hambledon, 1999).
Kruger, R. *Good-bye Dolly Gray* (Cassell, 1959).
Kuropatkin, A. *Russian Army and the Japanese War*, 2 vols (1909).
Laband, J. *Fight us in the Open* (University of Natal Press, Pietermaritzburg, 1985).
Laband, J. *Rope of Sand* (Jonathan Bull, Johannesburg, 1995).
Laband, J. *The Transvaal Rebellion – The First Boer War 1880–1881* (Longman, Harlow, 2005).
Laband, J. and Knight, I. *The War Correspondents – The Anglo-Zulu War* (Sutton Publishing, Stroud, 1996).
Laband, J. and Thompson, P. *Field Guide to the War in Zululand and the Defence of Natal 1879* (2nd edn, University of Natal Press, Pietermaritzburg, 1983).
Lambert, A. *The Crimean War. British Grand Strategy Against Russia, 1853–56* (Manchester University Press, 1991).
Leadley, S. *The Development of the Standard British Infantry Rifle 1815–1914* (private publication, 1983).
Lehmann, J. *All Sir Garnet: A Life of Field-Marshal Lord Wolseley* (Jonathan Cape, 1964).
Liddell Hart, B.H. *The Revolution in Warfare* (Faber & Faber, 1946).
Lloyd, A. *The Drums of Kumasi – The Story of the Ashanti Wars* (Longman, 1964).
Lock, R. and Qunatrill, P. *Zulu Victory* (Greenhill Books, 2002).
Luvaas, J. *The Education of an Army – British Military Thought, 1815–1940* (The University of Chicago Press, 1964).
McCourt, E. *Remember Butler – The Story of Sir William Butler* (Routledge, 1967).
Magnus, P. *Kitchener – Portrait of an Imperialist* (John Murray, 1958).
Malleson, Colonel G.B. *The Decisive Battles of India* (W.H. Allen, 1883).
Mallinson, A. *The Making of the British Army From the English Civil War to the War on Terror* (Bantam Press, 2009).
Manning, S. *Evelyn Wood V.C. Pillar of Empire* (Pen & Sword, Barnsley, 2007).
Manning, S. *Soldiers of the Queen* (Spellmount, Stroud, 2009).
Manning, S. *The Martini–Henry Rifle* (Osprey, Oxford, 2013).
Mansfield, H. *Charles Ashe Windham, A Norfolk Soldier (1810–1870)* (Terence Dalton, Lavenham, 1973).
Marjomaa, R. *War on the Savannah: The Military Collapse of the Sokoto Caliphate under the Invasion of the British Empire, 1987–1903* (University of Helsinki, Helsinki, 1998).
Massie, A. *The National Army Museum Book of the Crimea War* (Sidgwick & Jackson, 2004).
Maude, Colonel F.N. *Notes on the Evolution of Infantry Tactics* (Clowes & Son, 1905).
Mawson, M.H. (ed.). *Eyewitness in the Crimea – The Crimean War Letters of Lieutenant Colonel George Frederick Dallas* (Greenhill Books, 2001).

Maxwell, L. *The Ashanti Ring* (Leo Cooper, 1985).
Mercer, P. *Give Them a Volley and Charge! The Battle of Inkerman, 1854* (Spellmount, Staplehurst, 1998).
Meredith, J. *Omdurman Diaries 1898* (Greenhill, 1998).
Messenger, C. *History of the British Army* (Bison Books, 1986).
Miller, H.P. *A Guide to the Queen's Sixty OR Martini-Henry and Snider Rifles and How to Use Them* (1881).
Miller, S. *Volunteers on the Veld – Britain's Citizen-Soldiers and the South African War, 1899–1902* (University of Oklahoma Press, Norman, 2007).
Miller, S. (ed.). *Soldiers and Settlers in Africa, 1850–1918* (Brill, Boston, 2009).
Moodie, D. (ed.). *John Dunn, Cetywayo and the Three Generals* (Pietermaritzburg, 1886).
Morris, D. *The Washing of the Spears* (Simon & Schuster, New York, 1965).
Myatt, F. *The March to Magdala* (Leo Cooper, 1970).
Myatt, F. *The British Infantry 1660–1945 – The Evolution of a Fighting Force* (Blandford Press, Poole, 1983).
Nalson, D. *The Victorian Soldier* (Shire, Princes Risborough, 2000).
Nijjar, B.S. *Anglo-Sikh Wars* (K.B. Publications, New Delhi, 1976).
Norris Newman, C. *In Zululand with the British Throughout the War of 1879* (Greenhill, 1988).
Oakeley, R. *Oakeley's War 1899–1902* (private publication, 2005).
Pakenham, T. *The Boer War* (Abacus, 1992).
Pakenham, T. *The Scramble for Africa* (Weidenfeld & Nicolson, 1991).
Parry, E. Gambier. *Suakin 1885 – A Sketch of the Campaign* (Kegan, Paul, Trench & Co., 1885).
Pegler, M. *The Lee-Enfield Rifle* (Osprey, Oxford, 2012).
Pegler, M. *The Vickers-Maxim Machine Gun* (Osprey, Oxford, 2013).
Peterson, H., *The Book of the Gun* (Hamlyn, 1963).
Pollock, J. *Kitchener: The Road to Omdurman* (Constable, 1998).
Pridham, Major C. *Superiority of Fire – A Short History of Rifles and Machine-Guns* (Hutchinson, 1945).
Prior, M. *Campaigns of a War Correspondent* (1912).
Private Tucker's Boer War Diary (Elm Tree Books, 1980).
Rait, R. *The Life and Campaigns of Hugh First Viscount Gough Field Marshal*, Vol. II (Constable, 1903).
Raugh, H., Jr. *The Victorians at War, 1815–1914 – An Encyclopaedia of British Military History* (Clio, Oxford, 2004).
Ricketts, H. *Firearms* (Weidenfeld & Nicolson, 1964).
Roberts, F. *Forty-One Years in India* (Macmillan, 1897).
Ross, S. *From Flintlock to Rifle – Infantry Tactics, 1740–1866* (Frank Cass, 1996).
Royle, T. *Crimea – The Great Crimean War 1854–56* (Little Brown, 1999).
Russell, W.H. *Despatches from the Crimea* (Frontline Books, Barnsley, 2008).
Saunders, A. *Trench Warfare 1850–1950* (Pen & Sword, Barnsley, 2010).
Scott Daniell, D. *Cap of Honour – The 300 Years of the Gloucestershire Regiment* (3rd edn, Sutton Publishing, Stroud, 2005).
Sidhu, A.S. *The First Anglo-Sikh War* (Amberley Publishing, Stroud, 2010).
Simner, M. *The Sirdar and The Khalifa – Kitchener's Reconquest of Sudan, 1896–8* (Fonthill, 2017).
Skennerton, I. *A Treatise on the Snider – The British Soldier's Firearm 1866–c.1880* (Hollingsworth & Moss, Leeds, 1977).
Smith, Sir H. *Autobiography* (John Murray, 1901).
Smith, K. *Harry Smith's Last Throw – The Eighth Frontier War 1850–1853* (Frontline, Barnsley, 2012).
Smith, P. *Victoria's Victories* (Spellmount, Tunbridge Wells, 1987).
Smith-Dorrien, General Sir H. *Memories of 48 years Service* (John Murray, 1925).
Smithurst, P. *The Pattern 1853 Enfield Rifle* (Osprey Publishing, Oxford, 2011).

Snook, Lieutenant Colonel M. *Go Strong into the Desert – The Mahdist Uprising in Sudan 1881–5* (Perry Miniatures, Nottingham, 2010).
Spiers, E. *The Late Victorian Army, 1868–1902* (Manchester University Press, 1992).
Spiers, E. *Sudan, The Reconquest Reappraised* (Frank Cass, 1998).
Spiers, E. *The Victorian Soldier in Africa* (Manchester University Press, 2004).
Spiers, E. *The Scottish Soldier and Empire 1854–1902* (Edinburgh University Press, 2006).
Spilsbury, J. *The Thin Red Line* (Weidenfeld & Nicolson, 2005).
Stanley, H. *Coomassie and Magdala* (Sampson Low, Marston & Co., 1891).
Steevens, G. *With Kitchener to Khartoum* (William Blackwood, 1898).
Stone, J. and Schmidl, E. *The Boer War and Military Reforms* (University Press of America, New York, 1988).
Strachan, H. *From Waterloo to Balaclava – Tactics, Technology, and the British Army 1815–1854* (Cambridge University Press, 1985).
Strawson, J. *Beggars in Red: The British Army 1789–1889* (Pen & Sword, Barnsley, 2003).
Symons, J. *Buller's Campaign* (Cresset Press, 1963).
Temple, B. and Skennerton, I. *A Treatise on the British Military Martini – The Martini–Henry 1869–1900*, (B. Temple, Burbank, Australia, 1983).
Todd, P. *Private Tucker's Boer War Diary* (Elm Tree Books, 1980).
Travers, T. *The Killing Ground: The British Army, the Western Front and the Emergence of Modern Warfare, 1900–1918* (Pen & Sword, Barnsley, re-issue, 2003).
Vandervort, B. *Wars of Imperial Conquest in Africa 1830–1914* (UCL Press, 1998).
Wallis Budge, E. *A History of Ethiopia: Volume II* (Routledge, 2014).
Walter, J. (ed.). *Arms and Equipment of the British Army, 1866* (Greenhill, 1986).
Warner, P. *The Crimean War, A Reappraisal* (Arthur Baker, 1972).
Westwood, D. *Weapons and Warfare – An Illustrated History of their Impact – Rifles* (ABC-Clio, Oxford, 2005).
Wheeler, O. *The War Office Past & Present* (Methuen, 1914).
White, H. *One and All – A History of the Duke of Cornwall's Light Infantry 1702–1959* (Tabb House, Padstow, 2006).
Wilkinson-Latham, R. *Uniforms and Weapons of the Crimean War* (Batsford, 1977).
Wilson, B. *Heyday: Britain and the Birth of the Modern World* (Weidenfeld & Nicolson, 2016).
Wilson, H.W. *With the Flag to Pretoria*, 2 vols (1900–2).
Wolseley, Colonel Garnet, *The Soldier's Pocket Book for Field Service* (2nd edn, Macmillan, 1871).
Wolseley, Sir Garnet, *Ashantee Invasion – Latest Despatches* (Colonial Office, 1874).
Wolseley, Major General Sir Garnet. *The Soldier's Pocket Book for Field Service* (4th edn, Macmillan, 1882).
Wolseley, Field Marshal Viscount Wolseley. *The Story of a Soldier's Life*, 2 vols (Archibald Constable & Co., 1903).
Wood, E. *From Midshipman to Field Marshal: Vol. I* (Methuen, 1906).
Wood, Field Marshal Sir E. (ed.). *British Battles on Land and Sea*, Vols 1 and 2 (Cassell, 1915).
Woodend, H. *Catalogue of the Enfield Pattern Room British Rifles* (HMSO, 1981).
Woodham-Smith, C. *The Reason Why* (Constable, 1953).
Yate, A. *Lieutenant-Colonel John Haughton, Commandant of the 36th Sikhs; a hero of Tirah, a memoir* (John Murray, 1900).
Zulfo, I.H. (trans. from the Arabic by Peter Clark). *Karari: The Sudanese Account of the Battle of Omdurman* (Frederick Warne, 1980).

Pamphlets and Journal Articles

Bailes, H. 'Technology and Imperialism – A Case Study of the Victorian Army in Africa', *Victorian Studies*, 24 (1980), pp. 83–104.
Bailes, H. 'Patterns of Thought in the Late Victorian Army', *Journal of Strategic Studies*, 4 (1981), pp. 29–45.

Bailes, H. 'Technology and Tactics in the British Army', in R. Haycock and K. Neilson (eds), *Men, Machines and War* (Wilfrid Laurier University Press, Waterloo, Ontario, 1988).

Bailey, J. 'The First World War and the Birth of the Modern Style of Warfare', *Strategic & Combat Studies Institute Journal*, No. 22 (1996).

Da Costa Porter, Lieutenant R. 'Warfare against Uncivilised Races', Professional Papers 6 (1881), pp. 305–60.

Gawler, Colonel J.C. 'British Troops and Savage Warfare', *Journal of the Royal United Services Institution*, 17 (1873).

Gillings, K. 'Inyezane, Gingindlovu and the Relief of Eshowe; The Forgotten Battlefields of the Zulu War, 1879', *Military History Journal*, Vol. 4, No. 4 (Dec. 1978).

Guy, J.J. 'A Note on Firearms in the Zulu Kingdom with Special Reference to the Anglo-Zulu War of 1879', *The Journal of African History*, Vol. 12, No. 4 (1971), pp. 567–70.

Headrick, D. 'The Tools of Imperialism: Technology and the Expansion of European Colonial Empire in the Nineteenth Century', *The Journal of Modern History*, Vol. 51, No. 2 (June 1979), pp. 231–63.

Hutton, Lieutenant General Sir E. 'Some Recollections of the Zulu War, extracted from the unpublished reminiscences of the Late Lieut.-General Sir Edward Hutton', *The Army Quarterly*, XVI (April 1928), pp. 65–80.

Knight, I. '"Old Steady Shots" The Martini-Henry Rifle, Rates of Fire and Effectiveness in the Anglo Zulu War', *The Journal of the Anglo Zulu War Historical Society* XI (June, 2002), pp. 1–8.

McIntyre, W.D. 'British Policy in West Africa: The Ashanti Expedition of 1873–4', *The Historical Journal*, V, I (1962), pp. 19–45.

Marshall, W.P.P. 'The Comparative Merits of the Martini Rifle and the Westley Richards Rifle', *Engineering*, 27 April 1871.

Reynolds, P. 'The Man who Predicted This . . . History Today', Vol. 63, No. 5 (May, 2013), pp. 18–24.

Rogers, Captain E. 'The Gatling Gun: its Place in Tactics', *Journal of Royal United Services Institution*, 19 (1875).

Scarlata, P. 'The British Martini-Henry Rifle', *Shotgun News* (6 December 2004), pp. 36–40.

Spiers, E. 'The Use of the Dum Dum Bullet in Colonial Warfare', *Journal of Imperial and Commonwealth History*, 4 (1975), pp. 3–14.

Spiers, E. 'Reforming the Infantry of the Line', *Journal of the Society of Army Historical Research*, 59 (1981), pp. 82–94.

Storey, W. 'Guns, Race, and Skill in Nineteenth-Century Southern Africa', *Technology and Culture*, Vol. 45, No. 4 (2004), pp. 687–711.

Thomas, S. 'The Ashantee War: its causes and results', Bristol Select Pamphlets (1874).

Travers, T. 'The Offensive and the Problem of Innovation in British Military Thought, 1870–1915', *Journal of Contemporary History*, 13 (1978), pp. 531–53.

Travers, T. 'Technology, Tactics, and Morale: Jean de Bloch, the Boer War, and British Military Theory, 1900–1914', *Journal of Modern History*, 51 (1979), pp. 264–86.

Ukpabi, S.C. 'West Indian Troops and the Defence of British West Africa in the Nineteenth Century', *African Studies Review*, Vol. 17, No. I (1974), pp. 133–50.

War Office 40/1533, 'Maxim Gun and Small Arms, Compiled in the Field Artillery and Small Arms Branch, Ordnance College' (rev. edn 1911).

White, G. 'Firearms in Africa: An Introduction', *Journal of African History*, Vol. 12, No. II (1971), pp. 173–84.

Wood, Colonel E. 'The Ashanti Expedition of 1873–4', *Journal of the Royal United Services Institution*, Vol. XVII (June 1874), pp. 331–57.

Index

Abu Klea, Battle of, 129, 130, 133, 138–142, 146
Abu Kru, Battle of, 144–6
Alison, Archibald, 75, 81–3, 89
Aliwal, Battle of, 18, 25–7
Alma, Battle of, 48–50, 52, 57, 63
Amanquatia, Chief, 76, 77, 80, 87
Amery, Leo, 4, 201, 204
Amoaful, Battle of, 65, 79–87, 109
Aroge Plain, Battle of, 70–3
Atbura, Battle of, 163–4
Avitabile Regiment, 16, 18, 25, 26

Bailes, Howard, 3, 4, 65, 111, 125
Balaklava, Battle of, 2, 49, 50, 52, 53, 58
Belmont, Battle of, 180–1
Beresford, Lord Charles, 140–2, 144–5
Boer War (1881), 69, 175, 196
Boer War (1899–1902), 2, 5, 69, 178, 186, 191, 200, 201, 203–6, 208–11
Botha, Louis, 188, 193, 197–8
Boxer cartridge, 68, 86, 97, 99, 128
Brown Bess rifle, 8, 12, 15, 56, 101
Brunswick rifle, 12, 13, 41–4
Buller, Redvers, 75, 79, 110, 134, 177, 179–80, 186–198, 201, 203
Burleigh, Bennett, 135–6

Callwell, Colonel Charles, 3, 113, 117, 121
Campbell, Sir Colin, 48, 50–1
Centane, Battle of, 100–1, 103
Cetewayo, King, 103, 108, 119, 121
Chamberlain, Joseph, 176–7
Chassepot rifle, 66–7
Chelmsford, Lord, 101–5, 110–13, 115, 118–23, 125, 128
Churchill, Winston, 4, 153, 163, 169, 170, 179, 203
Colenso, Battle of, 5, 186–9, 191–2, 194, 195, 201

Colt, Samuel, 43–4
Cordite, 4, 151, 152, 178
Crimean War, 2, 45, 46, 47, 57, 62
Cromer, Lord, 159, 161–2
Cronje, Piet, 181–2, 197, 208

De La Rey, Koos, 181–2
Dongola, 159, 161
Dreyse rifle, 66–8
Dunn, John, 103, 113, 116

El Teb, Battle of, 129, 131–3
Emperor Tewodras II, 69–73
Esher, Lord, 204

Ferozeshah, Battle of, 14, 19–23, 26, 28
Firket, Battle of, 159
flintlock musket, 2, 12, 13, 15, 32, 41, 46, 48, 56, 70, 82, 109
French, John, 138, 179
Frere, Bartle, 101, 106
Fuller, John, 185–6, 210

Gardner machine gun, 128–30, 134, 139–43, 154, 156, 158
Gatacre, William, 164, 183
Gatling gun, 77–8, 91, 109, 113, 115, 118, 120–1, 127–8, 142, 154, 156
Gingindlovu, Battle of, 95, 106, 112–20, 122, 126, 128, 140, 173
Gordon, Charles, 127, 131, 136–8, 145, 158, 161
Gough, General Sir Hugh, 8, 10–12, 14, 17–24
    Sobroan campaign 26–39, 41–2
Gowan, Brigadier, 17, 30, 32
Gras rifles, 147

Hamilton, Ian, 179, 201, 207, 209
Hardinge, Sir Henry (later Viscount), 10, 21–4, 28, 32, 38, 44, 46–7
Hart, Fitzroy, 188–9, 192, 195–7, 199

Headrick, Daniel, 2, 65, 99, 210
Hicks-Beach, Sir Michael, 162

Inkerman, Battle of, 41, 52–7
Isandlwana, Battle of, 3, 103–8, 110, 111, 112, 116, 117, 125

Kerma, Battle of, 160–1
Khalifa Abdallahi, 158–9, 161, 163, 165–6, 168–9, 172, 174
Khalsa – the Sikh Army, 9–12, 18–20, 24–6
at the Battle of Sobroan, 28–37
Khambula, Battle of, 106, 112–13, 126, 173
Khartoum, 127, 129, 131, 137–8, 145, 158, 161–2, 174
Kimberley, 179–180, 182, 185
King Coffee Calcalli, 74, 78, 80
Kitchener, Herbert, 159–69, 172–5
Kruger, Paul, 176–7

Ladysmith, 5, 175, 178–80, 187, 189, 191, 192, 194–5, 200–1, 203
Lee, James Paris, 148–50
Lee–Enfield rifle, 153–4
Lee–Metford rifle, 148–9, 151–3, 158–9, 164, 169–70, 172, 177
lyddite, 4, 166, 178, 184, 189, 199, 201

machine guns, 2–5, 126, 130, 131, 134, 141, 147, 151, 154–8, 164, 177, 206, 207, 210
magazine rifles, 2, 4, 147, 177, 186, 206, 207
Magdala, 70–1, 73
Majuba Hill, Battle of, 175, 196–7
Marchand, Captain, 162
Martini–Henry rifle, 91, 93, 96–101, 103, 105–12, 114–23, 127, 130, 135, 139–41, 144–5, 147–9, 170
Matabale War, 157
Mauser rifle, 147, 179–84, 188–90, 200
Maxim, Hiram and the Maxim machine gun, 4, 154–60, 164, 168–71, 174, 177, 199
Metford, William, 148, 151
Methuen, Lord, 180–5
Milner, Sir Alfred, 177, 180
Minié, Claude, 42–4
Minié rifle, 43–9, 53, 56–9
Modder River, Battle of, 5, 180–2, 184

Napier, General Charles, 2, 41
Napier, General Robert, 69–73
Nordenfelt machine gun, 128–9, 154, 156–7

Omdurman, Battle of, 4, 146, 158, 161–3, 165–75
Osman Digna, 93, 127, 131–2, 134, 136, 166, 172
Owen Jones rifle, 148, 150

Penn Symons, William, 178–9
percussion cap, 2, 12–16, 38
percussion rifles, 41, 43, 46, 47, 53, 54, 56, 70
Pieter's Hill, Battle of, 5, 193, 196–201, 203
Prior, Melton, 102, 122

Raglan, Lord, 48–50, 52, 56
Rawlinson, Henry, 202
Reade, Winwood, 81, 83
Remington rifle, 69, 96–7, 126, 149–50, 168–9, 172
Rhodes, Cecil, 176, 179
rifled barrels, 97, 128, 152
Roberts, Frederick, 91–2, 188–9, 197, 208
Royal Small Arms Factory, Enfield, 148, 152
Rubini rifle and cartridge, 150–1
Russo-Japanese War, 207–9

Salisbury, Lord, 158, 161
Smith, Sir Harry, 24, 25, 29, 30, 33, 35, 38
Snider rifle, 68–74, 76, 79, 81, 82, 83–96, 99, 109
Sobroan, Battle of, 2, 7, 26–39
Spion Kop, Battle of, 189–91, 201
Stanley, Henry Morton, 65, 85–6
Stewart, Herbert, 132, 138–40, 142–3

Talana Hill, Battle of, 175, 179–80
Tamai, Battle of, 3, 129, 130, 133–6, 140, 146

Uitlanders, 176–7
Ulundi, 103, 104, 108, 120–2, 126, 128, 140

Vickers, Albert, 155–7
Vieille, Paul, 147–8, 151

Warren, Charles, 189–90
Waterloo, Battle of, 2, 7, 29, 111
Wauchope, Andrew, 173, 183–5
Wellington, Duke of, 7, 8, 43
White, Sir George, 178, 180, 187
Wolseley, Garnet, 8, 47
Ashanti Campaign 74–82, 86–9, 121–2, 125, 127, 130, 137, 155, 163
Wood, Evelyn, 75–8, 80–1, 85–6, 88, 103, 106, 110, 112, 120–1